Exam Ref 70-246 Monitoring and Operating a Private Cloud

Orin Thomas

PUBLISHED BY
Microsoft Press
A Division of Microsoft Corporation
One Microsoft Way
Redmond, Washington 98052-6399

Library of Congress Control Number: 2014943459
ISBN: 978-0-7356-8617-5

Printed and bound in the United States of America.

First Printing

Microsoft Press books are available through booksellers and distributors worldwide. If you need support related to this book, email Microsoft Press Book Support at mspinput@microsoft.com. Please tell us what you think of this book at http://www.microsoft.com/learning/booksurvey.

Microsoft and the trademarks listed at http://www.microsoft.com/about/legal/en/us/IntellectualProperty/Trademarks/EN-US.aspx are trademarks of the Microsoft group of companies. All other marks are property of their respective owners.

The example companies, organizations, products, domain names, email addresses, logos, people, places, and events depicted herein are fictitious. No association with any real company, organization, product, domain name, email address, logo, person, place, or event is intended or should be inferred.

This book expresses the author's views and opinions. The information contained in this book is provided without any express, statutory, or implied warranties. Neither the authors, Microsoft Corporation, nor its resellers, or distributors will be held liable for any damages caused or alleged to be caused either directly or indirectly by this book.

Acquisitions Editor: Anne Hamilton
Developmental Editor: Karen Szall
Editorial Production: Troy Mott, Martin Murtonen
Technical Reviewer: Telmo Sampaio
Copyeditor: Christina Rudloff
Indexer: Judy Hoer
Cover: Twist Creative • Seattle

Contents at a glance

Contents

What do you think of this book? We want to hear from you!

Microsoft is interested in hearing your feedback so we can continually improve our
books and learning resources for you. To participate in a brief online survey, please visit:

www.microsoft.com/learning/booksurvey/

Chapter 5:   Manage configuration and protection   **311**

What do you think of this book? We want to hear from you!

Microsoft is interested in hearing your feedback so we can continually improve our books and learning resources for you. To participate in a brief online survey, please visit:

www.microsoft.com/learning/booksurvey/

Introduction

The 70-246 exam deals with advanced topics that require candidates to have an excellent working knowledge of both Windows Server 2012 R2 and the products in the System Center 2012 R2 suite. Much of the exam comprises topics that even experienced systems administrators may rarely encounter unless they work with Virtual Machine Manager, Orchestrator, Service Manager, Data Protection Manager, and Operations Manager on a day-to-day basis. To be successful in taking this exam, a candidate not only needs to know how each of these products works when used by itself, but how the products in the System Center suite work together when used to monitor and operate a private cloud.

Candidates for this exam are Information Technology (IT) Professionals who want to validate their advanced Windows Server 2012 R2 operating system and System Center 2012 R2 management skills, configuration skills and knowledge. To pass this exam, candidates require a strong understanding of how to configure data process automation, deploy resource monitoring, configure and maintain service management, as well as managing configuration and protection for private cloud deployments. To pass, candidates require a thorough theoretical understanding as well as meaningful practical experience implementing the technologies involved.

This book covers every exam objective, but it does not cover every exam question. Only the Microsoft exam team has access to the exam questions themselves and Microsoft regularly adds new questions to the exam, making it impossible to cover specific questions. You should consider this book a supplement to your relevant real-world experience and other study materials. If you encounter a topic in this book that you do not feel completely comfortable with, use the links you'll find in text to find more information and take the time to research and study the topic. Great information is available on MSDN, TechNet, and in blogs and forums.

Microsoft certifications

Microsoft certifications distinguish you by proving your command of a broad set of skills and experience with current Microsoft products and technologies. The exams and corresponding certifications are developed to validate your mastery of critical competencies as you design and develop, or implement and support, solutions with Microsoft products and technologies both on-premises and in the cloud. Certification brings a variety of benefits to the individual and to employers and organizations.

> **MORE INFO** **ALL MICROSOFT CERTIFICATIONS**
>
> For information about Microsoft certifications, including a full list of available certifications, go to *http://www.microsoft.com/learning/en/us/certification/cert-default.aspx*.

Free ebooks from Microsoft Press

From technical overviews to in-depth information on special topics, the free ebooks from Microsoft Press cover a wide range of topics. These ebooks are available in PDF, EPUB, and Mobi for Kindle formats, ready for you to download at:

http://aka.ms/mspressfree

Check back often to see what is new!

Errata, updates, & book support

We've made every effort to ensure the accuracy of this book and its companion content. You can access updates to this book—in the form of a list of submitted errata and their related corrections—at:

http://aka.ms/ER246

If you discover an error that is not already listed, please submit it to us at the same page.

If you need additional support, email Microsoft Press Book Support at mspinput@microsoft.com.

Please note that product support for Microsoft software and hardware is not offered through the previous addresses. For help with Microsoft software or hardware, go to *http://support.microsoft.com*.

We want to hear from you

At Microsoft Press, your satisfaction is our top priority, and your feedback our most valuable asset. Please tell us what you think of this book at:

http://aka.ms/tellpress

The survey is short, and we read every one of your comments and ideas. Thanks in advance for your input!

Stay in touch

Let's keep the conversation going! We're on Twitter: *http://twitter.com/MicrosoftPress.*

Preparing for the exam

Microsoft certification exams are a great way to build your resume and let the world know about your level of expertise. Certification exams validate your on-the-job experience and product knowledge. While there is no substitution for on-the-job experience, preparation through study and hands-on practice can help you prepare for the exam. We recommend that you round out your exam preparation plan by using a combination of available study materials and courses. For example, you might use this Exam Ref and another study guide for your "at home" preparation and take a Microsoft Official Curriculum course for the class-room experience. Choose the combination that you think works best for you.

Note that this Exam Ref is based on publically available information about the exam and the author's experience. To safeguard the integrity of the exam, authors do not have access to the live exam.

CHAPTER 1

Configure data center process automation

There is a joke that I heard at the Microsoft Management Summit a few years back on the subject of datacenter automation. When asked how many people would work at a new datacenter, the designer replied, "Only two, a security guard and his dog. And the job of the dog is to bite the security guard if he tries to touch anything." The point that the presenter was trying to make is that the modern datacenter is so highly automated that it requires few actual physical staff to keep things running. Another benefit of automation is that complex repetitive tasks are handled by pre-configured workflows. Automating a complex process provides you with repeatable results. When you perform complex processes manually, there is always the chance that things will go off the rails should you get distracted. In this chapter you'll learn about data center process automation using System Center 2012 R2 and Windows Server 2012 R2.

> **IMPORTANT**
>
> *Have you read page xv?*
>
> It contains valuable information regarding the skills you need to pass the exam.

Objectives in this chapter:

- Objective 1.1: Implement workflows
- Objective 1.2: Implement service offerings

Objective 1.1: Implement workflows

Part of an effective private cloud deployment means automating any task that is repeatable using the tools at your disposal. In terms of the 70-246 exam, this means using products in the System Center 2012 R2 suite. In this section, you'll learn how you can leverage the System Center suite to create complex automation for your organization's private cloud.

This section covers the following topics:

- Implementing runbook automation
- Automating remediation of incidents
- Change and activity management workflows

Implementing runbook automation

With runbook automation you can automate complicated workflows. Runbooks represent a set of procedures that a server administrator performs on a regular basis. Originally, runbooks were actual physical books. These books contained documentation that described to the server administrator how to perform specific procedures. Today runbooks are software parts that, when triggered, actually perform the procedures with little or minimal direct input from the server administrator. Runbook automation is important in Microsoft private cloud environments because it allows you to automate complex tasks. The System Center product that you use to create runbook automation is System Center 2012 R2 Orchestrator.

Orchestrator

Unlike Windows PowerShell, which requires you to write scripts using an editor like Windows PowerShell ISE, Orchestrator allows you to build automation using a drag and drop interface called the Runbook Designer. Orchestrator can still call Windows PowerShell scripts, but it also integrates with many other products, including products within the System Center suite through integration packs. An integration pack is a collection of product-specific tasks that you can trigger through Orchestrator. You can download integration packs from the Internet, import them using the System Center 2012 R2 Orchestrator Deployment Manager as shown in Figure 1-1, and then deploy them to your runbook servers.

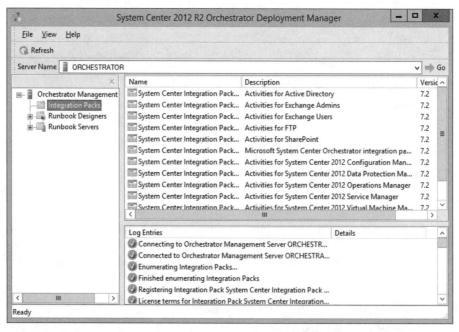

FIGURE 1-1 Orchestrator integration packs

An Orchestrator deployment consists of the following parts:

- **Management server**   This server manages the runbook servers. You use the management server to distribute integration packs to runbook servers and runbook designers. The management server also manages communication between the runbook designers, runbook servers, and the orchestration database. There is only one management server in an Orchestrator deployment

- **Runbook server**   This server runs Orchestrator runbooks. Each runbook server can run up to 50 runbooks concurrently. You can alter this number using the Runbook Server Runbook Throttling tools, but should monitor the runbook server's resource requirements. You can have multiple runbook servers in an Orchestrator deployment, with no maximum limit to the number of runbook servers specified in the Orchestrator documentation.

- **Runbook Designer**   This designer allows you to build and test runbooks. The interface allows you to build runbooks by dragging and connecting activities that are available in integration packs. The Runbook Designer is shown in Figure 1-2.

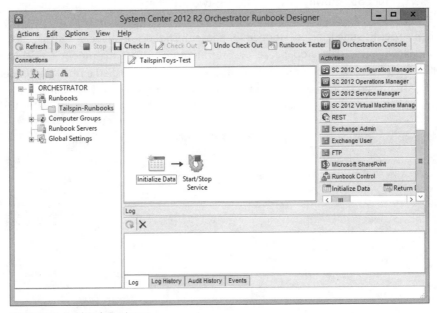

FIGURE 1-2 Runbook Designer

- **Orchestration database**   Hosted on a Microsoft SQL Server instance, the orchestration database stores configuration data, policies, and log information.

- **Orchestration console**   A web interface that users can use to list, control, and view runbooks.

- **Orchestrator Web Service** This web service allows custom applications, third-party tools, and other System Center items such as Service Manager, to connect to Orchestrator and to interact with runbooks.
- **Deployment Manager** The Deployment Manager allows you to deploy integration packs, Runbook Designers, and runbook servers. You use the Deployment Manager to import and deploy integration packs that you've downloaded from the Internet.

> *MORE INFO* ORCHESTRATOR
>
> You can learn more about Orchestrator at *http://technet.microsoft.com/en-us/library/hh237242.aspx*.

Runbooks

Runbooks are collections of linked activities that perform a procedure. You build runbooks in Orchestrator by dragging activities from integration packs to the designer workspace. For example, the runbook shown in Figure 1-3 uses two activities. The first activity, named Monitor Service, checks the state of a specific service on a specific computer and triggers if the service is in a specific state (started, stopped, or paused). The second activity, named Start/Stop Service, allows you to start, stop, pause, or restart a service. When the runbook is deployed, it will be triggered when the monitored service is in the state specified in the Monitor Service activity. After being triggered, the runbook will perform the task defined in the Start/Stop Service activity.

FIGURE 1-3 Simple runbook

This example is very basic. When creating Orchestrator runbooks to perform sophisticated automation tasks, you are likely to use multiple activities and include conditional branches, loops, and error handling tasks. Each integration pack that you import into Orchestrator increases the number of activities that you can include in your runbooks.

Keep the following in mind when creating Orchestrator runbooks:

- Provide meaningful names for activities. You can rename activities after you drag them to the designer workspace. By renaming activities with descriptive names, then you can quickly understand what tasks a runbook is designed to accomplish. For example, with the runbook in the example above, you might rename the Monitor Service activity "Is the VMM Service Stopped" and the Start/Stop Service activity "Start the VMM Service."

- Minimize the number of activities that are performed in a runbook. You can call runbooks from within runbooks. This modular approach to creating runbooks will simplify the process of troubleshooting them.

- Configure runbooks to write logs to external files rather than to the orchestration database.

Orchestrator runbooks run according to configured schedules. You create each run separately, and then assign the schedule to the runbook. You create runbook schedules in the Schedules node, under Global Settings, in the Runbook Designer as shown in Figure 1-4. Creating a runbook schedule involves assigning a name to the schedule, specifying what days of the week or days of the month the schedule applies to, and specifying which hours the schedule applies to.

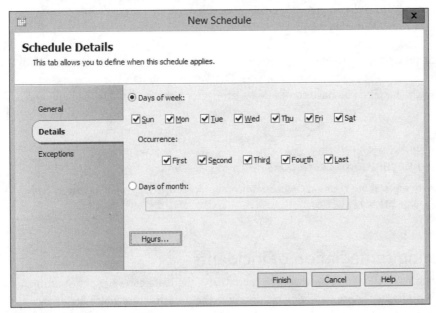

FIGURE 1-4 Runbook schedule

Once you've created the schedule, you can apply it to a runbook. You do this by selecting the schedule on the General tab of the runbook's properties, as shown in Figure 1-5.

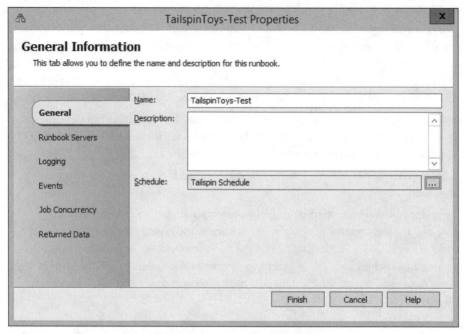

FIGURE 1-5 Apply runbook schedule

You check out a runbook to make changes to the runbook. When you check in a runbook, the runbook will be deployed to runbook servers. Checked-in runbooks will also synchronize to Service Manager if you have configured a connector between Service Manager and Orchestrator.

> **MORE INFO** ORCHESTRATOR RUNBOOKS
>
> You can learn more about creating Orchestrator runbooks at *http://technet.microsoft.com/ en-us/library/hh403790.aspx*.

Automating remediation of incidents

As anyone who has worked on a service desk can tell you, there are certain types of problems that users report to the service desk, or which occur in the infrastructure which are easily remediated by performing a specific set of actions. For example, a service might fail, just needing a manual restart. Using the capabilities of the System Center suite, it's possible to detect these commonly occurring problems and automatically perform the steps required to remediate them without requiring direct manual intervention by members of the IT team.

Incidents

Service Manager incidents, which you might call trouble tickets or service desk jobs in non-Service Manager environments, describe an issue with some aspect of the server, client, network, or software infrastructure that requires resolution. In the context of the 70-246 exam, a Service Manager incident would describe an issue with some aspect of the private cloud deployment that requires resolution by the IT team.

You can create an incident manually using the Service Manager console by performing the following steps:

1. In the Configuration Items workspace of the Service Manager console, select the Computer or User for which you want to manually create the incident.

2. In the Tasks pane, click Create Related Incident.

3. In the Tasks pane of the Incident, click Apply Template. Depending on the issue, you can select one of the default templates shown in Figure 1-6. The default templates are as follows:

   - Default Incident Template
   - Generic Incident Request
   - Hardware Issue Incident Template
   - High Priority Incident Template
   - Networking Issue Incident Template
   - Printing Issue Incident Template
   - Software Issue Incident Template

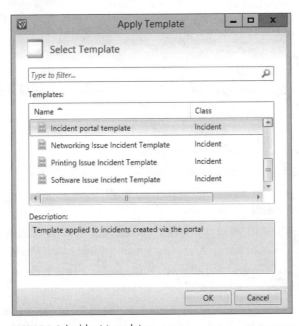

FIGURE 1-6 Incident templates

4. Click OK and the New Incident dialog box opens. The selection of the template causes certain fields of the incident to be automatically populated. For example, choosing the Networking Issue Incident Template causes the Classification category of the incident to be set to Networking Problems as shown in Figure 1-7.

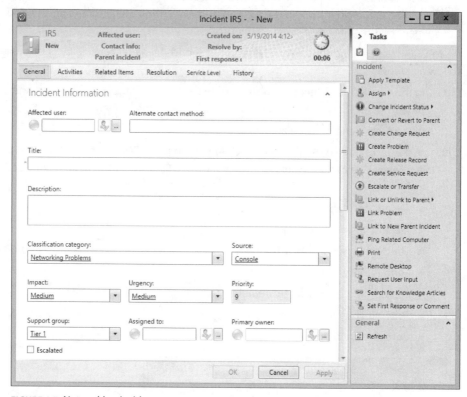

FIGURE 1-7 Networking incident

5. After selecting an incident template, you should provide the following additional information and then click OK:

   - **Affected User**   This is the user who reported the incident.
   - **Title**   Allows you to provide a name for the incident.
   - **Description**   A description of the incident.
   - Other information as necessary based on the incident itself. Some information will automatically be included with the template.

6. On the Activities tab of the New Incident dialog box, you can add activities such as Manual Activities or Runbook Automation Activities that are related to the incident.

7. On the Related Items tab, you can add Work Items, Configuration Items, Knowledge Articles, and Attached Files.

8. On the Resolution tab, you provide information about how the incident was resolved, how much time it took, and specify a resolution category.

9. The Service Level tab allows you to view service level information.

10. The History tab allows you to view the history of the incident.

You can also automate the Service Manager email messages sent by users indirectly by having the users submit a form through the Service Manager Self-Service Portal, or by configuring the Operations Manager Alert connector to automatically generate incidents based on Operations Manager alerts.

> *MORE INFO* **MANAGING INCIDENTS**
>
> You can learn more about managing incidents at *http://technet.microsoft.com/en-us/library/hh519697.aspx.*

Automatic incident creation

The Operations Manager alert connector for Service Manager allows you to automatically create Service Manager incidents based on Operations Manager alerts. An Operations Manager alert is created in Operations Manager when an object that Operations Manager monitors experiences a change that is deemed worthy of attention, such as a hardware or software failure occurring on a monitored server. There are two types of Operations Manager connectors for Service Manager: the alert connector, and the configuration item (CI) connector. The CI connector imports objects that Operations Manager has discovered into the Service Manager database. Alert connectors bring alert information into Service Manager.

To create the alert connector, perform the following steps:

1. In the Administration workspace of the Server Manager console, click Connectors.

2. On the Tasks pane, click Create Connector, and then click Operations Manager Alert Connector.

3. On the General page of the Operations Manager Alert Connector Wizard, provide a name for the alert connector.

4. On the Server Details page, shown in Figure 1-8, specify the name of the Operations Manager server and a Run As account that has permission to connect to Operations Manager. Ensure that you use the Test Connection button to verify that the account works and has appropriate permissions.

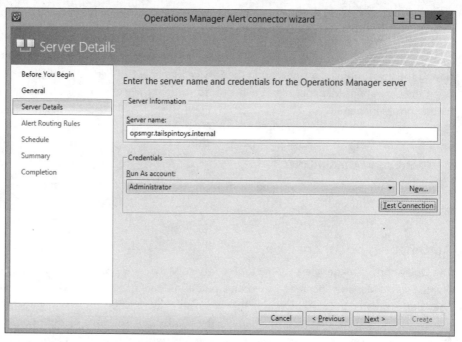

FIGURE 1-8 Alert connector configuration

5. On the Alert Routing Rules page, click Add to add an alert routing rule. An alert routing rule allows you to specify which Service Manager incident template will be used to create an incident based on an Operations Manager alert.

6. In the Add Alert Routing Rule dialog box, shown in Figure 1-9, provide the following information:

   - **Rule Name** The name of the alert routing rule.

   - **Template** The Service Manager incident template that will be used when creating the Service Manager incident.

   - **Criteria Type** Here you can select the conditions that trigger the alert routing rule. You can choose between the alert being generated by a specific Operations Manager management pack, being generated by a specific computer or security group, a custom field, or an Operations Manager monitoring class.

   - **Select Alert Severity And Priority** Allows you to specify the alert priorities and severities that will trigger the alert routing rule.

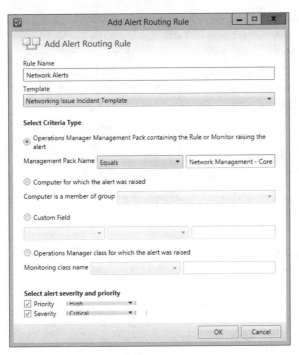

FIGURE 1-9 Alert routing rule

7. As Figure 1-10 shows, alerts that don't match any of your configured rules will automatically be created as incidents using the Operations Manager Incident Template.

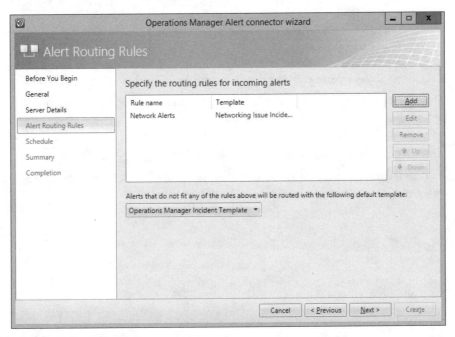

FIGURE 1-10 Routing rules

8. On the Schedule page, select the frequency at which Service Manager will query the Operations Manager server for alerts. You can also configure the connector so that alerts within Operations Manager will be closed when the incident that relates to the alert is resolved or closed in Service Manager. You can also configure Service Manager to automatically mark incidents as Resolved if the incident that triggered the alert in Operations Manager is closed. Figure 1-11 shows these settings.

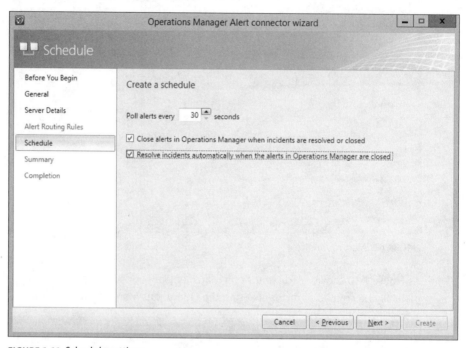

FIGURE 1-11 Schedule settings

9. On the Summary page, review the connector setup, and then create the connector.

Once the connector is created, you can modify the alert routing rules by editing the properties of the connector as shown in Figure 1-12.

> **MORE INFO OPERATIONS MANAGER CONNECTOR FOR SERVICE MANAGER**
>
> You can learn more about the Operations Manager Connector for Service Manager at *http://technet.microsoft.com/en-us/library/hh524325.aspx*.

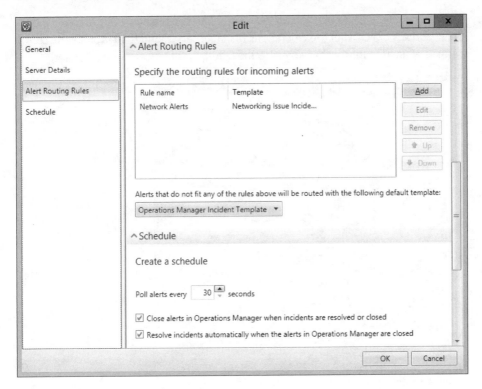

FIGURE 1-12 Connector properties

Integrating Orchestrator with Operations Manager and Service Manager

You can configure Orchestrator to integrate with Operations Manager by configuring a connection to the Operations Manager server from the Orchestrator Management server. When you do this, you can monitor and collect information from Operations Manager alerts, which you can use when building Orchestrator runbooks. To integrate Orchestrator with Operations Manager, first install the Operations Manager integration pack. You can download this integration pack from Microsoft's website. You'll also need to install the Operations Manager console on the server that hosts the Runbook Designer and verify that you can use it to make a connection to the Operations Manager server.

Once you've performed that step, you configure a connection from the Orchestrator Management server to the Operations Manager Management Group by performing the following steps:

1. In the Runbook Designer's Options menu, click SC 2012 Operations Manager.
2. On the Connections tab of the SC 2012 Operations Manager dialog box, click Add.

3. In the Connection dialog box, shown in Figure 1-13, type the name of the connection, the IP address or FQDN of the Operations Manager server, and then provide the credentials of an account that has access to the Operations Manager server.

FIGURE 1-13 Connection configuration

4. On the SC 2012 Operations Manager dialog box, shown in Figure 1-14, click Finish.

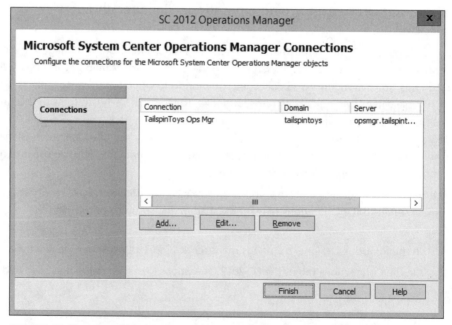

FIGURE 1-14 Operations Manager connections

Once you have configured the connection, you'll be able to use the activities that are included in the Operations Manager integration pack when building Orchestrator runbooks. These activities are shown in Figure 1-15, and have the following functionality:

- **Create Alert**   This activity allows you to create an alert in Operations Manager.
- **Get Alert**   This activity allows you to extract data from an Operations Manager alert. Use this activity as the basis of creating runbooks that create incidents in Service Manager by extracting relevant information from alerts and using that information when creating incidents.
- **Get Monitor**   Use this activity to collect monitoring data. You can take the data extracted from this activity and use it to populate incidents in Service Manager.
- **Monitor Alert**   Use this activity to watch for specific new or updated Operations Manager alerts. You might use this when configuring a runbook to have additional steps taken when specific alerts are raised in Operations Manager during runbook intiation.
- **Monitor State**   Use this activity to monitor and run when an object managed by Operations Manager has its state changed to Warning or Critical. You might use this when configuring a runbook to have additional steps taken when the state of specific Operations Manager monitored objects changes during runbook initiation.
- **Start Maintenance Mode**   This activity allows you to put an Operations Manager managed object into maintenance mode. Maintenance mode is a special state that suppresses alerting. For example, you would put a server into maintenance mode when applying software updates so that Operations Manager alerts aren't generated by the software update process.
- **Stop Maintenance Mode**   This activity allows you to take an Operations Manager managed object out of maintenance mode, so that Operations Manager alerts are no longer suppressed.
- **Update Alert**   Use this activity to update an Operations Manager alert with data. For example, you could update an Operations Manager alert with information provided in a Service Manager incident.

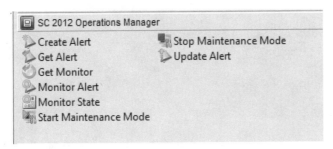

FIGURE 1-15 Operations Manager activities

You configure integration between Orchestrator and Service Manager by performing the following steps:

1. Ensure that the Service Manager integration pack is installed on the management server.

2. Click SC 2012 Service Manager in the Options menu of the Orchestrator Runbook Designer console.

3. On the Connections tab of the SC 2012 Service Manager dialog box, click Add.

4. In the Connection dialog box, shown in Figure 1-16, provide the following information. Ensure that you click Test Connection to verify that the connection to the Service Manager server functions correctly.

   - **Name** Name of the connection to the Service Manager server
   - **Server** FQDN of the Service Manager server
   - **Credentials** Credentials of an account that has permission to access the Service Manager server

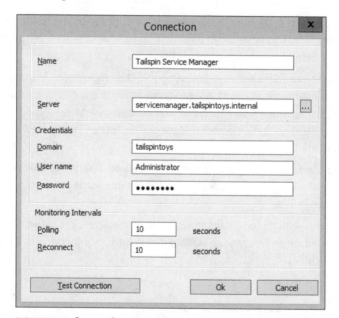

FIGURE 1-16 Connection properties

5. On the SC 2012 Service Manager dialog box, shown in Figure 1-17, click Finish.

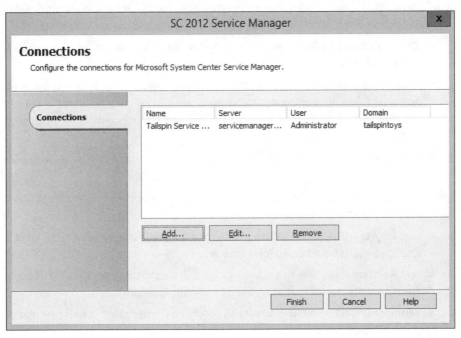

FIGURE 1-17 Service Manager connection

Once the connection between the Orchestrator and Service Manager server is established, you can use the integration pack activities, shown in Figure 1-18, to build workflows.

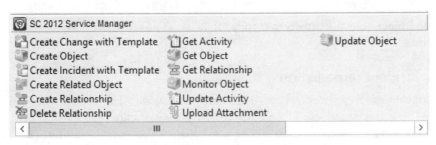

FIGURE 1-18 Service Manager integration pack activities

These activities allow you to do the following:

- **Create Change With Template**   Use this activity to create a change record using an existing change template. When you use this activity, mandatory fields in the service manager change record need to be configured using Orchestrator when you use this activity.
- **Create Object**   Use this activity to create a Service Manager object based on a defined class. For example, you could use this activity to create a Service Manager incident, change, or problem record.

- **Create Incident With Template**   Use this activity to create a Service Manager incident based on an existing template. When you use this activity, mandatory fields in the Service Manager incident record need to be configured using Orchestrator.

- **Create Related Object**   Use this activity to create new Service Manager objects that have relationships to existing Service Manager objects.

- **Create Relationship**   Use this activity to create relationships between Service Manager elements. For example, you could use it to create a relationship between an incident and a computer or user. You can also use it to relate multiple incidents with a Service Manager problem record.

- **Delete Relationship**   Use this activity to remove a relationship between Service Manager elements.

- **Get Activity**   Use this activity to instruct Orchestrator runbook to collect activity records based on specific criteria.

- **Get Object**   Use this activity to search for a Service Manager activity, incident, or change records based on specific criteria.

- **Get Relationship**   Use this activity to have Orchestrator generate a list of objects from separate classes that are related by specific criteria.

- **Monitor Object**   User this activity to configure Orchestrator to find new and updated records based on specific criteria.

- **Update Activity**   Use this activity to update Service Manager activity records.

- **Upload Attachment**   Use this activity to upload a file to an existing Service Manager object. For example, you might use this activity to upload a log file so that it can be stored with the incident generated automatically by an Operations Manager alert.

- **Update Object**   Use this activity to modify the values of a Service Manager object's properties.

Automatic incident remediation

Automatic incident remediation involves applying a specific solution to a known problem. You can configure Orchestrator runbooks triggered by specific Operations Manager alerts. Using some of the Orchestrator activities detailed earlier in this chapter, you can take the data contained in the alert and use it to populate a new Service Manager incident. The Orchestrator runbook can then perform the tasks necessary to automatically remediate the incident. For example, the Orchestrator runbook could run an activity that restarts the service that caused the original Operations Manager alert. Once the Operations Manager alert has been dealt with, the Orchestrator runbook could then update the Service Manager incident, closing both the incident and the Operations Manager alert once the issue that caused the alert has been resolved.

Change and activity management workflows

Workflows allow you to automate processes within Service Manager, making interactions with Service Manager more efficient. For example, you can configure workflows that will automatically close completed change requests, or configure workflows that will automatically notify Service Manager users when approvals are required. Using the Server Manager console, you can configure change management workflows that configure change request conditions and apply change request templates. You can also configure activity management workflows to configure activity management conditions and apply activity templates.

Change request templates

Change request templates store a common set of settings, applying these settings to new change requests. For example, you can create a change request template related to adding a new database to a SQL Server instance that includes commonly used properties, minimizing the amount of information that a user is required to enter when requesting such a change.

To create a change request template, perform the following steps:

1. In the Library workspace of the Server Manager console, click Templates, and then in the Tasks pane, click Create Template.

2. On the Create Template dialog box, specify a name for the template. Select the Change Request Class as shown in Figure 1-19, and select a Management Pack in which to store the new template.

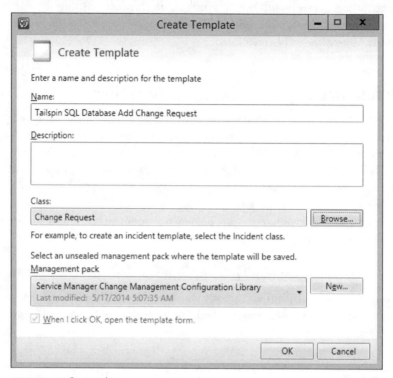

FIGURE 1-19 Create change request template

3. When you click OK, the Change Request Template form will be displayed. In this form, provide information that will be pre-populated on a change request template. As shown in Figure 1-20, this can include the area of the organization that the template applies to, the priority the change request should be assigned by default, as well as default impact and risk values.

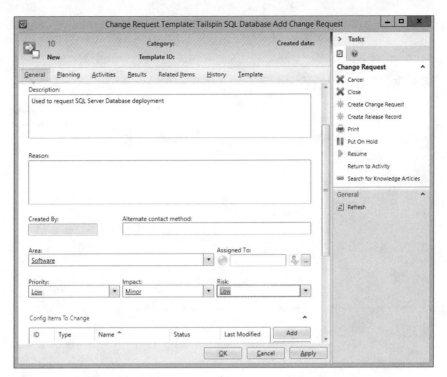

FIGURE 1-20 Configure change request template

4. On the Activities tab, you can add activities to the template. These additions can include any configured activity including runbook automation activities. Usually with Change Requests, you'd add a Default Review Activity as shown in Figure 1-21, which would allow another user to review and authorize the change request.

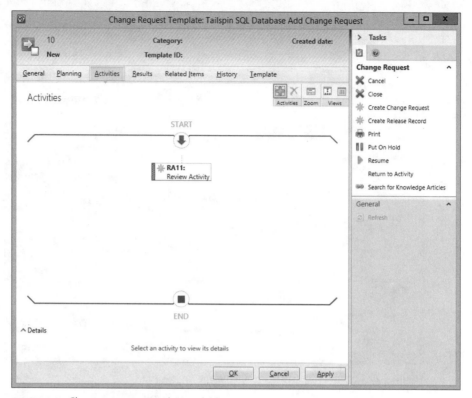

FIGURE 1-21 Change request template activities

Change management workflows

You can use change management workflows to automate the process of dealing with change management requests. To create a change management workflow, perform the following steps:

1. In the Administration workspace or the Service Manager console, expand the Workflows node, and click Configuration.

2. In the Configuration pane, click Change Request Event Workflow Configuration, and in the Tasks pane, click Configure Workflow Rules.

3. In the Configure Workflows dialog box, click Add.

4. On the Workflow Information page of the Configure Workflows For Objects Of Class Change Request dialog box, shown in Figure 1-22, specify a name, whether the event that triggers the workflow is when an object is created, or updated, and a management pack in which to store the workflow.

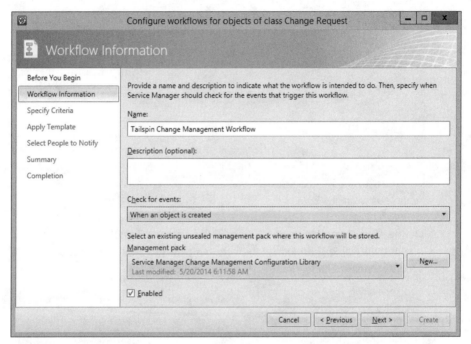

FIGURE 1-22 Workflow information

5. On the Specify Criteria page, ensure that Change Request is selected. In the list of available properties, select a criteria that will determine whether the change management workflow is applied. For example, in Figure 1-23, the change management workflow will be applied if the change request area is set to Security.

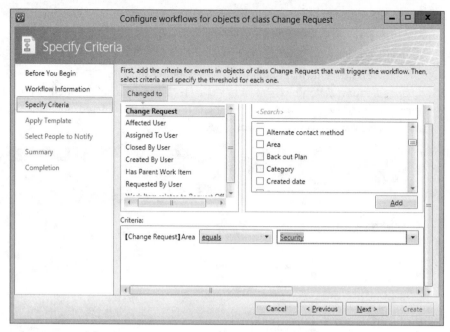

FIGURE 1-23 Workflow criteria

6. On the Apply Template page, click Apply The Selected Template. You can then choose one of the existing change management templates to apply. Figure 1-24 shows the Security Release Change Request template selected.

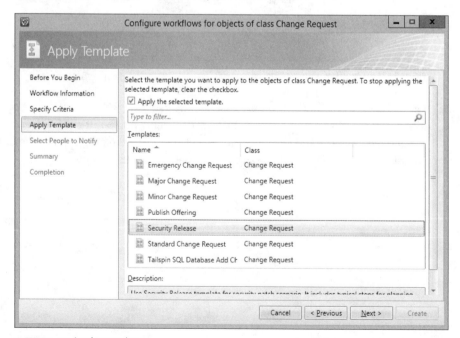

FIGURE 1-24 Apply template

7. On the Select People To Notify page, specify whether users should be notified when this change management workflow is triggered.

8. On the Summary page, review the settings, and click Create to create the change management workflow.

> **MORE INFO** **CHANGE MANAGEMENT WORKFLOWS**
>
> You can learn more about creating change management workflows in Service Manager by consulting the following TechNet article at *http://technet.microsoft.com/en-us/library/hh519653.aspx*.

Activity management workflows

Activity management workflows allow you to automate the management of activities based on the properties of the activity. For example, you might create a workflow to assign all unassigned manual activities to a particular member of the IT staff. To create an activity management workflow, perform the following steps:

1. In the Administration workspace of the Server Manager console, click Configuration under the Workflows node.

2. In the Configuration pane, select the Activity Event Workflow node, and then click Configure Workflow Rules in the tasks pane.

3. On the Select A Class dialog box, shown in Figure 1-25, click the activity class to which you want the workflow to apply.

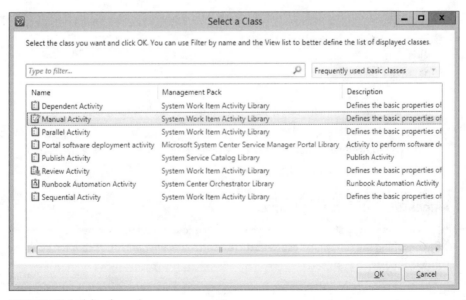

FIGURE 1-25 Activity class

4. On the Configure Workflows dialog box, click Add.

5. On the Workflow Information page of the Configure Workflows For Objects Of Class, specify a name for the activity management workflow, a management pack to store the workflow, and whether the workflow will be triggered upon object creation or object modification.

6. On the Specify Criteria page, select a property and criteria that will trigger the workflow. For example, in Figure 1-26, the criteria is that the Activity Status equals Failed.

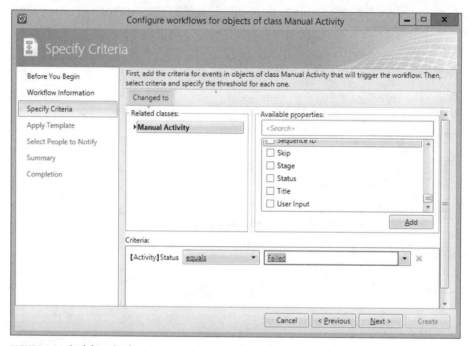

FIGURE 1-26 Activity criteria

7. On the Apply Template page, you can choose to apply a template.

8. On the Select People To Notify, you can choose to notify specific people. When you choose to notify a person, you select who is to be notified and the message template.

9. On the Summary page, click Create.

> **MORE INFO ACTIVITY WORKFLOWS**
>
> You can learn more about creating activity management workflows in Service Manager by consulting the following TechNet article at *http://technet.microsoft.com/en-us/library/hh495617.aspx.*

EXAM TIP

Remember that Operations Manager raises alerts, the cause of which can be resolved by running an Orchestrator runbook. Information about the alert and the resolution can be written to Service Manager by the Orchestrator runbook.

Thought experiment

Workflows at Tailspin Toys

You are in the process of configuring a private cloud trial deployment at Tailspin Toys. One of the aims of the eventual deployment is to empower users by allowing them to submit their own change requests through a web portal, rather than having them submit change requests using a more traditional pen and paper method. In the final deployment you want to have any alert raised by Operations Manager also raised as an incident in Service Manager. For the trial, you will restrict this to alerts raised in Operations Manager that are related to monitored SQL Servers.

You have the following goals for the trial:

- You want to have incidents automatically raised based on Operations Manager alerts generated by SQL Server management packs.

- You want users to be able to submit change requests through the Service Manager self-service portal.

- You want to have all change requests that the IT staff set to completed, automatically closed by Service Manager.

With this information in mind, answer the following questions:

1. Which System Center products do you need to deploy to support this solution?

2. Which connectors must you configure to support this solution?

3. What type of workflow must you configure to accomplish your goal?

Objective summary

- Orchestrator allows you to create runbook automation. You do this by linking activities from integration packs.
- You can configure Operations Manager to automatically create Service Manager incidents from alerts generated in Operations Manager.
- You can configure an Orchestrator runbook to create Service Manager incidents using the Service Manager integration pack.
- You can configure a Service Manager incident to trigger an Orchestrator runbook, which you can use to automatically resolve some types of issues.
- Change request templates store a common set of settings, applying these settings to new change requests.
- You can use change management workflows to automate the process of dealing with change management requests.

Objective review

Answer the following questions to test your knowledge of the information in this objective. You can find the answers to these questions and explanations of why each answer choice is correct or incorrect in the "Answers" section at the end of this chapter.

1. You want to create a runbook in System Center 2012 R2 Orchestrator that creates Service Manager incidents in response to Operations Manager alerts. Your organization has one Operations Manager server, one Orchestrator server, and one Service Manager server. Which of the following steps should you take?

    A. Configure a connection from the Operations Manager server to the Orchestrator server. Install the Orchestrator management pack on the Operations Manager server.

    B. Configure a connection from the Orchestrator server to the Operations Manager server. Install the Operations Manager integration pack on to the Orchestrator server.

    C. Configure a connection from the Orchestrator server to the Service Manager server. Install the Service Manager integration pack on to the Orchestrator server.

    D. Configure the Operations Manager connector on the Service Manager server. Configure alert routing rules for the connector on the Service Manager server.

2. You want to have alerts from any of the SQL Server 2012 instances monitored by your organization's Operations Manager deployment automatically assigned as Service Manager incidents to Barry the SQL Server administrator. All SQL Server alerts on the Operations Manager server are triggered by rules stored within a SQL Server 2012

management pack. Your organization has one Operations Manager server and one Service Manager server. You have not deployed any other System Center products. Which of the following steps would you take to accomplish this goal?

A. Configure the Operations Manager connector on the Service Manager server.

B. Deploy the Operations Manager agent on the Service Manager server.

C. Create an incident template for SQL Server events that assigns the incident to Barry. Create an Alert Routing rule for alerts generated by the SQL Server 2012 Management pack that applies this incident template.

D. Create an Orchestrator runbook that creates an incident on the Service Manager server when an alert is raised on the Operations Manager server related to the SQL Server 2012 management pack.

3. You want to configure Service Manager so that Barry the SQL Server Administrator is notified when a SQL Server related change request is entered into the Service Manager database. Which of the following would you configure in Service Manager to accomplish this goal?

A. Configure a change request workflow.

B. Configure an incident event workflow.

C. Configure an activity event workflow.

D. Configure a desired configuration management event workflow.

4. You are creating a new change request template in Service Manager. Which class should you select when creating the template?

A. Change Request

B. Incident

C. Problem

D. Knowledge Article

5. Which activity in the Operations Manager integration pack for Orchestrator do you use to extract data from an Operations Manager alert?

A. Create Alert

B. Get Alert

C. Monitor Alert

D. Update Alert

Objective 1.2: Implementing service offerings

Another important aspect of private cloud automation is implementing as much self-service functionality for users as possible. Rather than having to always ring the service desk to log a job, self-service allows many routine IT requests to be initiated by the user through a web browser interface. In some cases, these requests can be resolved without requiring the direct intervention of a member of the IT team, and in others they can be resolved subject to approval.

This objective covers how to:

- Creating custom workflows
- Self-Service Portal
- Service catalog
- Request offerings
- Service offerings
- Catalog item groups
- Orchestrator and Service Manager
- Using Orchestrator runbooks with Service Manager
- Self-service provisioning of virtual machines

Creating custom workflows

Earlier in this chapter you learned how to configure change management and activity management workflows, functionality for which is built into Server Manager 2012 R2. You can create new custom workflows for Service Manager using the System Center 2012 - Service Manager Authoring Tool. By building custom workflows, you can further automate Service Manager processes. You can download the Service Manager Authoring Tool from Microsoft's website.

> *MORE INFO* **CREATING CUSTOM WORKFLOWS**
>
> You can learn more about creating custom Service Manager workflows at *http://technet. microsoft.com/en-us/library/hh519585.aspx*.

To create a new workflow that runs on a scheduled basis, perform the following steps:

1. In the Service Manager Authoring Tool, select the management pack that will store the workflow or create a new management pack.

2. Right-click Workflows, and click Create. This will launch the Create Workflow Wizard as shown in Figure 1-27. Provide a name for the workflow. If you want to modify the default values for the workflow, retry intervals and time to run, click Advanced. The maximum time to run must be greater than 60 seconds and less than 24 hours.

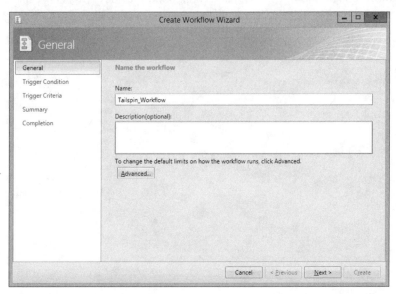

FIGURE 1-27 Create workflow

3. On the Trigger Condition page, select Run At A Scheduled Time Or At Scheduled Intervals as shown in Figure 1-28. You can also custom workflows to run in response to database object changes.

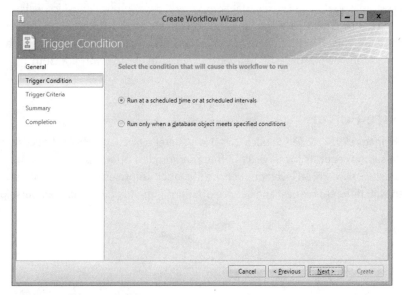

FIGURE 1-28 Trigger condition

4. On the Trigger Criteria page, configure the schedule for running the custom workflow.

5. On the Summary page, click Create.

Once you've created the workflow, you can use the Service Manager Authoring Tool to edit the workflow. You do this by dropping and configuring activities in a manner similar to configuring an Orchestrator runbook. Figure 1-29 shows the Service Manager Authoring Tool.

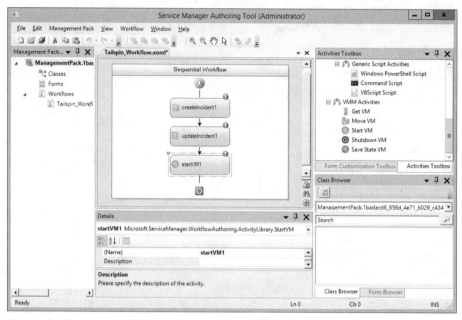

FIGURE 1-29 Custom workflow authoring

To add a custom workflow to Service Manager, copy the workflow files, which will have the name of the management pack with the .xml and .dll file name extensions, to the Service Manager installation folder. In the Service Manager console, import the management pack from the Administration workspace. Once imported, you can use the workflow with Service Manager.

Self-Service Portal

The Service Manager 2012 R2 Self-Service Portal is a SharePoint 2010 website that customers can use to submit requests for service offerings and request offerings using their web browser. The Self-Service Portal leverages Service Manager user roles, meaning that users will be presented with different request and service offerings depending on role membership. Users are able to submit requests and view the status of those requests using the portal. Figure 1-30 shows the Service Manager 2012 R2 Self-Service Portal.

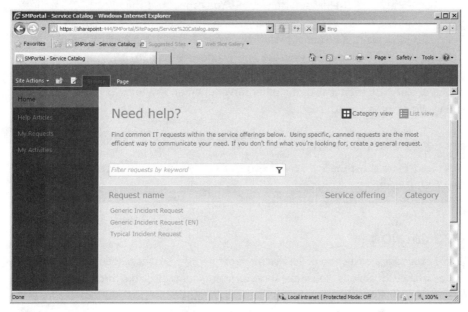

FIGURE 1-30 Self-Service Portal

When a user submits a request using the self-service website, the request is forwarded to the Service Manager server where the information submitted through the self-service website is processed. You can publish Service Manager requests and service offerings to the Self-Service Portal. Many organizations use the Self-Service Portal to allow users to submit their own incident tickets as an alternative to contacting the help desk.

This functionality is only the tip of the iceberg. If you integrate Service Manager with other System Center products, such as Operations Manager, Orchestrator, and Virtual Machine Manager, you can offer services that leverage these products through the Self-Service Portal. For example you could create a service offering that:

1. Allows users to request and deploy virtual machines through System Center Virtual Machine Manager, with the details of that request and subsequent deployment all logged within Service Manager.

2. Allows users to put SQL Server databases into protection, or perform self-service recovery by leveraging Service Manager integration with Data Protection Manager and Orchestrator.

3. Allows users to trigger Orchestrator runbooks. Since runbooks can be created to perform almost any task within your organization's Windows-based infrastructure, you can provide users with the ability, through the Self-Service Portal, to trigger any task for which you can build a runbook.

The Self-Service Portal can be hosted on a separate computer from the Service Manager server. One important thing to note is that you can only use SharePoint 2010 to host the Service Manager 2012 R2 RTM Self-service website. You cannot use SharePoint 2013 to host the Service Manager 2012 R2 RTM self-service website. This is important as you can deploy SharePoint 2010 on a computer running Windows Server 2008 R2, but cannot deploy it on computers running the Windows Server 2012 and Windows Server 2012 R2 operating systems. This means that you must deploy at least one computer running Windows Server 2008 R2 with SharePoint 2010 even if all of the other server operating systems in your environment are running Windows Server 2012 R2.

> **MORE INFO** **SELF-SERVICE PORTAL**
>
> You can learn more about the Self-Service Portal at *http://technet.microsoft.com/en-us/library/hh914195.aspx.*

Service catalog

The service catalog is a collection of Service Manager items, assistance, actions, or groupings of items, assistance, or actions. You make service catalog items available through the Self-Service Portal by publishing them either as request offerings or service offerings. Figure 1-31 shows the Service Catalog node of the Service Manager console.

FIGURE 1-31 Service catalog

You use the Request Offerings node to create service catalog items that are available to users. Request offerings allow you to specify what information you want to prompt the users to provide and any knowledge articles that you've created within Service Manager that might be related to the request offering. Service offerings allow you to create service catalog items that assign categories to request offerings.

> **MORE INFO** **SERVICE CATALOG**
>
> You can learn more about the service catalog at *http://technet.microsoft.com/en-us/library/hh495564.aspx*.

Request offerings

Request offerings are items or actions that you can make available to users through the service catalog. You usually collect request offerings in groups termed service offerings. You can publish service offerings and request offerings to the Self-Service Portal. To give users access to these service and request offerings, you need to assign them to Service Manager user roles that are associated with a catalog group that contains these items.

To create a request offering, perform the following steps:

1. In the Library workspace of the Service Manager console, expand the Service Catalog node, click the Request Offerings node, and in the Actions pane, click Create Request Offering.

2. On the Before You Begin page of the Create A Request Offering Wizard, click Next.

3. On the Create Request Offering page, shown in Figure 1-32, provide the following information:

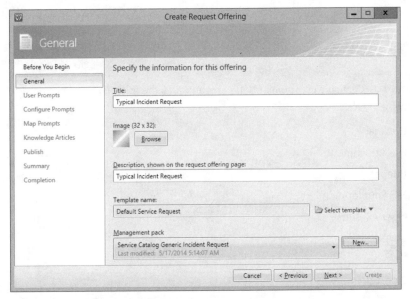

FIGURE 1-32 Create request offering

- **Title** Use this to specify the name of the request offering.

- **Image** Allows you to associate an image with the request offering. This image will be present with the request offering in the Self-Service Portal.

- **Description** Use this to provide a description of the request offering. This description will be present with the request offering in the Self-Service Portal.

- **Template** Use this drop-down menu to select an existing service request template.

- **Management Pack** Use this option to specify an unsealed management pack in which to store the request offering.

4. On the User Prompts page of the Create Request Offering Wizard, shown in Figure 1-33, provide prompts that users can respond to when accessing the request offering.

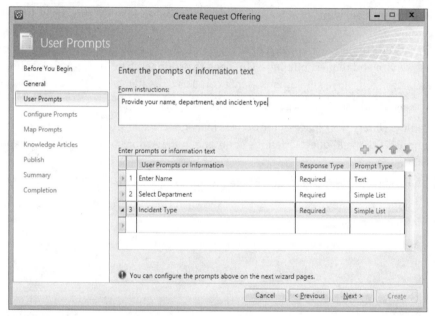

FIGURE 1-33 Configure user promptsYou can configure the following prompt types:

- Date
- Decimal
- File Attachment
- Integer
- MP Enumeration List
- Query Results
- Simple List
- Text
- True/False

5. On the Configure Prompts page, you specify additional required information to assist the user in providing information to the prompts. For example, if you specified one of the prompts as a simple list, you would create the list options that the user would be able to select from as shown in Figure 1-34.

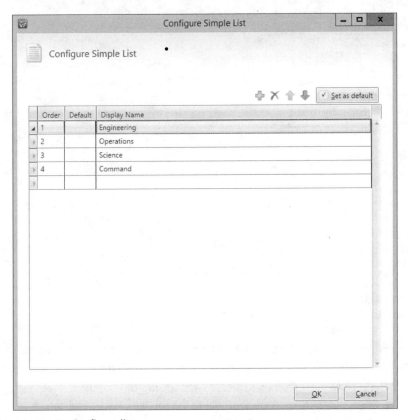

FIGURE 1-34 Configure lists

6. On the Map Prompts page, associate the prompts with the service request template. The prompts required will depend on the service request template.

7. On the Knowledge Articles page, you can specify knowledge articles that will appear with the request offering in the Self-Service Portal. This allows you to associate useful documentation with the service offering. For example, you might associate a knowledge article listing the top problems submitted as service requests by users and their solutions.

8. On the Publish page, shown in Figure 1-35, you can configure whether the Offering Status is Published, and the Offering Owner.

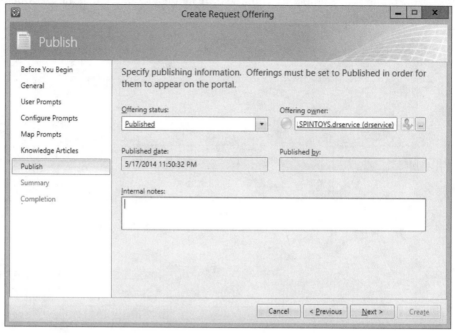

FIGURE 1-35 Publish settings

9. The Summary page provides summary information about the request offering. The completion page will confirm the creation of the request offering.

You can configure a request offering's status to either Draft or Published. A request offering assigned the draft status won't be available to the service catalog and cannot be requested by users. Setting a request offering's status to Published will make it appear in the catalog to users that have been granted access to the catalog item group that has the request offering as a member.

> *MORE INFO* **REQUEST OFFERINGS**
>
> You can learn more about creating request offerings at *http://technet.microsoft.com/en-us/library/hh519639.aspx*.

Service offerings

Service offerings are collections of request offerings. A single request offering can be associated with multiple service offerings. Self-service users are only able to access service offerings and their associated request offerings if:

■ Both the service offering and request offerings have their status set to Published.

- The end users are assigned to a user role associated with a catalog item group that contains the service offering and request offering catalog items.

To create a service offering, perform the following steps:

1. Click Service Offerings in the Library workspace of the Service Manger console.

2. In the Tasks pane, click Create Service Offering.

3. On the General page of the Create Service Offering Wizard, shown in Figure 1-36, provide the following information:

   - **Title**   The name of the service offering.

   - **Image**   An image that will be associated with the service offering on the Self-Service Portal.

   - **Category**   Allows you to specify a category to associate with the service offering. You can create your own custom categories.

   - **Language**   Allows you to specify a language for the service offering.

   - **Overview**   This short overview will be displayed on the Self-Service Portal home page.

   - **Description**   This lengthier description will be available on the service offering's page in the Self-Service Portal.

   - **Management Pack**   Allows you to specify the unsealed management pack in which the service offering will be stored.

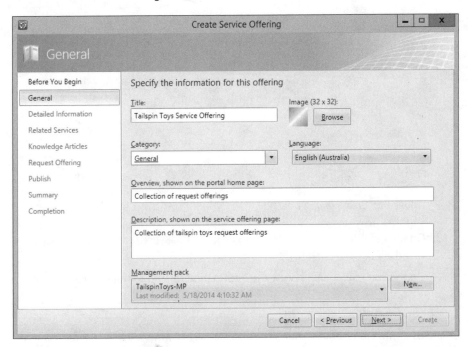

FIGURE 1-36 Create service offering

4. On the Detailed Information page, you can specify the following information:
   - Service level agreement information
   - Link for additional information
   - Cost information
   - Link for additional information
5. On the Related Service page you can specify business services associated with the service offering.
6. On the Knowledge Articles page, you can specify Service Manager knowledge articles associated with the service offering.
7. On the Request Offering page, shown in Figure 1-37, you specify the request offerings that self-service users will see grouped with this service offering.

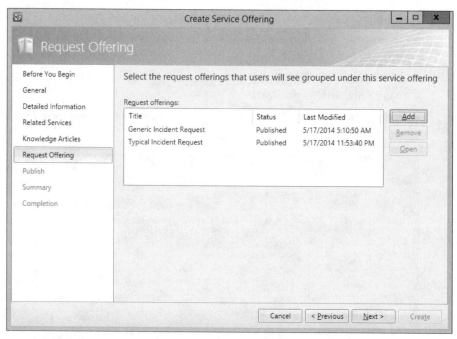

FIGURE 1-37 Create service offering

8. On the Publish page, select between assigning the service offering the Draft or Published status.
9. On the Summary page, review the information related to the service offering.

MORE INFO **SERVICE OFFERING**

You can learn more about creating service offerings at *http://technet.microsoft.com/en-us/library/hh519639.aspx.*

Catalog item groups

You use catalog item groups to restrict access to service manager catalog items. You add service manager catalog items to the catalog item group, and then configure access to the catalog item group by configuring a Service Manager user role. Service manager catalog items can be members of multiple catalog item groups. By default Service Manager has two catalog item groups:

- Generic Incident Request Catalog Items Group
- Global Operators Group

To create a catalog item group, perform the following general steps:

- In the Library workspace of the Service Manager console, click the Groups node.
- In the Tasks pane, click Create Catalog Group.
- On the General page of the Create Catalog Items Group Wizard, specify a group name, group description, and a management pack in which to save the group as shown in Figure 1-38.

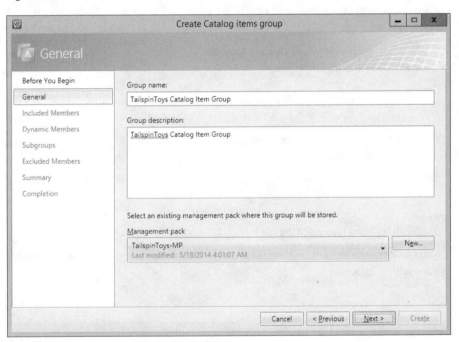

FIGURE 1-38 Catalog items group

1. On the Included Members page, specify the items that will be included as members of the group as shown in Figure 1-39. You can view by Catalog Item, Offering, Request Offering, or Service Offering.

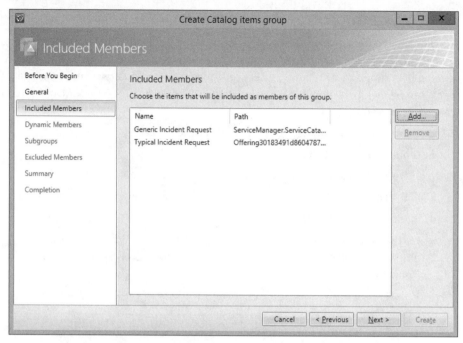

FIGURE 1-39 Included members

2. On the Dynamic Members page, you can have items added automatically on the basis of class and criteria.

3. On the Subgroups page, you can select existing groups as members of the new group that you are creating.

4. On the Excluded Members page, you can automatically exclude a class and specific objects based on class and criteria.

> **MORE INFO CATALOG GROUPS**
>
> You can learn more about creating service offerings at *http://technet.microsoft.com/en-us/library/hh519639.aspx*.

To provide access to members of a specific user role, edit the properties of that role and specify the catalog item groups to which the user role should have access as shown in Figure 1-40.

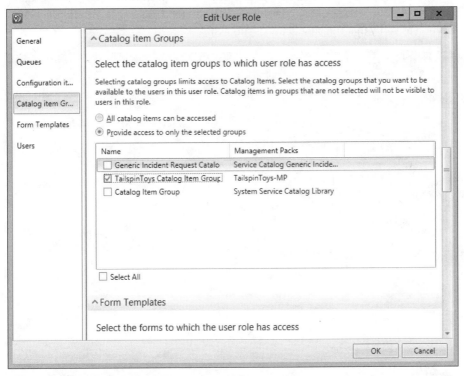

FIGURE 1-40 Edit user role

Orchestrator and Service Manager

Earlier in this chapter you learned how to connect Orchestrator to Service Manager, which allows you to use Orchestrator runbooks to perform tasks in Service Manager. You can also configure a connector that works the other way, between Service Manager and Orchestrator, which allows Service Manager to make reference to and utilize Orchestrator runbooks. To configure the connector between Service Manager and Orchestrator, perform the following steps:

1. In the Administration workspace of the Service Manager console, click Connectors.

2. In the Tasks pane, click Create Connector, and then click Orchestrator Connector.

3. On the General page of the Orchestrator Connector Wizard, enter a name for the connector.

4. On the Connection page, specify the Orchestrator Web Service URL as shown in Figure 1-41, and the operational database account. The URL of the Orchestrator web service will be *http://computer.fqdn:81/Orchestrator2012/Orchestrator.svc*. The Run As account you use must have the right to connect to Orchestrator. Ensure that you click Test Connection to verify that the connection is successful.

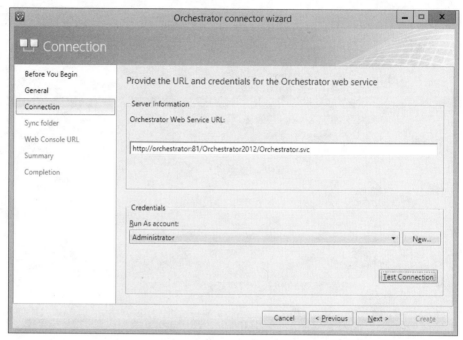

FIGURE 1-41 Orchestrator connector

5. On the Sync Folder page, select a Sync Folder, and click Next.
6. On the Web Console URL page, shown in Figure 1-42, specify the URL for the Orchestrator web console. The URL will be *http://computer.fqdn:82*.

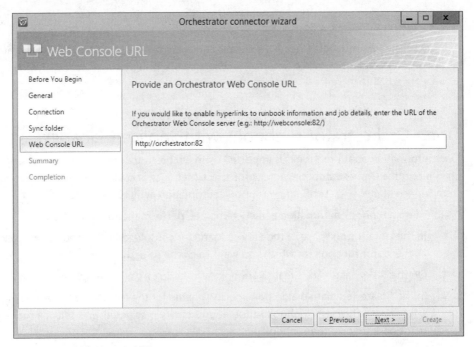

FIGURE 1-42 Web console URL

7. On the Summary page, review the settings, and click Create.

You will be able to verify that the process has worked by navigating to the Library workspace and clicking the Runbooks node. Any runbooks that you've created on the Orchestrator will be present in this node. Figure 1-43 shows this node with a runbook present.

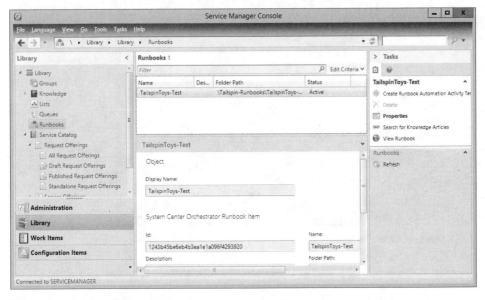

FIGURE 1-43 Synchronized runbooks

MORE INFO **CREATING ORCHESTRATOR CONNECTOR**

You can learn more about creating a connector between Service Manager and Orchestrator by consult the following article at *http://technet.microsoft.com/en-us/library/hh519779. aspx.*

Using Orchestrator runbooks with Service Manager

Once information about runbooks is imported from Orchestrator into Service Manager by configuring the Orchestrator connector for Service Manager, you can trigger the runbooks from Service Manager by configuring runbook automation activity templates.

To create a runbook automation activity template, perform the following steps:

1. In the Library workspace of the Service Manager console, click Runbooks, and click the Orchestrator runbook for which you want to create an activity template.

2. On the Tasks pane, click Create Runbook Automation Activity Template.

3. In the Create Template dialog box, specify a name for the template as shown in Figure 1-44, ensure the class Runbook Automation Activity is selected, and select a management pack to store the runbook in.

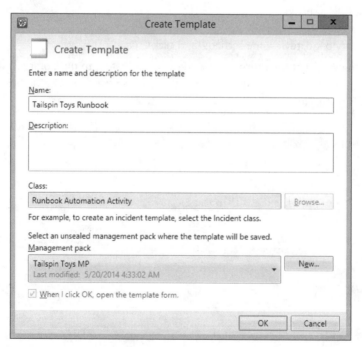

FIGURE 1-44 Create template

4. When you click OK, the Runbook Activity Template will open. Provide a title for the template and ensure that the Is Ready For Automation option is selected, as shown in Figure 1-45.

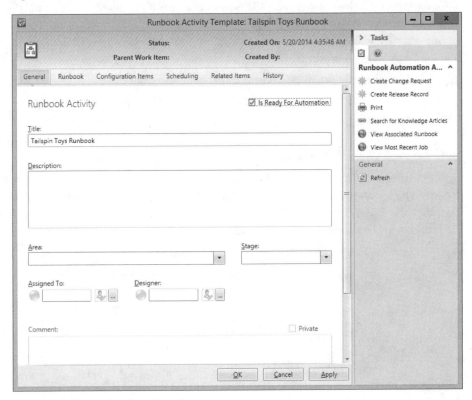

FIGURE 1-45 Runbook Activity Template

5. On the Runbook tab, there will be a list of parameters that are used for runbook input and output. You can edit mappings and specify default values to be used when Service Manager triggers the runbook.

6. Click OK to close and save the runbook automation activity template.

MORE INFO **USING RUNBOOKS WITH SERVICE MANAGER**

You can learn more about using Orchestrator runbooks with Service Manager at *http://technet.microsoft.com/en-us/library/hh519695.aspx.*

Self-service provisioning of virtual machines

When you enable self-service virtual machine provisioning, users are able to navigate to a specially configured portal and are able to use the portal to request virtual machines by filling out a form providing relevant details. The type of portal and the details required will depend on the self-service strategy that you choose. There are three basic strategies that you can pursue when providing self-service virtual machine provisioning to users when using Hyper-V and the System Center products. These are:

- Self-service with Virtual Machine Manager, and App Controller
- Self-service with Virtual Machine Manager, Service Manager, and Orchestrator
- Self-service with the Windows Azure pack

Self-service with VMM and App Controller

System Center App Controller provides users with self-service virtual machine deployment functionality for VMM 2012 SP1 and VMM 2012 R2. App Controller runs as a web application, shown in Figure 1-46. To perform self-service virtual machine deployment using App Controller, a user must be a member of a VMM self-service user role.

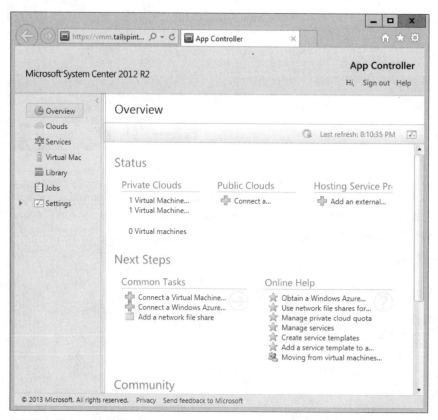

FIGURE 1-46 App Controller

To create a self-service user role in VMM, perform the following steps:

1. Click Create User Role on the ribbon when in the Settings workspace of the VMM console.

2. On the Name And Description page of the Create User Role Wizard, provide a name for the role and an optional description.

3. On the Profile page, click Application Administrator (Self-Service User), as shown in Figure 1-47.

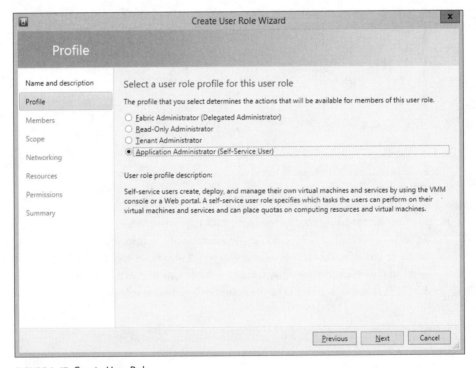

FIGURE 1-47 Create User Role

4. On the Members page of the Create User Role Wizard, click Add, and add an Active Directory security group that will host the user accounts of the people who you want to grant self-service privileges to.

5. On the Scope page, shown in Figure 1-48, select the private cloud into which self-service users will be able to deploy VMs.

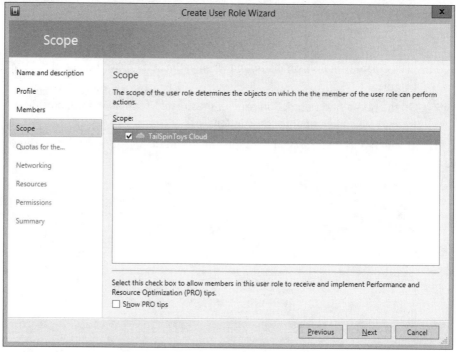

FIGURE 1-48 Create User Role

6. On the Quotas page, specify the quotas for the self-service user role. You can configure role level quotas, which apply to all users of the role, or individual quotas, that apply to individual users. For example, Figure 1-49 shows member level quotas configured so that each role member can use a maximum of 2 virtual CPUs, 8192 MB of RAM, 50 GB of storage, and deploy a maximum of 2 virtual machines.

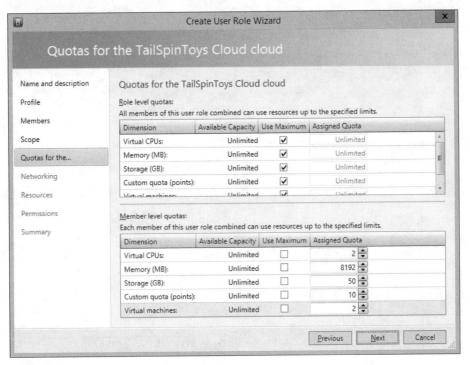

FIGURE 1-49 Member level quotas

7. On the Networking page, select which networks, if any, to which you will restrict the self-service users. If you don't specify any networks, self-service users can use any configured VM network.

8. On the Resources page, select which resources, if any, to which you will restrict the self-service users. If you don't specify any resources, self-service users can use any available VMM resources.

9. On the Permissions page, shown in Figure 1-50, configure the permissions that you want to assign to the users.

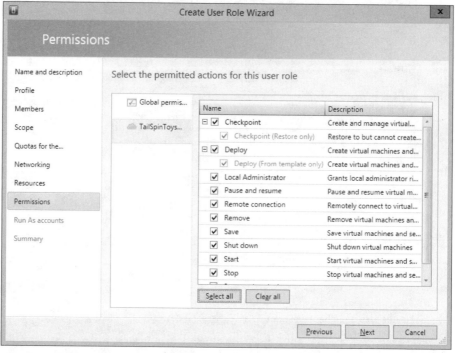

FIGURE 1-50 Permitted actions

10. On the Run As accounts page, select which VMM Run As Accounts that members of the user role can utilize.

Users assigned the appropriate permissions through the VMM role are able to sign in to the App Controller portal, connect to the private clouds hosted through VMM to which they have been assigned access, and deploy and manage virtual machines.

> **MORE INFO SYSTEM CENTER APP CONTROLLER**
>
> You can learn more about System Center App Controller by consulting the following article at *http://technet.microsoft.com/en-us/library/hh546834.aspx*.

Self-service with VMM, Service Manager, and Orchestrator

By integrating VMM, Service Manager, and Orchestrator, you can configure self-service virtual machines as Service Manager request offerings. To be able to perform this action, you'll need to configure the VMM Connector for Service Manager, and the VMM Connector for Orchestrator. When the user requests the VM through the Self-Service Portal, an Orchestrator runbook will start, which performs the necessary activities to trigger VMM tasks deploying the virtual machine.

Configuring the VMM connector for Service Manager will provide Service Manager with information about the VMM environment. To configure the VMM connector for Service Manager, perform the following steps:

1. In the Administration workspace of the Service Manager console, click Connectors.

2. In the Tasks pane, click Create Connector, and then click Virtual Machine Manager connector.

3. On the General page of the Virtual Machine Manager Connector Wizard, type the connector name.

4. On the Connection page, shown in Figure 1-51, typeenter the FQDN of the VMM server, and specify a Run As account. This account needs to have permissions to access VMM. Click Test Connection to verify this account.

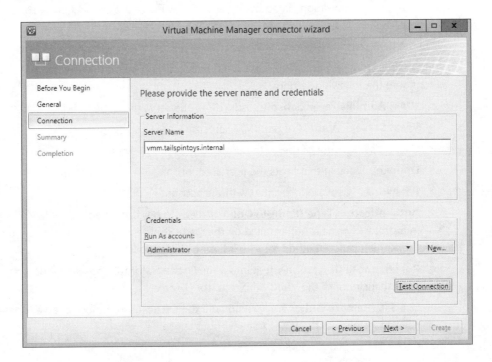

FIGURE 1-51 VMM connector

5. On the Summary page, review the configuration information, and click Create.

To create Orchestrator runbooks that can use activities that perform tasks in VMM, you configure VMM integration for Orchestrator. To configure the VMM connector for Orchestrator, perform the following steps:

1. Ensure that the VMM integration pack is installed on the Orchestrator server.

2. Ensure that the VMM Administration console is installed on the Orchestrator server. It is possible to configure the connector without a local deployment of the VMM console, but this is a more complicated process than installing the console on the Orchestrator server.

3. Ensure that the Windows PowerShell initiation policy on the Orchestrator server is set to Remote Signed.

4. In the Options menu of the Orchestrator Runbook Designer, click SC 2012 Virtual Machine Manager.

5. On the SC 2012 Virtual Machine Manager dialog box, click Add.

6. On the Add Configuration dialog box, specify the name of the connection. Next to type, click the ellipsis (...).

7. On the Item Selection page, click System Center Virtual Machine Manager.

8. In the Properties section of the Add Configuration dialog box, shown in Figure 1-52, configure the following settings:

   - **VMM Administrator Console** Address of the server with the VMM console
   - **VMM Server** Address of the VMM server
   - **User** User account of user with permissions to the VMM server
   - **Domain** Domain that hosts the user account
   - **Password** Password associated with the account
   - **Authentication Type (Remote Only)** Needs to be configured if the VMM Administrator console is not installed on the Orchestrator server. You need to enable the authentication method for WinRM using Group Policy.
   - **Port (Remote Only)** Only required if the Orchestrator runbook server doesn't have an instance of the VMM Administrator console.
   - **Use SSL (Remote Only)** Only required if the Orchestrator runbook server doesn't have an instance of the VMM Administrator console.
   - **Cache Timeout** Amount of time in minutes before the session times out

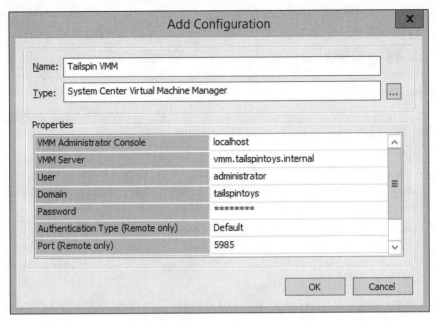

FIGURE 1-52 Connect VMM to Orchestrator

9. Click OK on the Add Configuration dialog box, and the SC 2012 Virtual Machine Manager dialog box.

As shown in Figure 1-53, the VMM integration pack contains 45 activities.

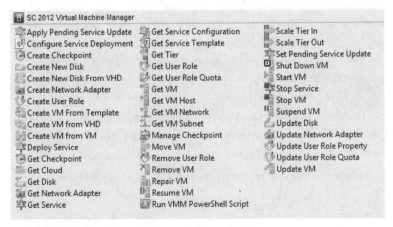

FIGURE 1-53 VMM activities for Orchestrator

These activities allow you to do the following:

- **Apply Pending Service Update**   Apply a pending service update to a VMM service.
- **Configure Service Deployment**   Configures a VMM service for deployment. Requires the service configuration name, service template name, and deployment target.
- **Create Checkpoint**   Create a VM checkpoint. Requires the GUID of the VM.
- **Create New Disk**   Creates a new virtual hard disk. Requires you specify IDE/SCSI, Dynamic or Fixed, File Name, Size, and VM GUID of VM to which the disk should be attached.
- **Create New Disk From VHD**   Creates a new virtual hard disk from an existing virtual hard disk. Requires you specify IDE/SCSI, Dynamic or Fixed, file name of new disk, path to original disk, VM GUID of VM to which the disk should be attached.
- **Create Network Adapter**   Creates a new network adapter and attaches it to a VM. Requires the VM GUID. You can also configure additional network adapter properties such as MAC Address, MAC Address Pool, Network Tag, Virtual Network ID, VLAN ID, and Logical Network.
- **Create User Role**   Creates a VMM user role. Requires that you specify a role name and the VMM user role profile that the role will use.
- **Create VM From Template**   Allows you to create a VM from an existing VMM template. Requires the Type Of VM, Destination, Path, Source Template Name, Cloud Capability Profile, and VM Name.
- **Create VM From VHD**   Use this activity to create a VM from an existing virtual hard disk. Requires you to specify IDE or SCI, name of destination VHD, path, location of VHD from which you will be creating the VM, the name of the VM host, and the VM name.
- **Create VM From VM**   Use this activity to create a new VM from an existing VM. Requires that you specify the type of VM to create, destination, VM path, the VM GUID of the source VM, and the name to apply to the newly created VM.
- **Deploy Service**   Use this activity to create a VMM service using a VMM service template. Requires that you specify the new service's name, and the VMM template name.
- **Get Checkpoint**   Use this activity to retrieve VM checkpoint information.
- **Get Cloud**   Get information to view information about clouds on the VMM management server.
- **Get Network Adapter**   View information about VMM virtual network adapters.
- **Get Service**   Use this activity to return data on all services on the VMM management server.
- **Get Service Configuration**   You use this activity to generate information about service configurations on the VMM management server.
- **Get Service Template**   This activity allows you to generate a list of all VMM service templates.

- **Get Tier**   Provides information about all VMM tiers.
- **Get User Role**   Use this activity to extract information about VMM user roles.
- **Get User Role Quota**   Use this activity to return information about all user role quotas on VMM management server.
- **Get VM**   This activity provides information on a specific VM.
- **Get VM Host**   Use this activity to extract information about a virtualization host.
- **Get VM Network**   This activity allows you to extract information about a VMM VM network.
- **Get VM Subnet**   Use this activity to provide Orchestrator with information about a VMM VM subnet.
- **Manage Checkpoint**   You can use this activity in an Orchestrator runbook to revert a VMM VM to a specific checkpoint, or to remove checkpoints that are no longer required.
- **Move VM**   This activity allows you to move a VM to a new location.
- **Remove User Role**   This activity deletes a user role from VMM.
- **Remove VM**   Use this activity to delete a VM. This activity can only target a VM that is in a shutdown state.
- **Repair VM**   Use this activity to issue a retry, undo, or dismiss action on a VMM VM.
- **Resume VM**   This activity allows Orchestrator to resume a VM that is in a paused state.
- **Run VMM PowerShell Script**   Use this activity to trigger a PowerShell script.
- **Scale Tier In**   This activity allows Orchestrator to remove a virtual machine instance from a specific service tier.
- **Scale Tier Out**   This activity allows Orchestrator to add a virtual machine instance to a specific service tier.
- **Set Pending Service Update**   Use this activity to set a specific VMM service template as the pending service update.
- **Shut Down VM**   This activity allows Orchestrator to shut down a stopped VM, taking the VM offline.
- **Start VM**   Use this activity in an Orchestrator runbook to start a VM that has been paused, shut down, or stopped.
- **Stop Service**   This activity will stop a VMM service.
- **Stop VM**   Use this activity in an Orchestrator runbook to place a VM into a stopped state.
- **Suspend VM**   This activity will place a VM into a suspended state.
- **Update Disk**   This activity allows an Orchestrator runbook to change the properties of an existing disk.

- **Update Network Adapter**   Use this activity to update the properties of an existing network adapter.
- **Update User Role Property**   Updates the properties of a VMM user role.
- **Update User Role Quota**   Updates the quota for a user role.
- **Update VM**   Use this activity in an Orchestrator runbook to update a VM.

MORE INFO **VMM INTEGRATION PACK**

Learn more about the VMM integration pack for Orchestrator by consulting the following article at: *http://technet.microsoft.com/en-us/library/hh830704.aspx.*

To configure self-service deployment using VMM, Service Manager, and Orchestrator, you need to perform the following general steps:

1. Create an Orchestrator runbook that takes inputs to create a VM. At a minimum this would involve the Create VM From Template Orchestrator Runbook activity, but more complex runbooks might extract more information about the VM, the template, and the Private Cloud to which the VM is deployed. You use the Initialize Data activity to collect parameters to be used with the runbook.

2. In Service Manager, create a runbook automation activity template, ensuring that the template is configured as Ready For Automation. Configure the runbook automation activity template to collect the parameters that will be used with the Orchestrator runbook. For example, this might be the VM template name and the private cloud name.

3. In Service Manager, create a service request template. In the template's Activities tab, link the runbook automation activity that you configured, which leverages the Orchestrator runbook that deploys the VM.

4. Create a Request Offering and use it to collect the parameters from the person using the request offering that will be passed to the Orchestrator runbook to perform VM deployment.

5. Create and publish a Service Offering that links the request offering. This will update the Self-Service Portal. When complete, a user will use the portal to enter the parameters needed by the Orchestrator runbook to leverage VMM to deploy the requested VM.

MORE INFO **AUTOMATING SELF-SERVICE VMM DEPLOYMENT**

Learn more about automating VMM deployment with Service Manager by consulting the following article at *http://technet.microsoft.com/en-us/magazine/jj933281.aspx.*

Self-service with Windows Azure Pack for Windows Server

An additional method to provide self-service virtual machine deployment to users in an organization is to deploy the Windows Azure Pack for Windows Server. Windows Azure Pack for Windows Server runs on top of Windows Server 2012 R2 and System Center 2012 R2, and provides a self-service multi-tenant cloud that uses the same interface as Microsoft's public cloud. Although not explicitly addressed by the 70-246 objectives, the Windows Azure Pack for Windows Server provides a pre-built alternative for organizations that want to provide on premises self-service virtual machine deployment.

> **MORE INFO** **WINDOWS AZURE PACK FOR WINDOWS SERVER**
>
> You can learn more about the Windows Azure Pack for Windows Server by consulting the following article at *http://technet.microsoft.com/en-us/library/dn296435.aspx*.

> **EXAM TIP**
>
> While Virtual Machine Manager 2012 RTM had a Self-Service Portal, this functionality was removed in Virtual Machine Manager 2012 SP1 and Virtual Machine Manager 2012 R2 in favor of App Controller.

> ## *Thought experiment*
> ### Self-service Virtual Machine deployment at WingTipToys
>
> You want to trial self-service virtual machine deployment as a way of providing people at WingTipToys with the necessary IT infrastructure to complete their projects. You have the following goals:
>
> - You want to provide users with the ability to deploy virtual machines. These users will be members of the Self-Service_VM security group in Active Directory.
> - Users should be only able to deploy a maximum of 2 virtual machines.
>
> With this information in mind, answer the following questions:
>
> 1. Which System Center products can you deploy to support virtual machine self-service deployment?
> 2. What should you configure in VMM to allow members of the Self-Service_VM security group to deploy and manage VMs using System Center App Controller?
> 3. What steps would you take to ensure that users are only able to deploy a maximum of 2 virtual machines?

Objective summary

- Custom workflows allow you to further automate Service Manager processes. You create custom workflows with the Service Manager Authoring Tool.
- The Service Manager 2012 R2 Self-Service Portal is a SharePoint 2010 website that customers can use to submit requests for service offerings and request offerings using their web browser.
- The service catalog is a collection of Service Manager items, assistance, actions, or groupings of items, assistance, or actions.
- Request offerings are items or actions that you can make available to users through the service catalog.
- Service offerings are collections of request offerings.
- You use catalog item groups to restrict access to service manager catalog items.
- You can configure a connector between Service Manager and Orchestrator, which allows Service Manager to make reference to and utilize Orchestrator runbooks.
- You can trigger the runbooks from Service Manager by configuring runbook automation activity templates.
- System Center App Controller provides users with self-service virtual machine deployment functionality for VMM 2012 SP1 and VMM 2012 R2.
- By integrating VMM, Service Manager, and Orchestrator, you can configure self-service virtual machines as Service Manager request offerings.

Objective review

Answer the following questions to test your knowledge of the information in this objective. You can find the answers to these questions and explanations of why each answer choice is correct or incorrect in the "Answers" section at the end of this chapter.

1. Which of the following Service Manager items do you use to collect together request offerings for publication on the Service Manager Self-Service Portal?

   A. Catalog item groups

   B. Incident templates

   C. Change Management workflows

   D. Service offerings

2. Which of the following server and software configurations support hosting the System Center 2012 R2 Service Manager Self-Service Portal?

   A. Windows Server 2012 R2

   B. Windows Server 2008 R2

   C. SharePoint Server 2010

   D. SharePoint Server 2013

3. You want to use an Orchestrator runbook as part of a Service Manager Change Management workflow. You have configured the Orchestrator connector for Service Manager. Which of the following must you also create to use the runbook with the workflow?

   A. Manual activity

   B. Review activity

   C. Runbook automation activity

   D. Sequential activity

4. Which of the following tools do you use to create a custom workflow for Service Manager?

   A. Service Manager Authoring Tool

   B. Orchestrator Runbook Designer

   C. Service Manager console

   D. Operations Manager console

5. Which of the following steps must you take prior to configuring a connection between Orchestrator server and a Virtual Machine Manager server?

   A. Install the VMM Management Console on the Orchestrator server.

   B. Install the Service Manager Authoring Tool on the Orchestrator server.

   C. Install the VMM integration pack on the Orchestrator server

   D. Install the Service Manager console on the Orchestrator server.

Answers

This section contains the solutions to the thought experiments and answers to the lesson review questions in this chapter.

Objective 1.1: Thought experiment

1. This solution can be configured using Operations Manager and Service Manager. Orchestrator is not required, though could also be used if more complicated automation is necessary.

2. To configure this solution, you only need to configure the Operations Manager connector for Orchestrator.

3. You need to configure a change management workflow to automatically close completed change requests.

Objective 1.1: Review

1. **Correct answers**: B and C

    A. **Incorrect:** You don't need to configure a connection from the Operations Manager server to the Orchestrator server with this proposed solution.

    B. **Correct**: You need to configure the connector from Orchestrator to Operations Manager so that you can then use the activities in the Operations Manager integration pack.

    C. **Correct:** You also need to configure a connection from the Orchestrator server to the Service Manager server so that you can have the Orchestrator workflow create incidents triggered by Operations Manager alerts.

    D. **Incorrect:** The solution mentions using an Orchestrator runbook. While it is possible to have incidents created using the Operations Manager connector for Service Manager, Orchestrator runbooks allow you to configure more complex automation.

2. **Correct answers**: A and C

    A. **Correct**: In this scenario, you should configure the Operations Manager connector for Service Manager as a way of extracting alert information.

    B. **Incorrect**: It is not necessary to deploy the Operations Manager agent on the Service Manager server to accomplish this goal.

    C. **Correct**: You need to create specific incident template and then configure an alert routing rule that leverages this template.

    D. **Incorrect**: According to the question text, Orchestrator has not been deployed in this environment.

3. **Correct answer**: A

   A. **Correct:** By configuring a change request workflow, you can configure certain users to be notified when change requests that meet specific criteria are entered into Service Manager.

   B. **Incorrect**: You would configure a change request, rather than an incident event workflow.

   C. **Incorrect**: You would configure a change request, rather than an activity event workflow.

   D. **Incorrect**: You would configure a change request, rather than a desired configuration management event workflow.

4. **Correct answer**: A

   A. **Correct**: You should select the change request class when creating a change request template.

   B. **Incorrect**: You should select the change request class when creating a change request template.

   C. **Incorrect**: You should select the change request class when creating a change request template.

   D. **Incorrect**: You should select the change request class when creating a change request template.

5. **Correct answer**: B

   A. **Incorrect**: This activity allows you to create alerts.

   B. **Correct:** The Get Alert activity allows you to extract data from Operations Manager alerts.

   C. **Incorrect**: Use this activity to watch for specific alerts, rather than to extract information from those alerts.

   D. **Incorrect**: Use this activity to update an alert.

Objective 1.2: Thought experiment

1. You can use System Center App Controller and Virtual Machine Manager, or a combination of Service Manager, Orchestrator, and Virtual Machine Manager.

2. You need to configure a VMM user role that uses the Application Administrator role profile and configure it to have the Self-Service_VM security group define its membership.

3. You'll need to configure a self-service user role with a quota limiting each user to a maximum of 2 virtual machines.

Objective 1.2: Review

1. **Correct answer:** D

   A. **Incorrect**: You use catalog item groups to collect together catalog items so that you can make them available to members of a specific user role.

   B. **Incorrect**: An incident template forms the basis of an incident in Service Manager.

   C. **Incorrect**: You use change management workflows to automate change management processes.

   D. **Correct**: You use service offerings to collect together request offerings for publication on the Service Manager Self-Service Portal.

2. **Correct answers:** B and C

   A. **Incorrect**: The System Center 2012 R2 Service Manager Self-Service Portal can only be hosted on SharePoint 2010, which can be deployed on Windows Server 2008 R2.

   B. **Correct**: The System Center 2012 R2 Service Manager Self-Service Portal can only be hosted on SharePoint 2010, which can be deployed on Windows Server 2008 R2.

   C. **Correct:** The System Center 2012 R2 Service Manager Self-Service Portal can only be hosted on SharePoint 2010.

   D. **Incorrect**: The System Center 2012 R2 Service Manager Self-Service Portal can only be hosted on SharePoint 2010.

3. **Correct answer:** C

   A. **Incorrect**: You need to create a runbook automation activity to use the runbook with the workflow.

   B. **Incorrect**: You need to create a runbook automation activity to use the runbook with the workflow.

   C. **Correct**: You need to create a runbook automation activity to use the runbook with the workflow.

   D. **Incorrect**: You need to create a runbook automation activity to use the runbook with the workflow.

4. **Correct answer:** A

   A. **Correct**: You use the Service Manager Authoring Tool to create custom workflows for Service Manager.

   B. **Incorrect**: You use the Service Manager Authoring Tool to create custom workflows for Service Manager.

   C. **Incorrect**: You use the Service Manager Authoring Tool to create custom workflows for Service Manager.

   D. **Incorrect**: You use the Service Manager Authoring Tool to create custom workflows for Service Manager.

5. **Correct answers**: A and C

  A. **Correct**: You need to deploy the VMM Management Console on the Orchestrator server and install the VMM integration pack on the Orchestrator server prior to configuring a connection between the Orchestrator server and a VMM server.

  B. **Incorrect**: You need to deploy the VMM Management Console on the Orchestrator server and install the VMM integration pack on the Orchestrator server prior to configuring a connection between the Orchestrator server and a VMM server.

  C. **Correct**: You need to deploy the VMM Management Console on the Orchestrator server and install the VMM integration pack on the Orchestrator server prior to configuring a connection between the Orchestrator server and a VMM server.

  D. **Incorrect**: You need to deploy the VMM Management Console on the Orchestrator server and install the VMM integration pack on the Orchestrator server prior to configuring a connection between the Orchestrator server and a VMM server.

CHAPTER 2

Deploy resource monitoring

Operations Manager functions as the senses for your organization's private cloud environment. Deploying the Operations Manager agent allows you to extract performance data and configuration information from the monitored computer, virtual machine, or device. In this chapter, you'll learn about: deploying agents to computers, how to monitor network devices, how to leverage management packs, how to monitor a variety of different services and applications, and how to view that monitoring data through dashboards and reports.

Objectives in this chapter:

- Objective 2.1: Deploy end-to-end monitoring
- Objective 2.2: Configure end-to-end monitoring
- Objective 2.3: Create monitoring reports and dashboards

Objective 2.1: Deploy end-to-end monitoring

End-to-end monitoring involves being able to monitor all aspects of a private cloud deployment, from the application running on a monitored server through to the functionality of network devices. To deploy end-to-end monitoring, you need to deploy the Operations Manager agent to the computers or virtual machines that you want to monitor. You can also configure Operations Manager to manage network devices. You enhance the functionality of Operations Manager by importing management packs.

> **This section covers the following topics:**
> - Deploying Operations Manager agents
> - Discovering network devices
> - Monitoring network devices
> - Using management packs

Deploying Operations Manager agents

The Operations Manager agent is a service that you deploy to computers and devices, usually termed "managed objects." You want to manage and monitor this service using Operations Manager. The Operations Manager agent collects information from the managed object.

The information that it collects depends on the rules and monitors that are included in the collection of management packs installed on the Operations Manager server. For example, the System Center Management Pack for SQL Server management pack will compare telemetry from the monitored instance of SQL Server against rules and thresholds defined in the management pack. In the event that one of these rules or thresholds is breached, the Operations Manager agent will transmit data to the Operations Manager management server, triggering an Operations Manager alert.

There are four general methods that you can use to deploy the Operations Manager agent to computers running Windows based operating systems:

- **Discovery Wizard** Part of the Operations Manager console. You can use this wizard to deploy agents to computers running Windows, UNIX, or Linux operating systems as shown in Figure 2-1. You can also use it to deploy agents to supported network devices.

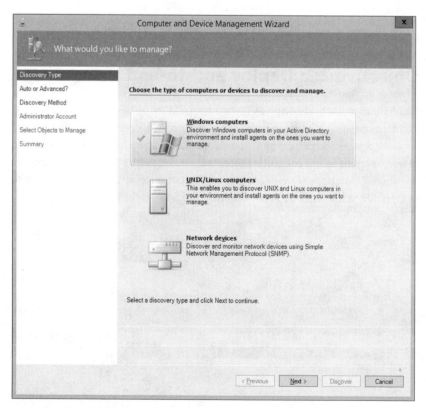

FIGURE 2-1 Discover Windows computers

- **Manual Installation**   While it's certainly possible to install the Operations Manager agent by signing on to a computer and running through the installation wizard, doing this consumes substantially more time than other methods. When you are considering deploying the Operations Manager agent across hundreds, if not thousands of devices, you'll need a method that requires less time than manual deployment.

- **Scripted Installation**   Scripting the installation of the agent is more efficient than manually installing the agent, as it doesn't require direct administrator intervention beyond launching the script.

- **Inclusion in OS Deployment Image**   Rather than install the agent after a computer or virtual machine has been deployed, you can instead include the Operations Manager agent in the deployment image. This is especially effective in environments where computers are members of an AD DS domain and are able to query AD DS for Operations Manager settings.

Windows agent deployment using the Discovery Wizard

The Discovery Wizard is part of the Operations Manager console and allows you to deploy agents to computers or devices. If you want to deploy the Operations Manager agent using the Operations Manager console, you'll need to use an account that is a member of the Operations Manager Administrator role.

To deploy the Operations Manager agent to Windows computers that are members of the same domain as the Operations Manager console, perform the following steps:

1. Right-click the Device Management node, located in the Administration workspace of the Operations Manager console. Then, click Discovery Wizard.

2. On the Discovery Type page of the Computer And Device Management Wizard, click Windows Computers.

MORE INFO **AGENT DEPLOYMENT**

You can learn more about deploying the Operations Manager agent at *http://technet. microsoft.com/en-us/library/hh551142.aspx*.

---

3. On the Auto Or Advanced page, click Automatic Computer Discovery as shown in Figure 2-2. Advanced Discovery gives you the option of specifying whether server or client operating systems will be discovered. You can also use this method to scan Active Directory for computers with particular names, owner, or with a particular description.

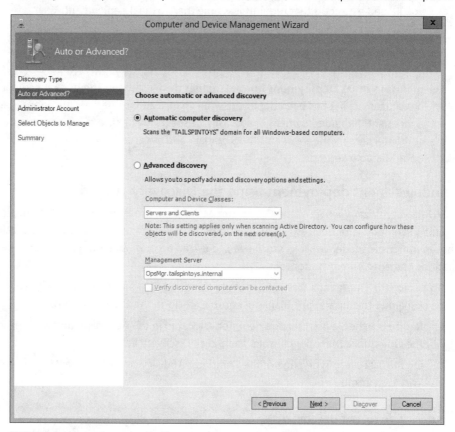

FIGURE 2-2 Automatic computer discovery

4. On the Administrator Account page, shown in Figure 2-3, select whether to use the Management Server Action Account, or a specific Active Directory user account that has the necessary privileges to install the agent on a managed computer. In most cases, this account will need to either be directly or indirectly a member of the local Administrators group on the target computer. When you click Discover, Operations Manager will query Active Directory for computer accounts. Depending on the number of objects within Active Directory, this might take some time.

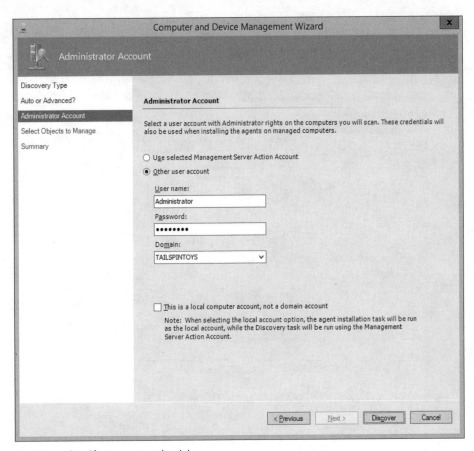

FIGURE 2-3 Specify account credentials

5. On the Discovery Results page, shown in Figure 2-4, select all of the hosts on which you want to deploy the Operations Manager agent. You can use this dialog box to choose between Agent and Agentless management. Agentless management allows you to collect performance and availability data from a computer, but not all management packs support agentless mode.

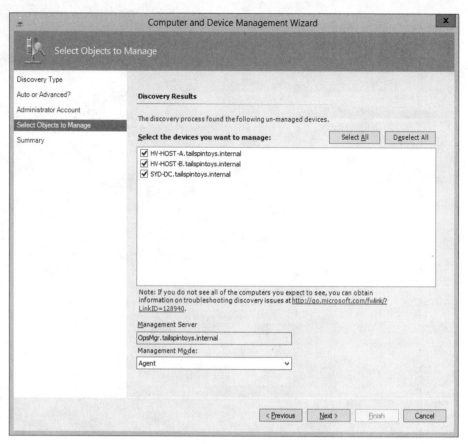

FIGURE 2-4 Discovery results

6. On the Summary page, shown in Figure 2-5, specify the credentials that the agent should use when performing actions on the managed computer, and the folder on the target computer into which the agent should be installed. The default is to use Local System. Clicking Finish will deploy the Operations Manager agent to the selected computers.

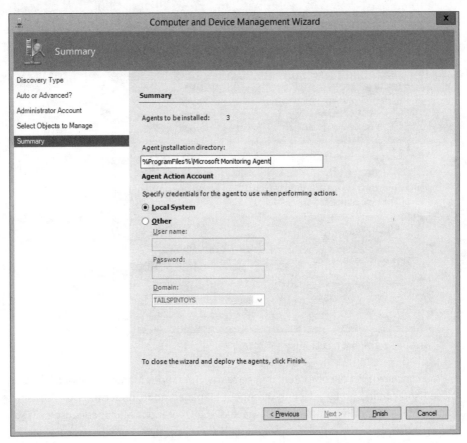

FIGURE 2-5 Agent installation directory

7. You will be able to view the progress of the installation on the Agent Management Task Status dialog box, shown in Figure 2-6.

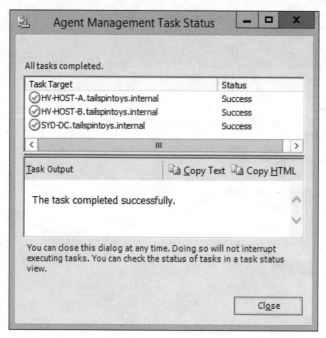

FIGURE 2-6 Agent task status

You can view a list of computers that have the Operations Manager agent already deployed and configured by selecting the Agent Managed node, under the Device Management node, in the Administration workspace of the Operations Manager console, as shown in Figure 2-7.

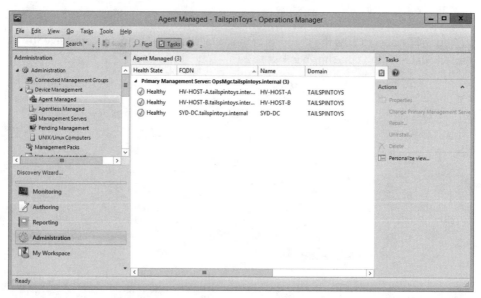

FIGURE 2-7 Agent managed computers

UNIX/Linux agent deployment using the Discovery Wizard

You can deploy the Operations Manager agent on computers running supported versions of UNIX or Linux by performing a local manual installation, or a remote installation using the Discovery Wizard. The Operations Manager agent is supported on the following versions of UNIX and Linux:

- CentOS 5 and 6 (x86/x64)

- Debian GNU/Linux 5,6, and 7 (x86/x64)

- HP-UX 11i v2 and V3 (PA-RISC and IA64)

- IBM AIX 5.3, AIX 6.1 (POWER), and AIX 7.1 (POWER)

- Novell SUSE Linux Enterprise Server 9 (x86), 10 SP1 (x86/x64), and 11 (x86/x64)

- Oracle Solaris 9 (SPARC), Solaris 10 (SPARC and x86), and Solaris 11 (SPARC and x86)

- Oracle Linux 5 and 6 (x86/x64)

- Red Hat Enterprise Linux 4, 5, and 6 (x86/x64)

- Ubuntu Linux Server 10.04 and 12.04 (x86/x64)

The first method is to transfer the appropriate installation packages from the Operations Manager server to the UNIX or Linux computer, and install them using an account that has sufficient privileges on that computer.

> **MORE INFO MANUAL UNIX/LINUX AGENT DEPLOYMENT**
>
> You can learn more about manually deploying the Operations Manager agent on computers running UNIX or Linux at *http://technet.microsoft.com/en-us/library/hh212686.aspx.*

The other option is to use the Discovery Wizard. Prior to deploying an agent to a computer running a supported version of UNIX or Linux using the Discovery Wizard, you need to configure a UNIX/Linux Action Account profile set up with a Monitoring Run As Account. To run the wizard to create this account, you'll need to have configured the following:

- Username and password for unprivileged access to the computer running UNIX or Linux. This account needs to be configured on the computer running UNIX or Linux so that it can elevate privileges using either su or sudo. If using 'su' to elevate privileges, you'll need to provide the 'su' password. Sudo will also need to be specially configured with appropriate TTY and password settings to support the Discovery Wizard. You can configure these using the visudo command. While it is also possible to configure an account that already has privileged access and doesn't require su or sudo to elevate privilege, this presents a security risk and should be avoided.

- The computer will need to be configured so that an SSH connection can be made using this account and that appropriate ports are open on the computer's firewall. You should verify that an SSH connection can be established from the management server to the computer running UNIX or Linux prior to attempting installation using the Discovery Wizard.

> **MORE INFO** TROUBLESHOOTING UNIX/LINUX AGENT DEPLOYMENT
>
> You can learn more about troubleshooting the deployment of the Operations Manager agent for Linux and UNIX at *http://social.technet.microsoft.com/wiki/contents/articles/4966. troubleshooting-unixlinux-agent-discovery-in-system-center-2012-operations-manager. aspx.*

To create the account profile used by Operations Manager for installation of the agent on computers running UNIX or Linux, perform the following steps:

1. In the Administration workspace of the Operations Manager console, select UNIX/ Linux accounts under Run As Configuration, and click Create Run As Account in the Tasks pane.

2. On the Account Type page of the Create UNIX/Linux Run As Account Wizard, click Agent Maintenance Account, as shown in Figure 2-8, and click Next. If you were creating an account to monitor a UNIX or Linux computer on which an agent was already installed, you would select the Monitoring Account option.

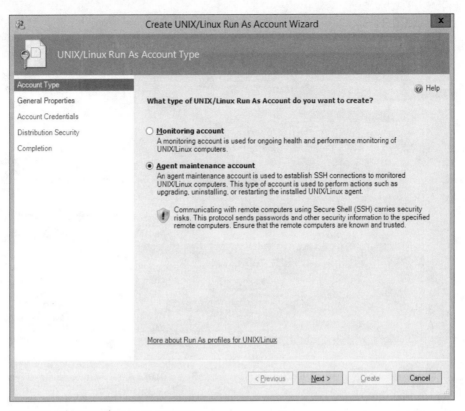

FIGURE 2-8 Agent maintenance account

3. On the General Properties page, provide a name and a description for the account.

4. On the Account Credentials page, shown in Figure 2-9, specify the username and password used to connect to the computer running UNIX or Linux. This connection will be made over SSH. You can choose a privileged account, which is assumed already have root privileges, or an unprivileged account. In that case su or sudo will be used to elevate privileges once a session is established.

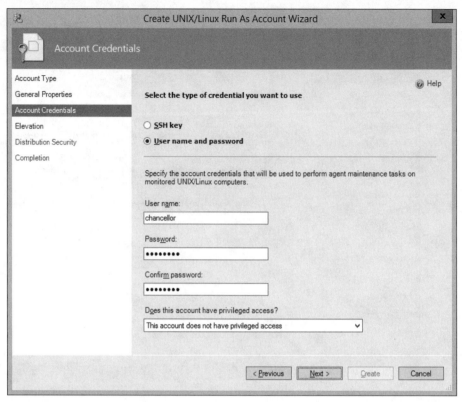

FIGURE 2-9 Run As Account credentials

5. On the Elevation page, shown in Figure 2-10, select the method used to elevate privileges once the credentials specified in the previous step have been used to establish a connection.

6. On the Distribution Security page, select how credentials will be transmitted to managed computers, and then create the Run As Account.

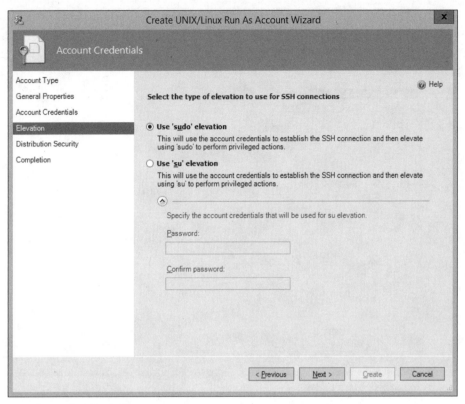

FIGURE 2-10 Elevation options

Once the Run As Account is created, you'll need to create a Run As Profile. To create a Run As Profile, perform the following steps:

1. In the Administration workspace of the Operations Manager console, select Profiles under Run As Configuration, and click Create Run As Profile in the Tasks pane.

2. On the General Properties page of the Run As Profile Wizard, provide a name for the Run As profile, and select a management pack in which to store the management pack.

3. On the Run As Accounts page, add the Run As Accounts that will be used with this profile. This will include the Agent Maintenance account described earlier and any Monitoring accounts that you have also configured to interact with computers running UNIX or Linux operating systems. This page is shown in Figure 2-11.

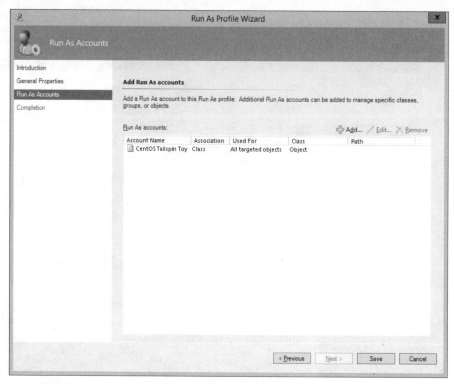

FIGURE 2-11 Run As Accounts

4. Complete the wizard to create the Run As Profile.

Once the Run As Profile is configured for supported Linux-based and UNIX-based computers, you'll be able to deploy the Operations Manager agent to these computers using the Discovery Wizard by performing the following steps:

1. Right-click the Device Management node in the Administration Workspace of the Operations Manager console, and then click Discovery Wizard.

2. On the Discovery Type page of the Computer And Device Management Wizard, click UNIX/Linux computers.

3. On the Discovery Criteria page, select a target resource pool and click Add. This specifies where the monitored computers will be placed. Use the All Management Servers Resource Pool unless you have configured another option. A resource pool is a collection of Operations Manager management servers that share an Operations Manager workload.

4. On the Discovery Criteria dialog box, enter the IP address or FQDN of the computers running UNIX or Linux that you wish to deploy the agent on. Use the Set Credentials button to configure the credentials used for discovery and agent installation. This dialog box is shown in Figure 2-12. After you have configured the discovery criteria, save these criteria, and then click Discover on the Discovery Criteria page.

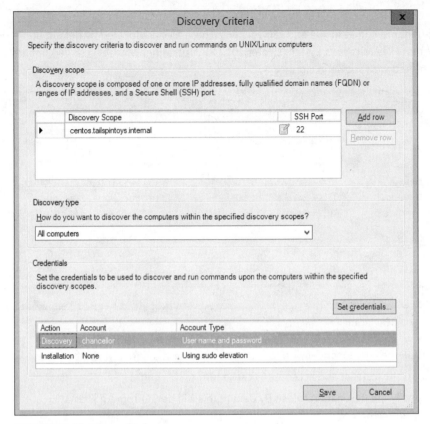

FIGURE 2-12 Discovery criteria

5. On the Computer Selection page, select the discovered computers that you want to manage, and click Manage. The agent will be deployed.

Manual agent installation

You'll need to install the Operations Manager agent manually if you need to monitor computers located on a perimeter or isolated network, or if you need to monitor computers that are not members of an AD DS domain. You can perform manual installation in one of two ways:

- Double-clicking the MOMAgent.msi installer and answering the questions posed in the wizard
- Using the command line options to perform the installation

USING THE MOMAGENT.MSI SETUP WIZARD

MOMAgent.msi comes in x64 and x86 versions. These files are located by default under the C:\Program Files\Microsoft System Center 2012 R2\Operations Manager\Server\AgentManagement folder, as shown in Figure 2-13.

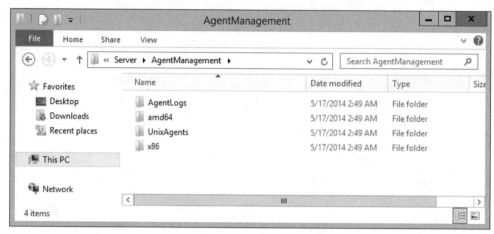

FIGURE 2-13 Agent location

To install the agent manually using the wizard, perform the following steps:

1. Start the installer and accept the license terms.

2. Specify the destination folder. By default this will be C:\Program Files\Microsoft Monitoring Agent.

3. On the Agent Setup page, select whether you want Active Directory to configure the agent. This requires that you have configured a container in AD DS using MOMAD-Admin.exe. You can also configure the agent to connect to Operations Manager to determine management group information.

4. On the Management Group Configuration page, specify the Management Group Name, the Management Server Name, and the Management Server Port. Figure 2-14 shows this page configured to connect to the management group named Tailspintoys on the management server Opsmgr.tailspintoys.internal.

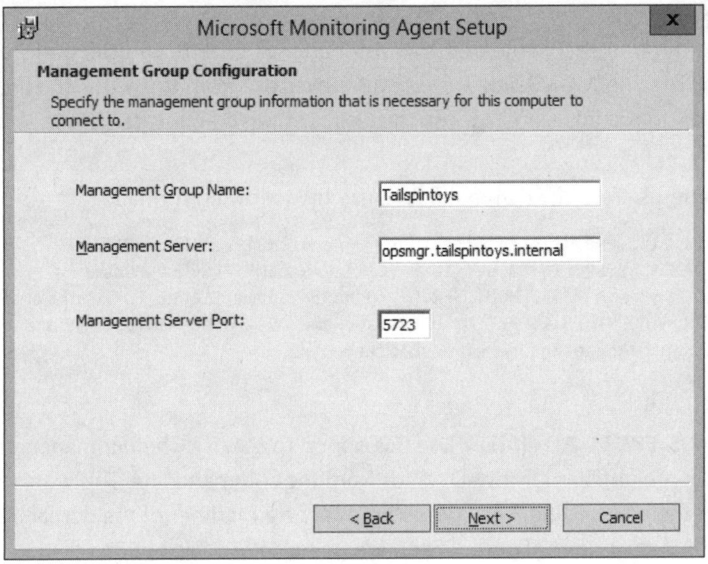

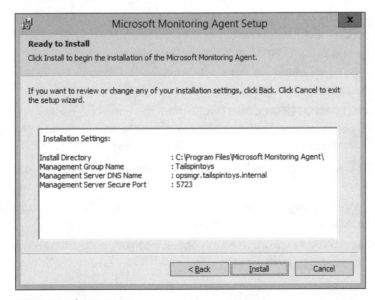

FIGURE 2-14 Management group configuration

5. On the Agent Action Account page, choose whether actions performed by the Operations Manager agent are completed using the Local System account, a Domain account, or a Local account.

6. On the Microsoft Update page, choose whether Microsoft Update will be used to provide automatic updates.

7. Review the summary, like the one shown in Figure 2-15, and click Install to complete the agent installation.

FIGURE 2-15 Agent setup

USING THE COMMAND LINE

Rather than walking through each page of the MOMAgent.msi Wizard, you can perform agent installation by running MOMAgent.msi using Msiexec.exe from the command line. Msiexe.exe allows you to run installers that use the .msi format and is located in the %WinDir%\System32 folder.

To run MOMAgent.msi from the command line, use the following format:

```
%WinDir%\System32\msiexec.exe /i path\Directory\MOMAgent.msi /qn USE_SETTINGS_
FROM_AD={0|1} USE_MANUALLY_SPECIFIED_SETTINGS={0|1} MANAGEMENT_GROUP=MGname
MANAGEMENT_SERVER_DNS=MSname MANAGEMENT_SERVER_AD_NAME=MSname SECURE_PORT=PortNumber
ACTIONS_USE_COMPUTER_ACCOUNT={0|1} ACTIONSUSER=UserName ACTIONSDOMAIN=DomainName
ACTIONSPASSWORD=Password AcceptEndUserLicenseAgreement=1
```

Where:

- **USE_SETTINGS_FROM_AD={0|1}**   Use this option to specify whether management group settings are obtained from AD DS, or from the command line. This works in conjunction with the next setting. The computer must be a member of the domain, and Active Directory must be configured if you are going to use this option.

- **USE_MANUALLY_SPECIFIED_SETTINGS={0|1}**   Use this option to specify whether management group settings are specified from the command line. This works in conjunction with the previous setting.

- **MANAGEMENT_GROUP=MGname**   Use this option to specify the Operations Manager Management Group name, when you are using the command line to specify the options.

- **MANAGEMENT_SERVER_DNS=MSname**   Use this option to specify the Operations Manager management server FQDN, when using the command line to specify the options.

- **MANAGEMENT_SERVER_AD_NAME =MSname**   Use this option to specify the Active Directory computer account name of the Operations Manager Management Server, when using the command line to specify the options.

- **SECURE_PORT=PortNumber**   Use this option to specify the health service port number. The default port number is 5723.

- **ACTIONS_USE_COMPUTER_ACCOUNT={0|1}**   Use this option to specify whether the LOCAL SYSTEM account or a specified user account, specified using the ACTIONSUSER, ACTIONSDOMAIN, and ACTIONSPASSWORD settings, is used.

- **ACTIONSUSER=UserName**   Use this option when using a custom account to specify the user name of the account.

- **ACTIONSDOMAIN=DomainName**   Use this option when using a custom account to specify the domain name used with the account.

- **ACTIONSPASSWORD=Password**   Use this option when using a custom account to specify the password associated with the account.

- **AcceptEndUserLicenseAgreement=1** Use this option to agree to the Microsoft Software License Terms. This option is required when installing the Operations Manager agent from the command line.

Before a manually installed agent can be used, you'll need to authorize it from the Operations Manager console.

MORE INFO **MANUAL AGENT INSTALLATION**

You can learn more about manual agent installation at *http://technet.microsoft.com/en-us/library/hh212915.aspx*.

Automatic agent assignment

You can use AD DS to assign computers with the Operations Manager agent installed to Operations Manager management groups. For example, you would do this when you have deployed the agent manually using the option to get management server and group settings from AD DS, or when you've deployed the Operations Manager agent as part of an operating system image.

To configure automatic agent assignment, perform the following steps:

1. Create a domain security group and add it to the Operations Manager Administrators security role. Figure 2-16 shows the TailspinMOMAdmin security group added to this security role.

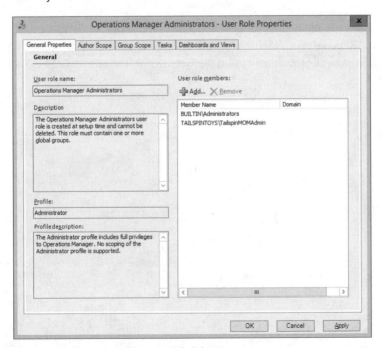

FIGURE 2-16 Operations Manager Administrators

2. A member of the Domain Admins AD DS group must then run the following command MOMADADMIN.exe <ManagementGroupName> <MOMAdminSecurityGroup> <RunAsAccount> <Domain> where

  - **<ManagementGroupName>** is the name of the Operations Manager management group.

  - **<MOMAdminSecurityGroup>** is the name of the domain security group that has been added to the Operations Manager Administrators security role.

  - **<RunAsAccount>** is an account that has the permission to read and write information to the newly created container in Active Directory.

  - **<Domain>** is the domain that the container is created in.

3. Running this command also adds the <RunAsAccount> to the <MOMAdminSecurityGroup>.

MORE INFO **ACTIVE DIRECTORY ASSIGNMENT**

You can learn more about Active Directory assignment at *http://technet.microsoft.com/en-us/library/hh212922.aspx.*

For example, to create the container for the TailspinToys management group, using the TAILSPINTOYS\TailspinMOMAdmin group as the security group, and TAILSPINTOYS\Administrator as the runas account, start the command:

```
MOMADAdmin.exe tailspintoys TAILSPINTOYS\TailspinMOMAdmin TAILSPINTOYS\Administrator
tailspintoys
```

The MOMADAdmin.exe utility is located by default in the C:\Program Files\Microsoft System Center 2012 R2\Operations Manager\Server folder. You can determine your Operations Manager management group name using the Get-SCOMManagementGroup Windows PowerShell cmdlet.

Once the container has been created, you run the Agent Assignment And Failover Wizard to assign agents to specific management servers within the management group. You can start the Agent Assignment And Failover Wizard by clicking Add on the Auto Agent Assignment tab of the Management Server Properties dialog box of the management server that you want to assign agents to, in the Administration workspace shown in Figure 2-17.

FIGURE 2-17 Auto Agent Assignment

You must run the Agent Assignment And Failover Wizard in each domain where you want to use it to perform auto assignment. To complete the wizard, perform the following steps:

1. On the Domain page, specify the domain for which you are configuring automatic agent assignment. Figure 2-18 shows the selection of the Tailspintoys.internal domain.

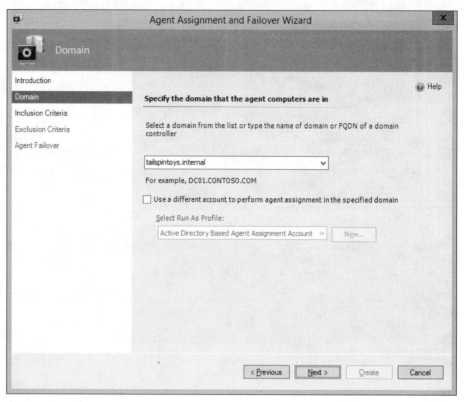

FIGURE 2-18 Domain selection

2. On the Inclusion Criteria page, you can create an LDAP query, or use the dialog box to configure a search based on criteria including name, description, managed by, operating system, and operating system version. Figure 2-19 shows the inclusion criteria that will include all of the computers that have names starting with the characters SYD.

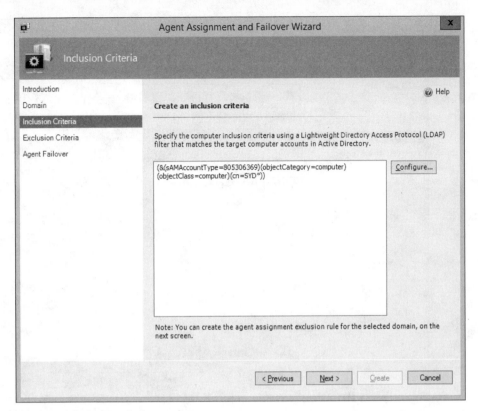

FIGURE 2-19 Inclusion criteria

3. On the Exclusion Criteria page, you can enter a list of computers to be excluded from agent assignment. You should list computers using FQDNs, separating each by a semi-colon, comma, or new line. Figure 2-20 shows the computer Excluded.tailspintoys. internal in the list of excluded computers.

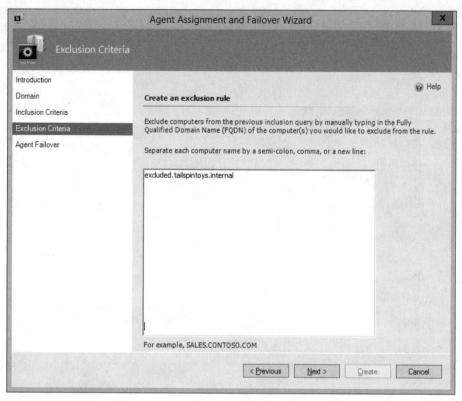

FIGURE 2-20 Exclusion rule

4. On the Agent Failover page, you can specify whether agents will contact another management server in the same management group automatically, or manually fail over to specific management servers. Figure 2-21 shows the Agent Failover page of the Agent Assignment And Failover Wizard, with the Automatically Manage Failover option page.

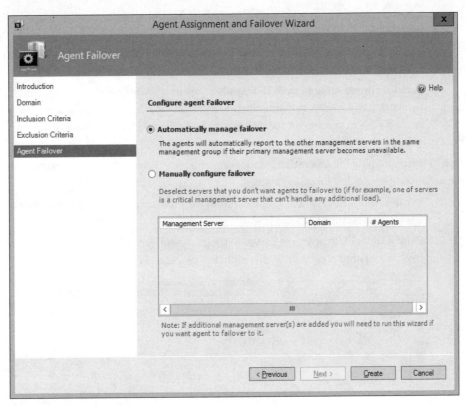

FIGURE 2-21 Automatic failover management

Authorizing agents

If you are planning on installing the Operations Manager agent onto a computer manually, using the MOMAgent.msi installer, or plan to deploy the agent as part of an image, you'll need to configure how the Operations Manager management deals with the agents once it is contacted.

You can configure one of the following options:

- **Reject New Manual Agent Installations**   When you select this option, any requests from a manually deployed agent, or agent deployed as part of an image will automatically be rejected by the Operations Manager management server.

- **Review New Manual Agent Installations In Pending Management View** When you select this option, all requests from manually deployed agents or agents deployed as part of an image will be placed in a list, visible through the Pending Management queue. Administrators are able to use this list to perform approval.

- **Auto-Approve New Manually Installed Agents** When you select this option (only available if the Review option is already selected) any Operations Manager agent that contacts the management server will automatically be joined to the management group.

To configure how the Operations Manager management server responds to manual agent installation, perform the following steps:

1. In the Settings node of the Administration workspace, right-click Security under Type: Server, and click Properties.

2. On the Global Management Server Settings - Security dialog box, select the option that you want to configure, as shown in Figure 2-22.

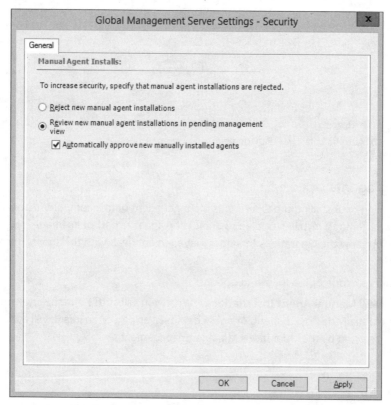

FIGURE 2-22 Global Management Server Settings

EXAM TIP

You'll need to be familiar with the different ways in which you can deploy the Operations Manager agent. You'll also need to know in which cases you will need to authorize an agent and when you need to perform a manual installation

Discovering network devices

Operations Manager discovers network devices by running discovery rules that the Operations Manager Administrator configures. Network discovery rules include the following information:

- IP address or FQDN of the devices that you want to discover.
- The SNMP (Simple Network Management Protocol) version used by each device. Operations Manager supports SNMP v1, v2, and v3.
- The SNMP community string of any SNMP v1 or v2 compatible devices to be discovered.
- User name, context, authentication protocol, authentication key, privacy key, and privacy protocol for each SNMP v3 device.
- The management server that will monitor the discovered network devices.

When performing network discovery, any firewalls between the Operations Manager management server and the network devices to be discovered must allow SNMP (UDP) and ICMP bidirectionally. SNMP usually uses 161 (UDP) and 162 (TCP/UDP). If you are going to be discovering devices that use SNMP v1 or v2, you'll need to configure the Run As account to use for this purpose. You can do this before creating the discovery rule, or during the discovery rule creation process.

To create a network discovery rule, perform the following steps:

1. Right-click the Network Management node in the Administration workspace of the Operations Manager console, and click Discovery Wizard.
2. On the Discovery Type page of the Computer And Device Management Wizard, click Network Devices, as shown in Figure 2-23, and click Next.

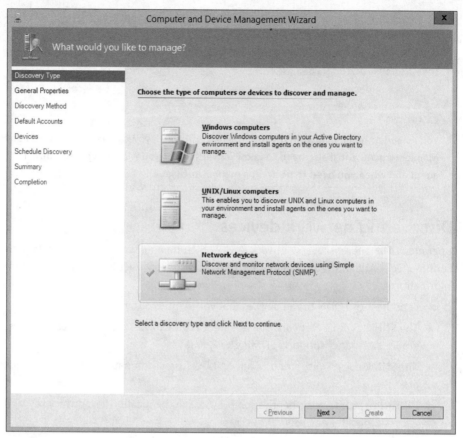

FIGURE 2-23 Network devices

3. On the General Properties page, shown in Figure 2-24, provide the following information:

   - The name for the rule. An informative name for the Rule.

   - The management server from which network discovery will be performed.

   - The resource pool. You can create a new resource pool, or select an existing resource pool that will be responsible for monitoring discovered network devices.

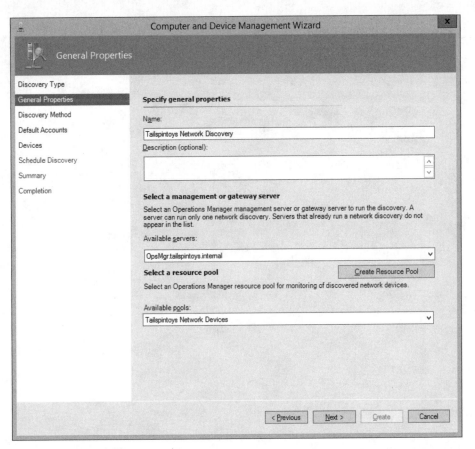

FIGURE 2-24 Network Discovery rule

4. On the Discovery Methods page, shown in Figure 2-25, choose between Explicit Discovery and Recursive Discovery. You should select Explicit Discovery when you know the address of each network device that you want Operations Manager to manage. Recursive Discovery provides a more thorough discovery of network devices, but this process is likely to take longer and is likely to discover devices that you may not be interested in having Operations Manager monitor.

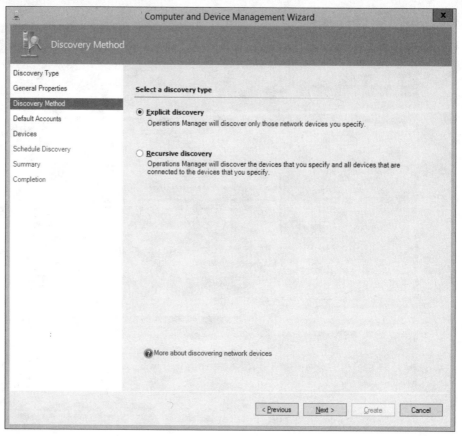

FIGURE 2-25 Explicit Discovery

5. If you are discovering devices that support SNMP v1 or SNMP v2, either select an existing Run As account, or create a new Run As account for this purpose. This Run As account includes the SNMP v1 or v2 community string.

EXAM TIP

Remember what you need to include when configuring a Run As account for network device discovery for devices that use SNMP v1 or v2.

6. On the Devices page, shown in Figure 2-26, you can either add the devices that you want to discover manually, or import them from a text file that contains a list of IPv4 addresses.

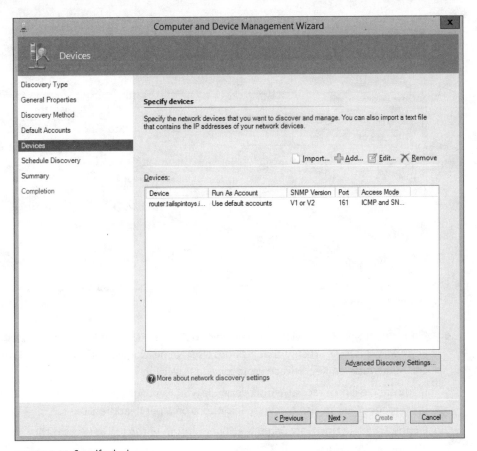

FIGURE 2-26 Specify devices

7. When adding devices manually, provide the following information as shown in Figure 2-27:

   ■ IPv4 address or FQDN of the device.

   ■ Access mode. This can be ICMP, SNMP, or ICMP and SNMP. If you choose ICMP and SNMP, the device must be accessible using both protocols.

   ■ Port number. The default is UDP port 161, but if you are using another port for SNMP you can change this.

   ■ SNMP version. This allows you to specify whether to use SNMP v1 or v2, or SNMP v3. If using SNMP v1 or v2, specify the Run As account that contains the community string.

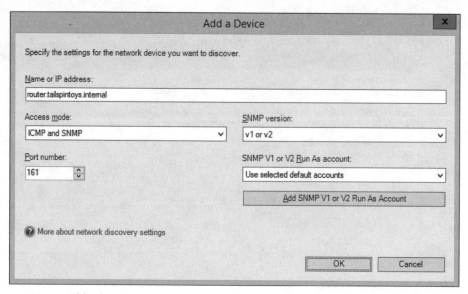

FIGURE 2-27 Add a device

8. If adding an SNMP v3 device, you will need to add the FQDN or IP address, as well as an SNMP v3 Run As account that includes User Name, Context, Authentication Protocol, Authentication Key, Privacy Protocol, and Privacy Key.

9. If you are creating a recursive discovery rule, you can configure filters based on IP address range. You can also configure exclusions on a per IP address basis.

10. On the Schedule Discovery page, specify how often to run the network device discovery rule. Figure 2-28 shows this page.

11. On the Summary page, review the settings, and click Create.

You can confirm successful discovery of network devices by viewing the Network Devices node, under Network Management in the Administration workspace of the Operations Manager console.

> **MORE INFO** **NETWORK DEVICE DISCOVERY**
>
> You can learn more about how Operations Manager can discover network devices at *http://technet.microsoft.com/en-us/library/hh278846.aspx*.

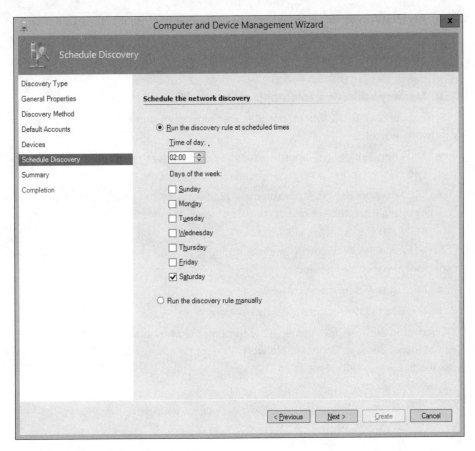

FIGURE 2-28 Network discovery schedule

Monitoring network devices

You can use Operations Manager to monitor physical and virtual network routers and switches, including the ports on those devices, VLANs (virtual local area network) and Host Standby Router Protocol (HSRP) groups that they are members of, as well as the status of supported firewall and load balancing devices. Specifically, you can use Operations Manager to monitor the following aspects of network devices:

- **Connection health** Monitor from the perspective of the network device and devices connected to the monitored network device.

- **VLAN health** Allows you to view the health state of switches that participate in a specific VLAN.

- **HSRP group health** View the health state of the devices that participate in a HSRP group.

- **Port/Interface**   Monitor the operational and administrative status of device ports and interfaces.
- **Processor utilization**   Monitor the processor utilization of supported network devices.
- **Memory utilization**   Monitor the memory utilization of supported network devices.

System Center 2012 R2 Operations Manager supports monitoring the following numbers of network devices:

- 2000 network devices (approximately 25,000 monitored interfaces/ports) managed by two resource pools.
- 1000 network devices (approximately 12,500 monitored interfaces/ports) managed by a single resource pool that consists of three or more Operations Manager management servers.

To perform network discovery and monitoring, you need to ensure that the following management packs are installed:

- Microsoft.Windows.Server.NetworkDiscovery
- Microsoft.Windows.Client.NetworkDiscovery

Discovered network devices are visible through the Monitoring workspace of the Operations Manager console. Under the Network Monitoring node, shown in Figure 2-29, you can view the following information:

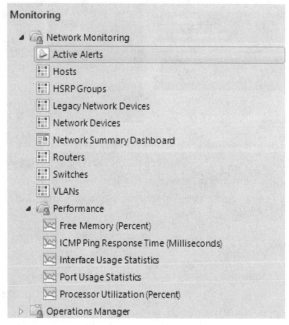

FIGURE 2-29 Network Monitoring categories

- Active Alerts
- Hosts
- HSRP Groups
- Legacy Network Devices
- Network Devices
- Network Summary Dashboard
- Routers
- Switches
- VLANS

You can also view the following device-related performance information:

- Free Memory (Percent)
- ICMP Ping Response Time (Milliseconds)
- Interface Usage Statistics
- Port Usage Statistics
- Processor Utilization (Percent)

You can also use the following Operations Manager dashboard views when monitoring network devices:

- **Network Summary Dashboard** Provides summary information, including which network devices are experiencing the highest processor utilization, or which interfaces are encountering the most errors.
- **Network Node Dashboard** Provides information about each network device. Includes alerts generated by each device and information including processor utilization.
- **Network Interface Dashboard** Provides information about network device interfaces/ports, including alerts generated by interfaces/ports and traffic statistics.
- **Network Vicinity Dashboard** Provides information on the relationship between discovered network devices and computers with the Operations Manager agent installed. This is useful for determining the cause of network outages.

MORE INFO **NETWORK DEVICE MONITORING**

You can learn more about network device monitoring at *http://technet.microsoft.com/en-us/library/hh212935.aspx.*

Using management packs

An Operations Manager management pack is a collection of elements that allow you to use Operations Manager to perform tasks, gather, and display important information about computers, applications, services, and devices. Management packs are often specific to a particular product, device, application, role, or service, and contain elements that extend Operations Manager's ability to integrate with that service. For example, the Microsoft Exchange Server 2013 management pack contains elements that allow Operations Manager to monitor important aspects of an Exchange Server 2013 deployment, just as the System Center Management Pack for SQL Server contains elements that allow Operations Manager to monitor important aspects of a SQL Server 2012 deployment. Individuals or organizations with detailed knowledge about how the managed object functions, write management packs. You can view the list of management packs imported into Operations Manager from the Management Packs node of the Administration workspace, as shown in Figure 2-30.

> **MORE INFO MANAGEMENT PACKS**
>
> You can learn more about Operations Manager management packs at *http://technet. microsoft.com/en-us/library/hh212794.aspx*.

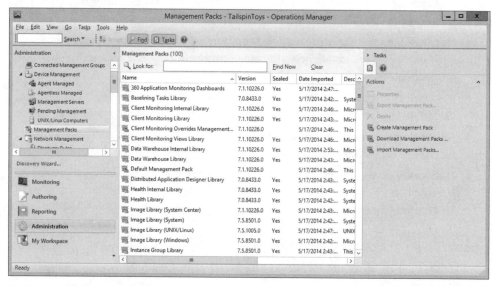

FIGURE 2-30 Management Packs

Management packs can include some or all of the following elements:

- **Monitors**   Provides information to the Operations Manager agent about which aspects of the managed object it should track. For example, which logs to monitor.

- **Rules** Determines which performance and discovery data the agent collects. It also determines which situations trigger alerts. For example, which event in a specific log should generate an Operations Manager alert.

- **Tasks** Allows an activity to be performed either through the agent or the Operations Manager console. For example, a task might restart a particular service. Tasks are triggered either by alerts or manually through the Operations Manager console. Tasks are performed by the Operations Manager agent or by the console (for example, when you trigger a ping task).

- **Views** Provides a customized interface for viewing information and managing managed objects.

- **Reports** Display insightful and meaningful data about the managed object. Customized reports come from the management pack authors to display information about the managed objects.

- **Object Discoveries** Identify objects that Operations Manager can monitor.

- **Run As profiles** Allows rules, tasks, monitors, and discoveries to be run using an alternate set of credentials.

- **Knowledge** These are helpful articles that provide Operations Manager administrators with diagnostic and problem resolution advice.

Management packs come as either sealed or unsealed. A sealed management pack is read-only. Sealed management packs are digitally signed by the management pack authors and use the .mp extension. This digital signature gives you confidence that a third party hasn't modified the contents of the management pack. You can make modifications to sealed management packs using overrides, described later in this chapter. Unsealed management packs usually use the .xml extension and can be created and modified by the Operations Manager Administrator.

EXAM TIP

Remember the difference between sealed and unsealed management packs.

Some management packs are designated libraries. Library management packs provide a set of classes on which other management packs build. Dependencies exist where one management pack makes references to content in another management pack. To view a management pack's dependencies, right-click the management pack and select the Dependencies tab, as shown in Figure 2-31. The information displayed on this tab will also provide you with a list of management packs that depend on this management pack.

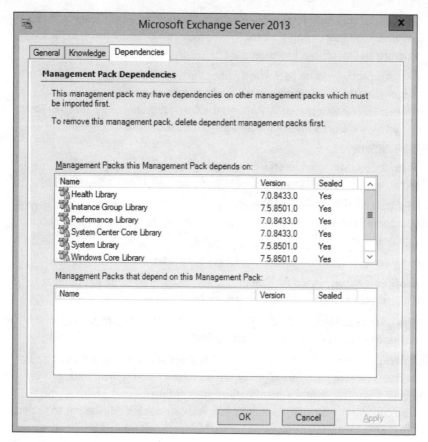

FIGURE 2-31 Management pack dependencies

Importing management packs

While Operations Manager ships with a collection of management packs, to get the most out of the product, you'll need to import management packs that are specific to the type of objects that you want to monitor. You can use several methods to obtain Operations Manager management packs.

The simplest method is to download and import management packs from the Microsoft System Center Marketplace using the Operations Manager console. Figure 2-32 shows searching for and selecting a SQL Server 2012 related management pack from the online catalog. System Center Marketplace stores a very large number of management packs and should be the first place you look when you need an Operations Manager management pack.

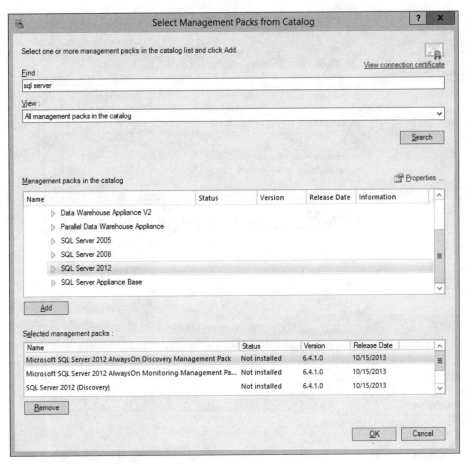

FIGURE 2-32 Management pack catalog

You can use the Operations Manager console to download management packs from the online catalog to import at a later point in time. Figure 2-33 shows the Operations Manager console interface for downloading management packs. This allows you to store important management packs in a separate location for easy import into other Operations Manager management groups.

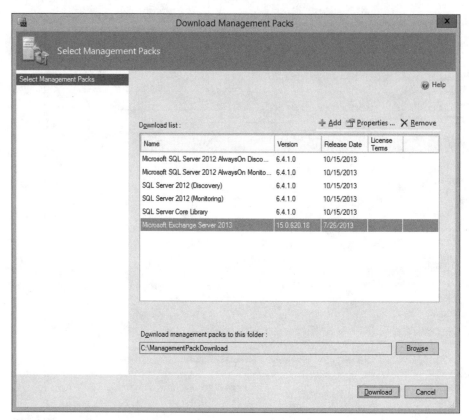

FIGURE 2-33 Management pack download

If you've obtained the management pack files already, you can import them from local storage using the Operations Manager console. When importing sealed management packs, you must ensure that the Operations Manager server trusts the CA that issued the signing certificate used to sign the sealed management pack. If the Operations Manager server doesn't trust the CA that issued the signing certificate that was used to sign the sealed management pack, you won't be able to import the sealed management pack. Prior to attempting to import management packs, ensure that you've imported any management pack dependencies. You won't be able to import a management pack if dependency management packs are not present on the Operations Manager server. Figure 2-34 shows importing SQL Server 2012 and Exchange Server 2013 management packs.

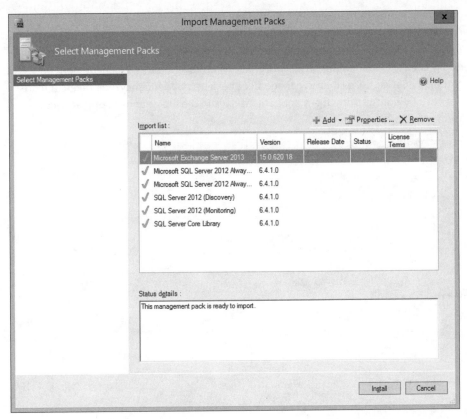

FIGURE 2-34 Import management pack

Important to note is that once you have imported a management pack, Operations Manager will automatically begin monitoring relevant objects based on the default management pack configurations and thresholds. This can lead to an increase in alerts, depending on the configuration of the management pack that you have imported.

> **MORE INFO** **IMPORTING MANAGEMENT PACKS**
>
> You can learn more about importing management packs at *http://technet.microsoft.com/en-us/library/hh212691.aspx.*

Removing management packs

Removing a management pack eliminates all of the settings and thresholds associated with the management pack. For example, if you've upgraded all of the SQL Server instances in your organization to SQL Server 2014, you might choose to remove management packs that were used to monitor previous versions of SQL Server.

You can only remove a management pack if any dependent management packs have also been removed. For example, Figure 2-35 shows that the SQL Server Core Library management pack is required for three other management packs. Before you are able to remove the SQL Server Core Library management pack, you'll have to remove the three management packs that list the SQL Server Core Library management pack as a dependency. You delete a management pack by right-clicking the management pack in the Operations Manager console, and clicking Delete.

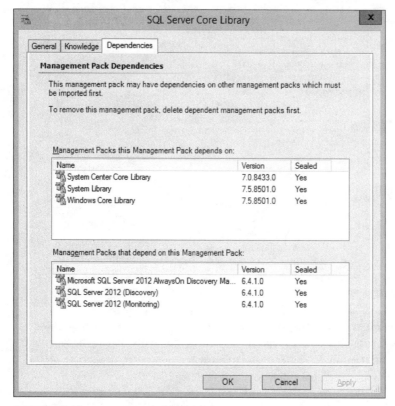

FIGURE 2-35 Management pack dependencies

MORE INFO **REMOVING MANAGEMENT PACKS**

You can learn more about removing management packs at *http://technet.microsoft.com/ en-us/library/hh230746.aspx*.

Objective summary

- You can deploy the Operations Manager agent to computers that are members of a trusted Active Directory domain using the Discovery Wizard. You can also manually install the agent, or include it in an operating system image.

- You can deploy the Operations Manager agent to supported versions of UNIX and Linux using the Discovery Wizard, or by manually installing the agent.

- When manually installing the agent, or including it in an image, you'll need to configure agent authorization.

- You can use Operations Manager to manage network devices that support the SNMP v1, v2, or v3 protocols.

- Management packs allow you to enhance the functionality of Operations Manager.

- You can only import a management pack if the management pack dependencies are already installed.

- You can only remove a management pack if no other management packs exist, that have the management pack you want to remove as a dependency.

Objective review

Answer the following questions to test your knowledge of the information in this objective. You can find the answers to these questions and explanations of why each answer choice is correct or incorrect in the "Answers" section at the end of the chapter.

1. You are creating a Run As account to be used with a network device discovery rule. All network devices in your organization support SNMP v2. Which of the following must you include when configuring the Run As account?

   A. Community string.

   B. Device name.

   C. Device IP address.

   D. Authentication key.

2. You want to ensure that all newly deployed servers in your organization have the Operations Manager agent installed and connected to the single management server. All newly deployed servers are automatically joined to an AD DS domain. Which of the following must you configure to accomplish this goal?

   A. Configure Active Directory automatic agent assignment.

   B. Configure the Global Management Server additional setting Automatically Approve New Manually Installed Agents.

   C. Configure the Global Management Server settings to Reject New Manual Agent Installations.

   D. Configure the Global Management Server settings to Review New Manual Agent Installations In Pending Management View.

3. Which of the following utilities do you use to configure Active Directory automatic agent assignment?

   A. MOMADadmin.exe.

   B. Cmtrace.exe.

   C. MOMAgent.msi.

   D. GPedit.msc.

Objective 2.2: Configure end-to-end monitoring

Once you have imported management packs, you'll need to tune them so that they provide you with useful monitoring information. Another form of monitoring is synthetic transactions, which allow you to configure monitoring for a variety of different objects, from websites, through to UNIX processes, network ports, and Windows Services. If you want to verify the functionality of your organization's web applications from external locations, you can configure Global Service Monitor. If you want to monitor complex multi-tier applications, you can configure a distributed application model.

Managing management packs

Subject matter experts create Operations Manager management packs so that Operations Manager will provide you with useful information about a particular application, service, role, or device. However, while the experts who created the management pack know a large amount about the subject of the management pack, they don't know anything about your specific private cloud environment. Importing the management pack is only the first part of the management pack's lifecycle. You also need to test, tune, and alter each management pack so that it provides you with the information that you actually need to know to perform your job.

> **MORE INFO MANAGEMENT PACK LIFECYCLE**
>
> You can learn more about the management pack lifecycle at *http://technet.microsoft.com/ en-us/library/hh212732.aspx*.

Microsoft describes the management pack lifecycle in the following manner:

- **Review and evaluate in pre-production environment**   Before deploying a management pack into your organization's production environment, you should evaluate the management pack in a test or development environment.
- **Tune the management pack settings**   Use overrides to tune the management pack. Save these overrides in a separate unsealed management pack.
- **Deploy the management packs into production environment**   When you do this, you'll also import the separate, unsealed management packs that contained the overrides that you created in your test or development environment.
- **Maintain the management pack**   Once the management pack has been deployed, you may still need to perform additional tuning. The following changes in circumstances should lead you to retune the management pack:
- **Changing business needs**   Your organizational requirements might change in terms of the monitoring of the object that is the subject of the management pack. This may necessitate reevaluating how the management pack has been tuned.
- **The environment changes**   For example, there is a change in computer hardware, operating system, or virtual machine configuration that impacts the monitored object.

- **Additional applications**   You add a new application to the environment that interacts with the monitored object in a substantive way.

- **Application upgrade**   You should tune the management pack if the management pack monitors an application that you've upgraded, or to which you've applied a service pack.

- **Updated management pack**   If the vendor releases an updated version of the management pack, you may need to begin the process again. Management pack upgrades provide a great example as to why you should document the management pack tuning process. If you've created documentation explaining how you've tuned the management pack, you'll be able to refer to it when tuning a new version of the management pack.

Overrides

When you first import a management pack, you may find that while it tells you many useful things about the product, service, device, or object that you should know, it also tells you many things about the product, service, device, or object that you aren't interested in. Overrides allow you to alter the settings of a rule or a monitor in a sealed management pack without changing the rule or monitor itself.

To configure an override for a rule, perform the following steps:

1. In the Authoring workspace of the Operations Manager console, expand Management Pack Objects, and click the Rules node.

2. Locate the rule for which you want to create the override. Figure 2-36 shows a rule named MSSQL 2012: Logins Per Second.

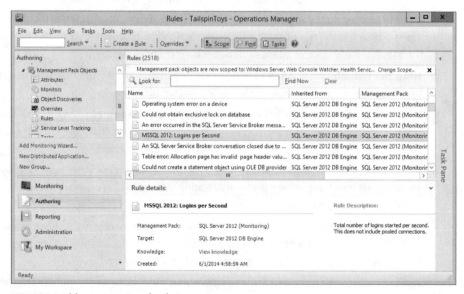

FIGURE 2-36 Management pack rules

3. Right-click the rule, and click Properties. On the Overrides tab, shown in Figure 2-37, click Disable to disable the rule, or click Override to change the parameters of the rule.

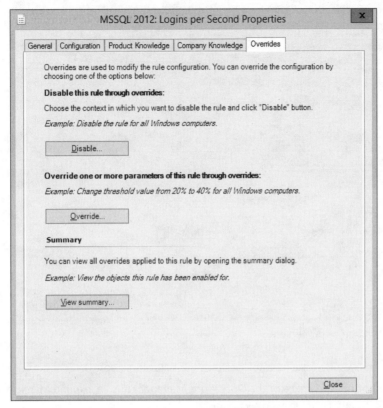

FIGURE 2-37 Configure overrides

4. When you click Override, you'll be asked to choose between all objects of the class that the override applies to, to a group, to a specific object of the class, or for all objects of another class. If you only wanted to configure the override on logins per second for one SQL Server instance, you'd choose the Specific Object Of The Class option.

5. On the Override Properties dialog box, you then select the parameter name that you want to override, provide a new override value, select the option to enforce the override, and select an unsealed management pack in which to store the override. You should create a management pack to store for overrides of a specific management pack, otherwise it will be stored in the default management pack. Figure 2-38 shows that the Frequency parameter of the MSSQL 2012: Logins Per Second rule has been altered to 500.

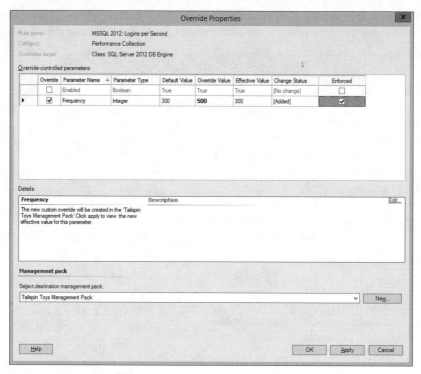

FIGURE 2-38 Override properties

To configure an override for a monitor, perform the following steps:

1. In the Authoring workspace of the Operations Manager console, expand Management Pack Objects, and click the Monitors node.

2. Select the monitor that you want to configure the override for. Figure 2-39 shows the Server Resources monitor in the Exchange Server Management pack.

FIGURE 2-39 Monitors

3. Right-click the monitor that you want to configure the override for, and click Properties.

4. On the Overrides tab, shown in Figure 2-40, click the Monitor that you wish to configure the override for, and click Override. Click Disable if you want to disable the monitor instead.

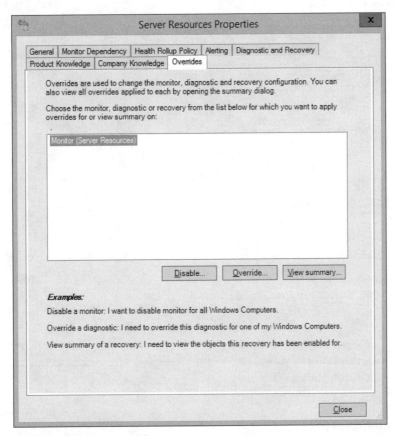

FIGURE 2-40 Monitor overrides

5. When you click Override, you'll be given the option of creating an override for all objects in the class, for a group, for a specific object, or for objects in another class. If you only want to configure an override for a specific monitored object, rather than all objects the monitor is used with, select Specific Object. You can only select a specific object if Operations Manager already monitors that object.

6. On the Override Properties dialog box, select the parameter that you want to modify, set the Override value, ensure that the Enforced checkbox is selected, and choose the unsealed management pack in which to store the override. For example, in Figure 2-41, the Alert Priority is set to Medium, from Low.

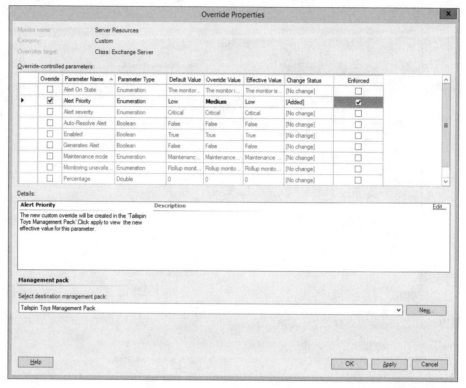

FIGURE 2-41 Override options

> **MORE INFO OVERRIDES**
>
> You can learn more about Operations Manager management pack overrides at *http://tech-net.microsoft.com/en-us/library/hh212869.aspx.*

Tuning management packs

Tuning a management pack is the process of adjusting what the management pack is telling you so it provides you with the information that you want to know, rather than the information that the management pack authors think you need to know. When tuning management packs, you should consult with the service owner, subject matter experts, and the operations team members who are responsible for monitoring and responding to alerts.

You can use the following approach when tuning management packs:

- Start by tuning the highest severity alerts first, and then work through towards the lowest.

- Remember that rules generate alerts that do not auto-close when the issue that caused the alert is resolved. Alerts generated by monitors close, then the issue is fixed.

- Evaluate how actionable an alert is. Actionable alerts are those where you are informed what event occurred to trigger the alert, and where there are clear steps to resolve the cause of the alert. Consider disabling alerts for rules where no action is required.

- Evaluate the validity of the alert. Some alerts will inform you that they were triggered by a particular event, such as a service failing. If you investigate and find that the service that supposedly triggered the alert hasn't failed, assess whether you should disable the alert.

- Evaluate whether multiple alerts are informing you about the same issue. You can suppress those alerts that are providing you with duplicate notification about the same issue.

Microsoft provides the following recommendations for management pack tuning:

- Only import a single management pack at a time. This gives you a chance to concentrate on tuning one management pack. Tuning more than one management pack concurrently consumes substantially more time.

- Review alerts reported for servers monitored by the newly imported management pack. Use the Alerts and Most Common Alerts reports to determine which alerts are being created the most often, and use this as a starting point for tuning.

- Disable monitors or rules when you determine that you don't need to be notified about a particular issue.

- Alter the threshold of the monitor generating the alert if you want the underlying issue to be monitored, but not at the sensitivity at which the current monitor is configured.

- Save overrides to an unsealed management pack that uses the name Management-Pack_Overrides. For example, call the management pack that stores the overrides for the Microsoft Exchange Server 2013 management pack, Microsoft Exchange Server 2013_Overrides. This simplifies the process of keeping track of overrides.

> **MORE INFO MANAGEMENT PACK TUNING**
>
> You can learn more about tuning Operations Manager management packs at *http://tech-net.microsoft.com/en-us/library/hh230704.aspx*.

Exporting management packs

Exporting a management pack allows you to create a backup of that management pack. This can be useful for management packs that store overrides and customizations as exporting that management pack allows you to save all of the overrides and customizations that you configured. This allows you to then import the custom unsealed management pack to a management server in another management group so that you can use the overrides and customizations with the sealed management pack in that management group. For example, you might spend time tuning a new sealed management pack in a development-monitoring environment before introducing it into a production-monitoring environment. Prior to importing the management pack into the production environment, you would export the customizations into a separate unsealed management pack, importing both the sealed and unsealed management pack.

If you are using the Operations Manager console, you're only able to export unsealed management packs. If necessary, you can export a sealed management pack using the Export-SCOMManagementPack Windows PowerShell cmdlet, though it is usually simpler to reimport the sealed management pack from the location from which you originally obtained it.

> **MORE INFO EXPORTING MANAGEMENT PACKS**
>
> You can learn more about exporting management packs at *http://technet.microsoft.com/en-us/library/hh320149.aspx*.

Configuring synthetic transactions

Synthetic transactions are a form of outside-in monitoring which do not require an agent on the monitored object. Synthetic transactions are performed by a third computer, with the Operations Manager agent installed, called a watcher node. Synthetic transactions are tests that are performed to determine the availability or performance of one of the following items:

- OLD DB Data Source
- Process
- TCP Port
- UNIX or Linux Log File
- UNIX or Linux Process
- Web Application Availability
- Web Application Transaction
- Windows Service

You can configure Operations Manager to run tests against these items by configuring one of the management pack templates, available through the Authoring workspace of the Operations Manager console, and shown in Figure 2-42. The Application Performance Monitoring template, also listed here, is covered later in the chapter.

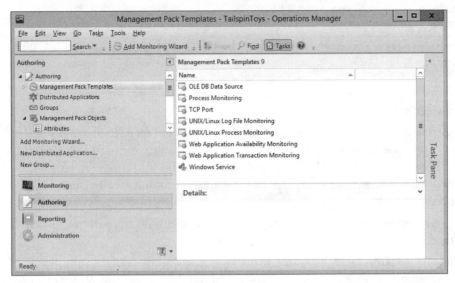

FIGURE 2-42 Management pack templates

The tests that form the basis of synthetic transactions are initiated from a computer termed a watcher node. A watcher node can be a management server, a computer or device that hosts an Operations Manager agent. When configuring certain synthetic transactions, you specify which computers will function as watcher nodes, as shown in Figure 2-43.

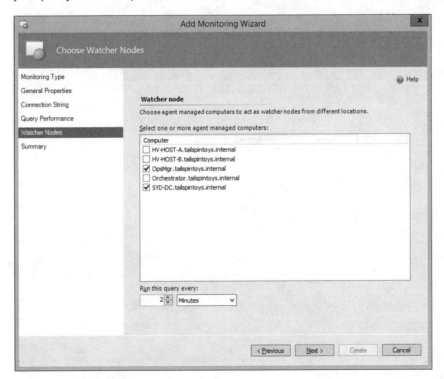

FIGURE 2-43 Watcher nodes

MORE INFO WATCHER NODES

You can learn more about watcher nodes at *http://technet.microsoft.com/en-us/library/ hh457584.aspx*.

OLE DB data source

You can use the OLE DB data source template to create a synthetic transaction to monitor the performance and availability of any database, not just those running Microsoft's SQL Server, that you can establish a connection to through OLE DB. It's possible to create this synthetic transaction even when the computer that hosts the database does not have an Operations Manager agent installed.

To create a synthetic transaction using the OLE DB Data Source Wizard, perform the following steps:

1. Under Management Pack Templates, in the Authoring workspace of the Operations Manager console, click OLE DB Data Source, and click Add Monitoring Wizard on the ribbon.

2. On the Monitoring Type page, select OLE DB Data Source, as shown in Figure 2-44, and click Next.

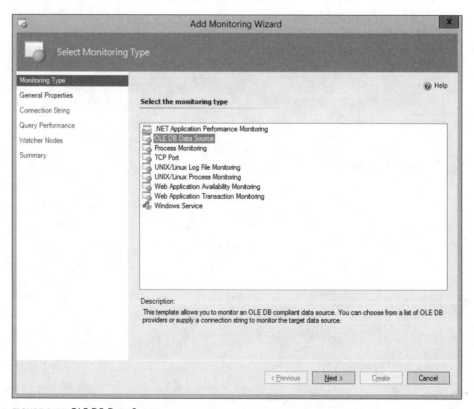

FIGURE 2-44 OLE DB Data Source

3. On the General Properties page, provide a name for the monitor, and select an unsealed management pack in which to store the monitor.

4. On the Connection String page, provide the connection string to the database that you will be connecting to with the monitor. Provide a query that will be used to perform the test and specify a timeout. Figure 2-45 shows a query against the Operations Manager database.

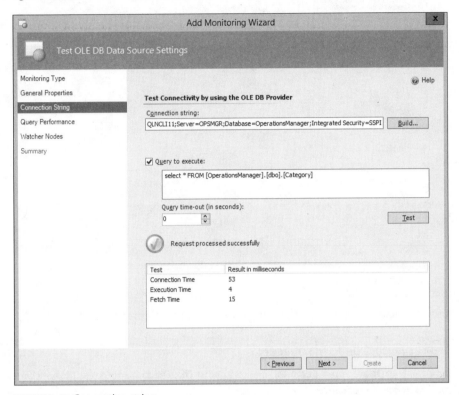

FIGURE 2-45 Connection string

5. On the Query Performance page, select the measurements that you want to monitor, the error threshold, and the warning thresholds, as shown in Figure 2-46.

6. On the Watcher Nodes page, specify the computers with the Operations Manager agent installed from which the OLE DB test will be performed.

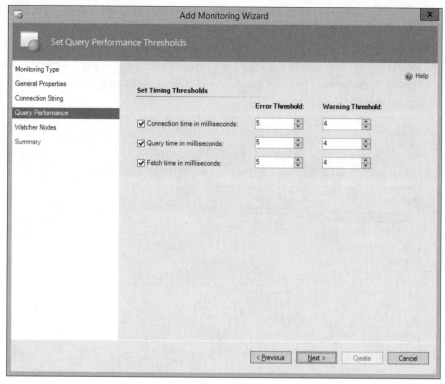

FIGURE 2-46 Query performance

7. Complete the wizard to create the OLE DB synthetic transaction.

> **MORE INFO OLE DB DATA SOURCE**
>
> You can learn more about performing tests against OLE DB data sources at *http://technet. microsoft.com/en-us/library/hh457575.aspx*.

Process

A process monitoring synthetic transaction allows you to monitor whether a specific process is running on a computer. You can use a process monitoring synthetic transaction to determine the following information:

- Number of processes running
- Amount of time that the process has been running
- Processor utilization of the process
- Process memory utilization

When configuring a process monitoring synthetic transaction, you can also configure an alert to be raised if the processor or memory utilization exceeds a specific threshold, as shown in Figure 2-47.

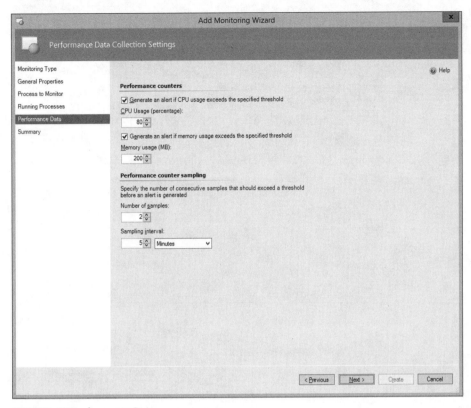

FIGURE 2-47 Performance Data

> **MORE INFO PROCESSES**
>
> You can learn more performing tests against processes at *http://technet.microsoft.com/ en-us/library/hh457551.aspx.*

TCP Port

A TCP Port-based synthetic transaction allows you to perform a test to determine if a service, host, or device is contactable over the network. When creating a TCP Port-based synthetic transaction, you can determine the following:

- Can the target host be contacted?
- Is the connection to the target host accepted?
- Has the connection to the target host timed out?
- Can the FQDN of the target host be resolved?

When configuring the TCP Port-based synthetic transaction, you specify the computer name or IP address, and the port that you want the transaction to connect to. Figure 2-48 shows a synthetic transaction that will connect to host Smtp.tailspintoys.internal on port 25.

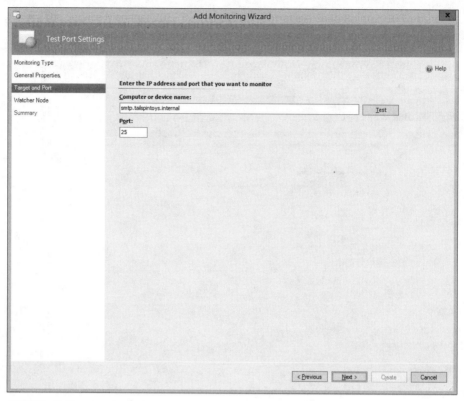

FIGURE 2-48 Target and port

> **MORE INFO** **TCP PORTS**
>
> You can learn more about performing tests against TCP Ports at *http://technet.microsoft. com/en-us/library/hh457544.aspx.*

UNIX or Linux log file

The UNIX or Linux log file synthetic transaction type allows you to check whether specific text is detected in a certain log file residing on a computer running the UNIX or Linux operating systems. When configuring the synthetic transaction, you must provide the following information:

- **Computer Name** This is the name of a computer running UNIX or Linux that has the Operations Manager agent installed and which hosts the log file that you want to monitor. As an alternative, you can specify a Computer Group, which will allow you to use the synthetic transaction to monitor multiple computers with the UNIX or Linux operating system.

- **Log file path**   The path to, and name of, the log file
- **Regular expression**   This is a regular expression to detect the text that must occur in the log file to trigger an alert. If the text is a simple string, you don't have to use a regular expression.

MORE INFO **UNIX OR LINUX LOG FILES**

You can learn more about performing tests on UNIX or Linux log files at *http://technet. microsoft.com/en-us/library/hh457589.aspx*.

UNIX or Linux Process

You can use the UNIX or Linux Process synthetic transaction type to determine if a particular process is currently running on a computer running the UNIX or Linux operating systems that have the Operations Manager agent installed. When configuring a synthetic transaction type to determine if a process is running on a computer with a supported UNIX or Linux operating system installed, you must provide the following information:

- **Process name**   The name of the process.
- **Computer group**   The Operations Manager computer group that contains the UNIX or Linux hosts that you want to check for the process.
- **Alert sensitivity**   The sensitivity of the alert to raise if the process is not running.

You can also configure a regular expression to filter process arguments to separate multiple instances of a process with the same name.

MORE INFO **UNIX OR LINUX PROCESSES**

You can learn more about performing tests against UNIX or Linux Processes at *http://technet.microsoft.com/en-us/library/hh457572.aspx*.

Web application availability

A web application availability synthetic transaction allows you to create a monitoring test for one or more web application URLs to determine that they respond to basic requests. To create a web application availability synthetic transaction, perform the following steps:

1. Click the Management Pack Templates node in the Authoring workspace of the Operations Manager console, and then click Add Monitoring Wizard on the ribbon.
2. On the Monitoring Type page, select Web Application Availability Monitoring, as shown in Figure 2-49, and click Next.

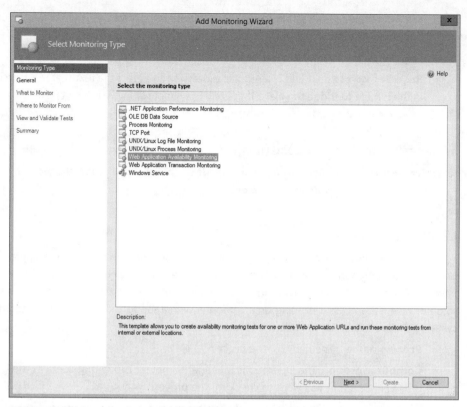

FIGURE 2-49 Web application availability monitoring

3. On the General page of the Add Monitoring Wizard, provide a name for the synthetic transaction monitor, and specify an unsealed management pack in which to store the transaction's settings.

4. On the Enter URLs To Be Monitored page, specify the website name and the website address. Figure 2-50 shows the default IIS site of the server named Orchestrator.tail-spintoys.internal.

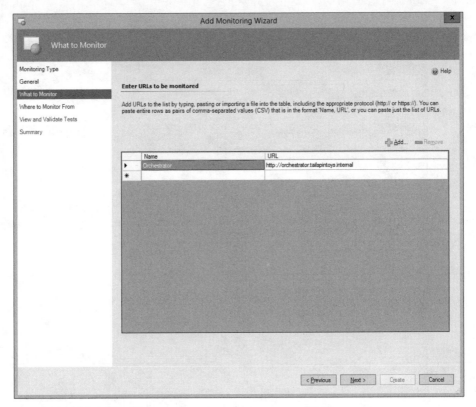

FIGURE 2-50 URLs to monitor

5. On the Where To Monitor From page, specify which computers that have the Operations Manager agent installed will function as watcher hosts.

6. On the View And Validate Tests page, click Run Test to verify that the synthetic transaction works, as shown in Figure 2-51.

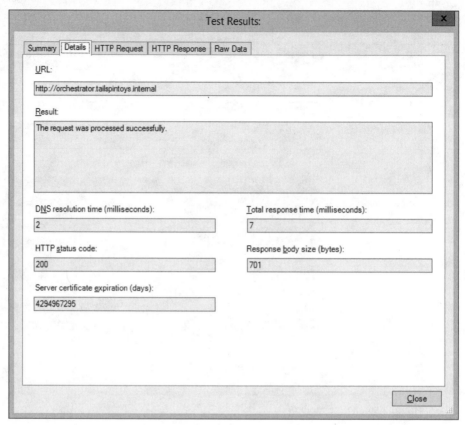

FIGURE 2-51 Test results

7. Complete the wizard to create the synthetic transaction.

> **MORE INFO** **WEB APPLICATION AVAILABILITY**
>
> You can learn more about performing tests against web application availability at *http://technet.microsoft.com/en-us/library/hh881883.aspx.*

Web application transaction

A web application transaction synthetic monitor goes further than a web application availability synthetic transaction as it not only verifies that the target web application is available, but that the web application responds to specific prompts and inputs, including authentication.

You can use the Web Recorder to record a browser session that includes multiple requests to a target web application. You can then use the information generated by the Web Recorder as the transaction used in the synthetic monitor.

To record a web application session and then create a synthetic monitor based on that information, perform the following steps:

1. In the Authoring workspace of the Operations Manager console, select Web Application Transaction Monitoring under Management Pack Templates.

2. In the Tasks menu, click Custom Actions, and then click Record A Browser Session.

3. On the Web Application Editor, shown in Figure 2-52, provide a name and select an unsealed management pack in which to store the session information.

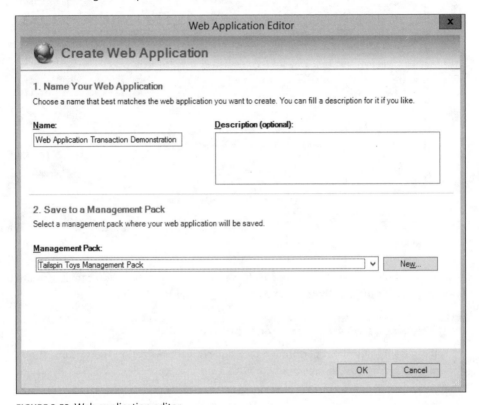

FIGURE 2-52 Web application editor

4. On the Web Application Editor - Browsing Session dialog box, click Start Capture. Internet Explorer will launch. Browse to the web application and perform the interaction that you want to test.

5. When you complete the browsing session, close the browser, click Stop Capture, click Apply on the Web Application Editor, then select a watcher node, and click Apply again. Verify that the Web Application Data Imported Successfully message is displayed, as shown in Figure 2-53, and then close the Web Application Editor dialog box.

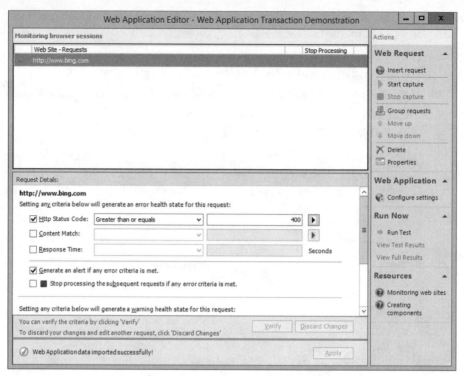

FIGURE 2-53 Web application editor

Clicking Apply creates the web application synthetic transaction. You can also create the web application synthetic transaction by performing the steps in the wizard.

> **MORE INFO** **WEB APPLICATION TRANSACTIONS**
>
> You can learn more about performing tests against web application Transactions at *http://technet.microsoft.com/en-us/library/hh457553.aspx*.

Windows Service

You can create a Windows Service synthetic transaction to determine the state of a service running on a Windows-based computer. When configuring the transaction, you need to provide the following information:

- Service name
- Operations Manager computer group

Once the service is selected, you can configure alerts to be triggered if specific CPU and memory thresholds are exceeded. Figure 2-54 shows a Windows Service synthetic transaction where an alert will be triggered if the CPU utilization exceeds 80 percent and the memory utilization exceeds 150 MB.

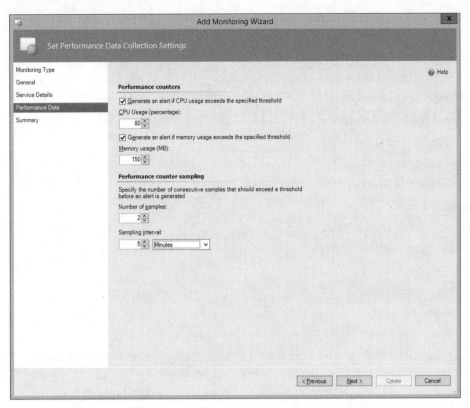

FIGURE 2-54 Performance data

MORE INFO WINDOWS SERVICE

You can learn more about performing tests against Windows Services at *http://technet.*
microsoft.com/en-us/library/hh457595.aspx.

EXAM TIP

Remember the different types of synthetic transactions that you can configure.

Using Global Service Monitor

System Center Global Service Monitor is a cloud service that allows you to perform outside-in monitoring of your organization's external web-based applications. Outside-in monitoring is a type of monitoring that checks the availability and functionality of the monitored web-based application from a location external to your organization's internal network. Rather than checking whether a web-based application is functioning from the perspective of a user and host on your organization's internal network, a series of tests are performed against the web application from multiple locations around the world including:

- Amsterdam, Netherlands
- Chicago, United States
- London, United Kingdom
- Los Angeles, United States
- Miami, United States
- Moscow, Russia
- Newark, United States
- Paris, France
- San Antonio, United States
- Sao Paulo, Brazil
- Singapore
- Stockholm, Sweden
- Sydney, Australia
- Zurich, Switzerland

Global Service Monitor runs tests against the web application, rather than just verifying that the web server that hosts the application is responding to traffic requests. You can configure tests using Global Service Monitor where a test user signs on to the web application and performs certain tasks, such as ordering an item from an online store.

Global Service Monitor has the following conditions:

- System Center 2012 Operations Manager or later must be deployed in your environment.
- You must have a System Center Global Service Monitor subscription.
- The Operations Manager servers in the management server pool that will be used with Global Service Monitor must be able to communicate with hosts on the Internet using the HTTP protocol.
- Windows Identity Foundation must be installed on the management server that communicates with the Global Service Monitor servers in the cloud.

Global Service Monitor provides the following dashboards:

- **Summary Dashboard**   This dashboard provides simple availability information through a world map showing the locations that monitoring is being performed from. It also displays rollup test status for each location.
- **Detailed Dashboard**   This dashboard allows you to view the results of specific tests and alerts. For each web application that you are monitoring, you can check a location, and the tests performed from that location that you want to investigate.

- **Health Explorer**   This allows you to view the health status of a web application avail-ability test on a per-location basis.
- **Test Visualization Dashboard**   This allows you to view Global Service Monitor web test results, including performance data.

> *MORE INFO* **GLOBAL SERVICE MONITOR**
>
> You can learn more about System Center Global Service Monitor at *http://technet. microsoft.com/en-us/library/jj860368.aspx.*

Application Performance Monitoring

Application Performance Monitoring (APM) allows you to monitor Internet Information Services (IIS) hosted .NET and Windows Communication Foundation (WCF) applications from both the server and client side perspectives. This allows you to use Operations Manager to collect detailed information about a specific application's performance of reliability.

You use the .NET Application Performance Monitoring Template, available through the Authoring workspace of the Operations console, to configure Application Performance Monitoring. To view Application Performance Monitoring event details, it is necessary to have installed an instance of the Operations Manger web console. You'll also have to import the following management packs and their dependencies:

- Windows Server 2008 IIS 7.0
- Operations Manager APM Web IIS 7

If monitoring Windows Server 2012 or Windows Server 2012 R2, you'll need to import the following management packs and their dependencies:

- Microsoft Windows Server 2012 IIS 8
- Microsoft System Center APM Web IIS 8

Once these management packs are installed, you'll be able to view the ASP.NET applica-tions that Operations Manager finds in the Monitoring workspace, under Application Moni-toring, under the .NET Monitoring node in the ASP.NET Web Application Inventory node. You'll be able to view WCF applications under the IIS Hosted WCF Web Service Inventory node. Once APM discovers an application, IIS will usually need to be restarted. This allows the application pools to recycle, enabling the APM extensions, and allowing the APM function, to be registered with the application.

The server-side monitoring capabilities of APM include:

- Performance event monitoring and alerting
- Exception event monitoring and alerting
- Modifying performance event threshold
- Configuring performance event monitoring thresholds and sensitivity on a per-namespace or per-method basis

- Configuring exception event monitoring types on a per-exception or per-exception handler basis.

The client-side monitoring capabilities of APM include:

- Performance event monitoring and alerting
- Exception event monitoring and alerting
- Performance event thresholds for:
  - Page load
  - Asynchronous JavaScript and XML
  - WCF
- Collecting data related to images, scripts, CSS, HTML, global variables, and exception stack
- Collecting load balancer header data

To configure Application Performance Monitoring, perform the following steps:

1. In the Authoring workspace of the Operations Manager console, click Management Pack Templates, and then click Add Monitoring Wizard on the ribbon.

2. On the Monitoring Type page, shown in Figure 2-55, click .NET Application Performance Monitoring.

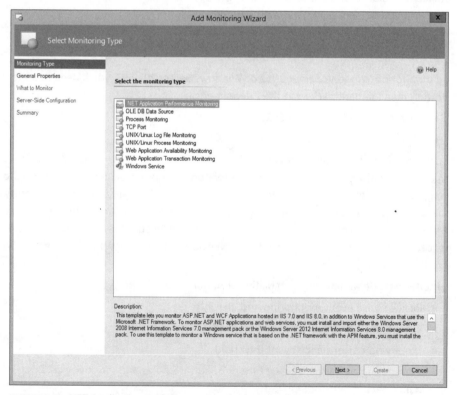

FIGURE 2-55 .NET Application Performance Monitoring template

3. On the General Properties page, provide the name of the monitor and specify an un-sealed management pack in which to store the monitor files.

4. On the What To Monitor page, click Add. On the Object Search page, click Search. A list of web applications and services that have been discovered on servers that host the Operations Manager agent will be displayed. Select the applications that you want to manage, and click Add. This dialog box is shown in Figure 2-56.

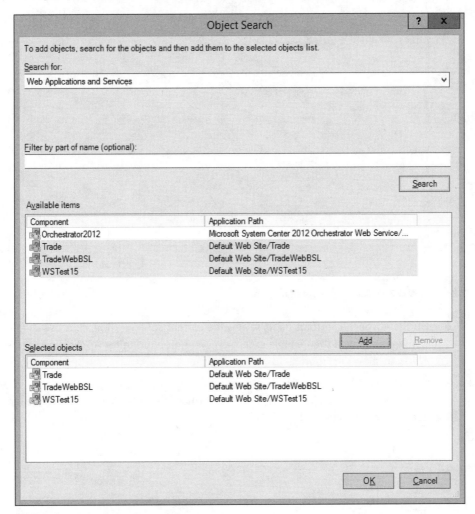

FIGURE 2-56 Web application search

5. On the Server-Side configuration, select Enable Additional Configuration Options For Server-Side And Client-Side Monitoring, as shown in Figure 2-57, and then click Advanced Settings.

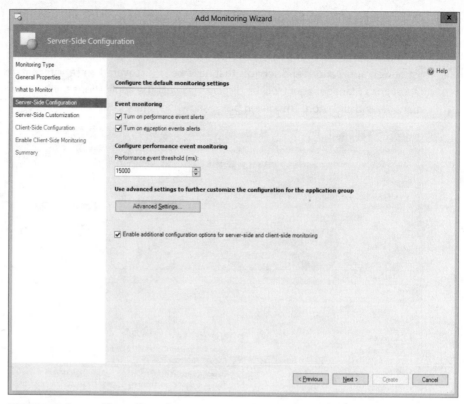

FIGURE 2-57 Server-side configuration

6. On the Advanced Settings page, review the current configuration, click Use Default Configuration, and then enable exception event monitoring for Application Failure Alerts, as shown in Figure 2-58.

7. On the Server-Side Customization page, select the first segment, and click Customize. Verify that you can configure separate performance event monitoring settings for each application segment, and then click OK.

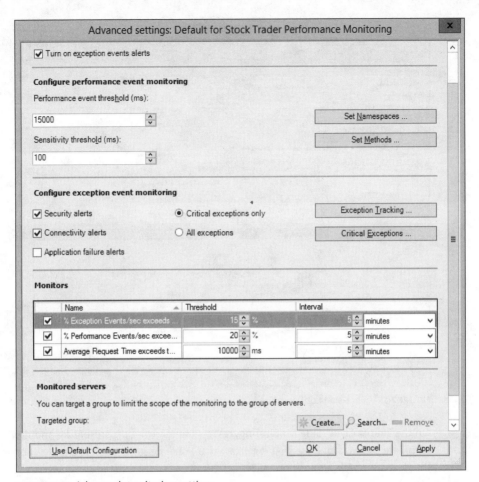

FIGURE 2-58 Advanced monitoring settings

8. On the Client-Side Configuration page, enable performance event alerts and exception event alerts, as shown in Figure 2-59. Review the page load threshold, and Ajax and WCF threshold settings.

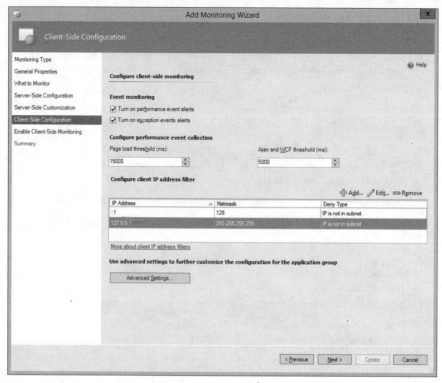

FIGURE 2-59 Client-side configuration

9. On the Enable Client-Side Monitoring, review the information presented, and then complete the wizard. Note that it is likely that you'll need to restart IIS on the server that hosts the web application.

> **MORE INFO** APPLICATION PERFORMANCE MONITORING
>
> You can learn more about Application Performance Monitoring at *http://technet.microsoft. com/en-us/library/hh457578.aspx*.

Creating distributed application models

A distributed application is one that consists of multiple objects. For example, a distributed application could comprise a database running on one monitored computer, a web server running on another computer, and a device that functions as a network load balancer. In Operations Manager, you can monitor each of the disparate objects that comprise the distributed application as a way of monitoring the overall health of the application. To be included in a distributed application, Operations Manager must already monitor each of these objects before you can add them to a distributed application using the Distributed Applications Designer, a tool available from the Operations Manager console.

The Distributed Application Designer allows you to create distributed applications using a graphical tool. This graphical tool is shown in Figure 2-60. The figure shows three groups named Databases, Management Servers, and Infrastructure.

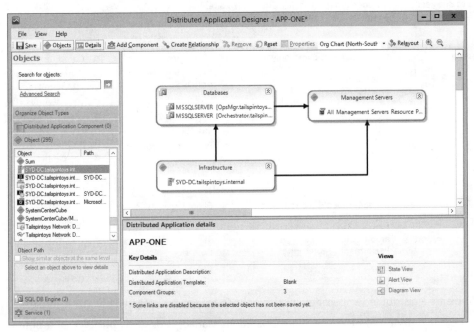

FIGURE 2-60 Distributed Application Designer

You create distributed applications with the distributed application designer by using the following:

- **Objects**   Any object that has been discovered by Operations Manager can be used when building a distributed application.

- **Component Groups**   These are collections of objects. Before you can add an object to a distributed application, you need to add that object to the component group. Component groups can contain any type of object, though it's also possible to restrict component groups to objects of a specific class.

- **Relationships**   These allow you to express that a relationship exists between two different component groups.

You can build a distributed application in the Distributed Application Designer from a blank template, or use one of the following built-in templates listed in Table 2-1.

TABLE 2-1 Distributed application templates

Template Name	Description	Container Groups	Contained Classes
Line of Business Web Application	Includes groups that describe a common web application	Web Sites Databases	Web Sites Database
Messaging	Includes groups commonly used by messaging services. This template is shown in Figure 2-61.	■ Messaging clients ■ Messaging components ■ Directory Services ■ Network Services ■ Storage ■ Physical Network	■ Computer Role ■ Distributed Application segment ■ Logical Application ■ Logical Hardware segment ■ Network Device ■ Perspective ■ Physical Entity ■ Service
.NET 3-Tier Application	Includes objects and data from synthetic transactions as well as data generated through Application Performance Monitoring	■ Client Perspective ■ Presentation Tier ■ Business Tier ■ Data Tier	■ Perspective ■ ASP.NET application ■ .NET application segment ■ Database

To create a distributed application, perform the following general steps:

1. In the Authoring workspace of the Operations Manager console, right-click Distributed Applications, and click Create A New Distributed Application.

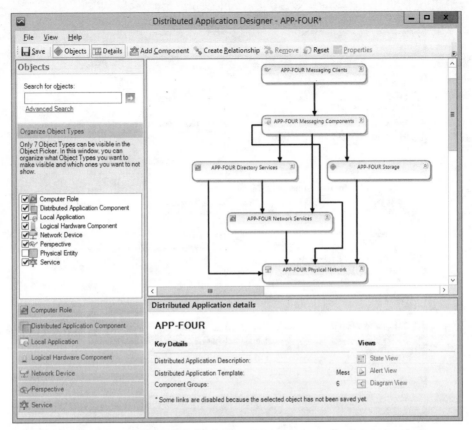

FIGURE 2-61 Messaging distributed application

2. On the Create A Distributed Application dialog box, shown in Figure 2-62, provide a name for the distributed application, choose a template, and choose an unsealed management pack in which to store the application.

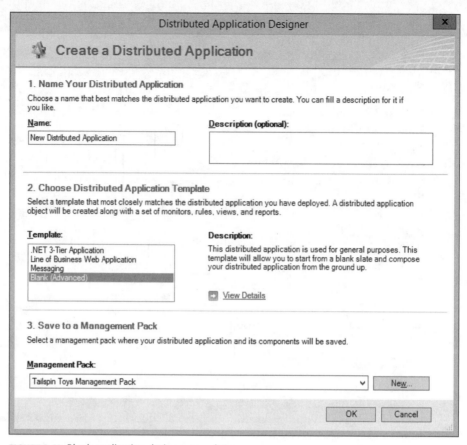

FIGURE 2-62 Blank application designer template

3. Click Add Component, to add a new component to the distributed application.

4. In the Create New Component Group, shown in Figure 2-63, specify the object classes that you want to include in the component group.

MORE INFO **DISTRIBUTED APPLICATIONS**

You can learn more about distributed applications at *http://technet.microsoft.com/en-us/ library/hh457612.aspx.*

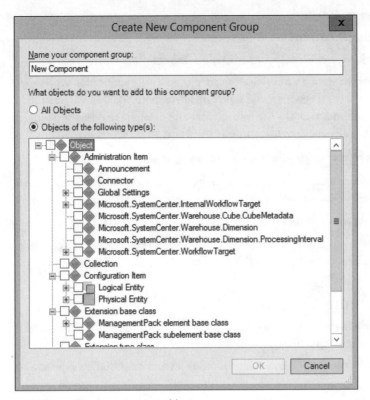

FIGURE 2-63 Component group objects

5. Populate the component group by dragging objects to it from the sidebar. Create relationships between component groups by clicking Create Relationship, and selecting the source and destination component groups.

EXAM TIP

Remember that objects in the Distributed Application Designer must be members of component groups.

Thought experiment

Travel booking application at Margie's Travel

The developers at Margie's Travel have just deployed a .NET application across several virtual machines on your organization's perimeter network. One VM hosts the IIS segment, and another hosts the web application's database tier. This application is supposed to be available to users around the world.

With this information in mind, answer the following questions:

1. Which service should you configure to verify that the external web application is available to people around the world?

2. What would you configure to monitor the web application as a single entity?

3. What would you configure so that you can assess and monitor the performance of the web application?

Objective summary

- You can tune a management pack so that it presents you with information that is relevant for your particular environment.

- Tuning involves configuring overrides for monitors and rules that change how each of these work.

- When tuning a sealed management pack, you store the overrides in a separate unsealed management pack

- Synthetic transactions allow you to create monitors for a variety of items, including UNIX and Linux processes, Windows Services, web applications, and OLE DB data sources

- Global Service Monitor allows you to configure remote monitoring of externally available web applications

- Application Performance Monitoring allows you to configure advanced monitoring for .NET and WCF applications

- Distributed application models allow you to create models of applications that depend upon multiple disparate segments.

Objective review

Answer the following questions to test your knowledge of the information in this objective. You can find the answers to these questions and explanations of why each answer choice is correct or incorrect in the "Answers" section at the end of the chapter.

1. Which type of synthetic transaction would you configure to verify that a SQL Server database was responding to remote queries?

   A. Windows Service.

   B. TCP Port.

   C. OLE DB data source.

   D. Web application availability.

2. Which type of synthetic transaction would you configure to verify that a specific web application was available? (choose the best answer)

   A. TCP Port.

   B. Windows Service.

   C. OLE DB data source.

   D. Web application availability.

3. Which type of synthetic transaction would you configure to verify that your ISP's SMTP Smart Host was available to route outgoing email traffic?

   A. OLE DB data source

   B. Windows Service

   C. Web application availability

   D. TCP Port

Objective 2.3: Create monitoring reports and dashboards

Once you've configured the monitoring of the objects in your organization, you can view the monitoring data in a variety of ways. Service level tracking allows you to configure performance and availability benchmarks as a way of measuring whether the services that you are monitoring are meeting the availability and performance expectation of the stakeholders who use them. Reports allow you to generate visual representations of the information gathered by Operations Manager. Dashboards allow you to configure at-a-glance representations of important information.

This section covers the following topics:
- Service-level tracking
- Reports
- Dashboards

Service level tracking

You can use Operations Manager to monitor how well your organization is meeting service level agreements (SLA) and/or operating level agreements (OLA). This is done by configuring Operations Manager to track service availability and performance against agreed upon benchmarks between the organizations participating in the SLA or OLA.

To perform service level tracking in Operations Manager, you define a specific service level objective (SLO) in terms of a set of monitors, such as performance and availability. You then schedule and access regular reports to verify that the SLOs are being met, or, if they aren't, change processes so that the SLOs will be met.

> **MORE INFO** **MONITORING SERVICE LEVEL OBJECTIVES USING OPERATIONS MANAGER**
>
> You can learn more about monitoring service level objectives using Operations Manager at *http://technet.microsoft.com/en-us/library/hh212753.aspx.*

Application SLOs

Monitoring an application SLO with Operations Manager involves ensuring that availability and performance goals are being met. To define a SLO against an application, in this case the SQL Server 2012 database engine, which requires a SQL Server management pack, using Operations Manager, perform the following steps:

1. In the Authoring workspace of the Operations Manager console, click Service Level Tracking under Management Pack Objects.

2. On the ribbon, click Create.

3. On the General page of the Service Level Tracking Wizard, type the name **SQL Server 2012 OpsMgr SLO**.

4. On the Object To Track page, ensure that an unsealed management pack is selected, and then click Select.

5. On the Select A Target Class dialog box, click Distributed Application, and then click All. In the list of results, click SQL DB Engine, as shown in Figure 2-64, and then click OK.

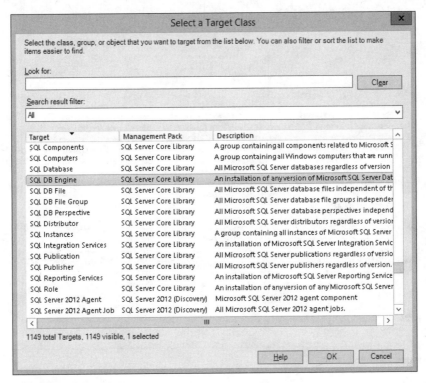

FIGURE 2-64 Target class

6. On the Object To Track page, click a group or object that contains objects of the targeted class, and then click Select. On the Select An Object dialog box, select the SQL Server instance on the operations manager server that is of the class SQL 2012 DB Engine, as shown in Figure 2-65. This will ensure that the SLA only applies to this specific instance of the database engine.

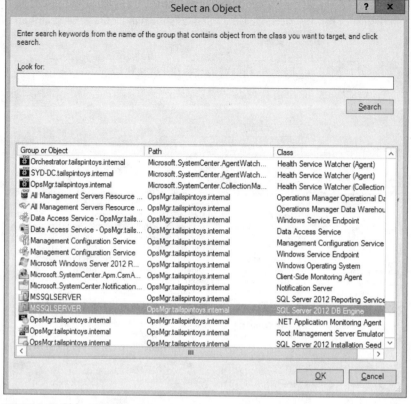

FIGURE 2-65 Object selection

7. On the Service Level Objectives page, click Add, and then click Monitor State SLO. Monitor state SLOs allow you to track the availability of the application.

8. On the Service Level Objective (Monitor State) dialog box, provide a name for the objective, and list the states that qualify as downtime for the objective. The states that you select will be dependent on the agreement made between the stakeholders. Figure 2-66 shows a 99.99 percent service level objective goal where Unplanned Maintenance, Unmonitored, Monitoring Unavailable, and Monitoring Disabled count as downtime. Click OK.

9. On the Service Level Objectives page, click Add, and then click Collection Rule SLO. Collection rule SLOs allow you to track the performance of the application.

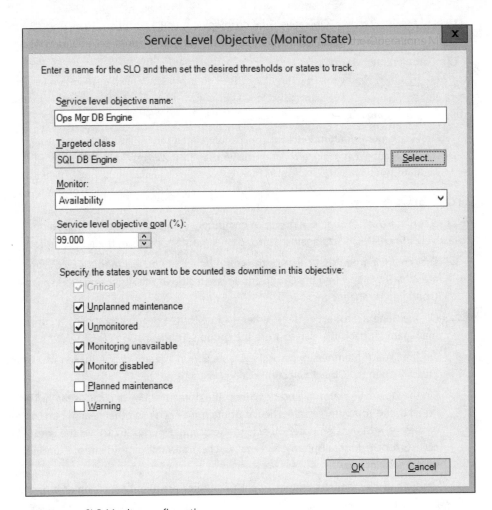

FIGURE 2-66 SLO Monitor configuration

 EXAM TIP

Remember the difference between Monitor State SLOs and Collection rule SLOs.

10. On the Service Level Objective (Collection Rule) dialog box, provide a name. Next to Performance Collection Rule, click Select. You can only select an existing performance collection rule. You can create rules from the Authoring workspace of the Operations Manager console. For example, if the SLO were about ensuring that the SQL Server DB engine never exceeded 90 percent processor utilization, you'd use a performance collection rule related to processor utilization.

11. On the Service Level Objective Goal drop down menu, select Less Than, and specify 90. This means that the engine should not exceed 90 percent processor utilization.

12. Complete the wizard.

MORE INFO APPLICATION SLOs

You can learn more about monitoring application related service level objectives using Operations Manager at *http://technet.microsoft.com/en-us/library/hh212753.aspx*.

Group SLOs

You can configure a SLO against a group of computers by monitoring the computer objects collectively. To create an SLO against a group of computers, perform the following tasks:

1. First create a group that contains the computers that you will monitor by clicking Create A New Group when the Groups node is selected in the Authoring workspace of the Operations Manager console.

2. On the General Properties page, enter a name for the group and specify an unsealed management pack in which to store the group settings.

3. On the Explicit Members page of the Create Group Wizard, click Add/Remove Objects. This will open the Object Selection dialog box.

4. On the Object Selection dialog box, enter the domain suffix, and click search. This will list all of the computers in a particular domain. You can use other search parameters as necessary. Add the Computer objects to the group. Figure 2-67 shows the computer objects for OpsMgr.tailspintoys.internal, Orchestrator.tailspintoys.internal, and SYD-DC.tailspintoys.internal.

5. Verify that the members that you want to monitor are members of the group, and complete the wizard.

6. In the Authoring workspace of the Operations Manager console, select Service Level Tracking under Management Pack Objects and on the ribbon, click Create.

7. Provide a name for the group SLO you are creating.

8. On the Objects To Track page, click Select.

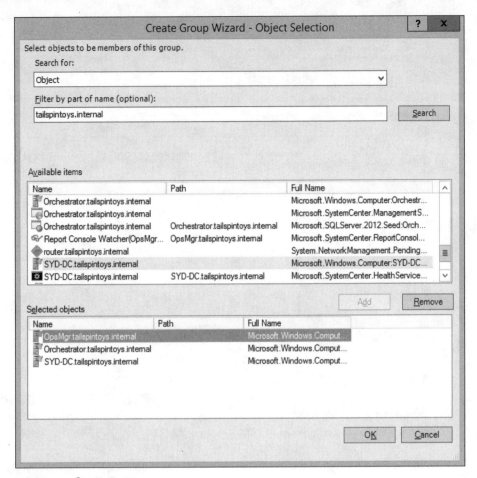

FIGURE 2-67 Create group

9. On the Select A Target Class page, click Distributed Application, and click All. Type the name of the group that you created, and select that group, shown in Figure 2-68, and click OK.

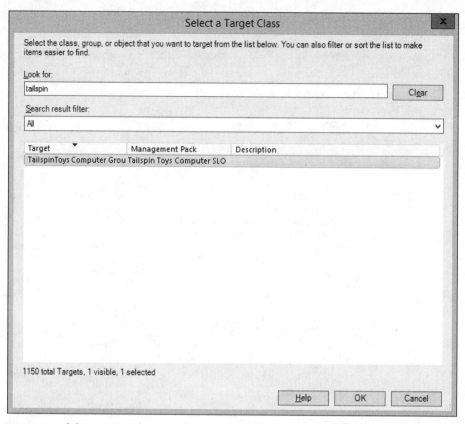

FIGURE 2-68 Select a target class

10. On the Service Level Objectives page, click Add, and then click Monitor State SLO.

11. On the Service Level Objective (Monitor State) dialog box, provide the following information as shown in Figure 2-69.

- **Service Level Objective Name**   A name for the SLO.
- **Monitor**   In this scenario, this will be set to Availability.
- **Service Level Objective Goal**   The availability goal.
- **What counts as downtime**   Allows you to specify which states count as downtime towards measuring the SLO.

12. Click OK and complete the wizard.

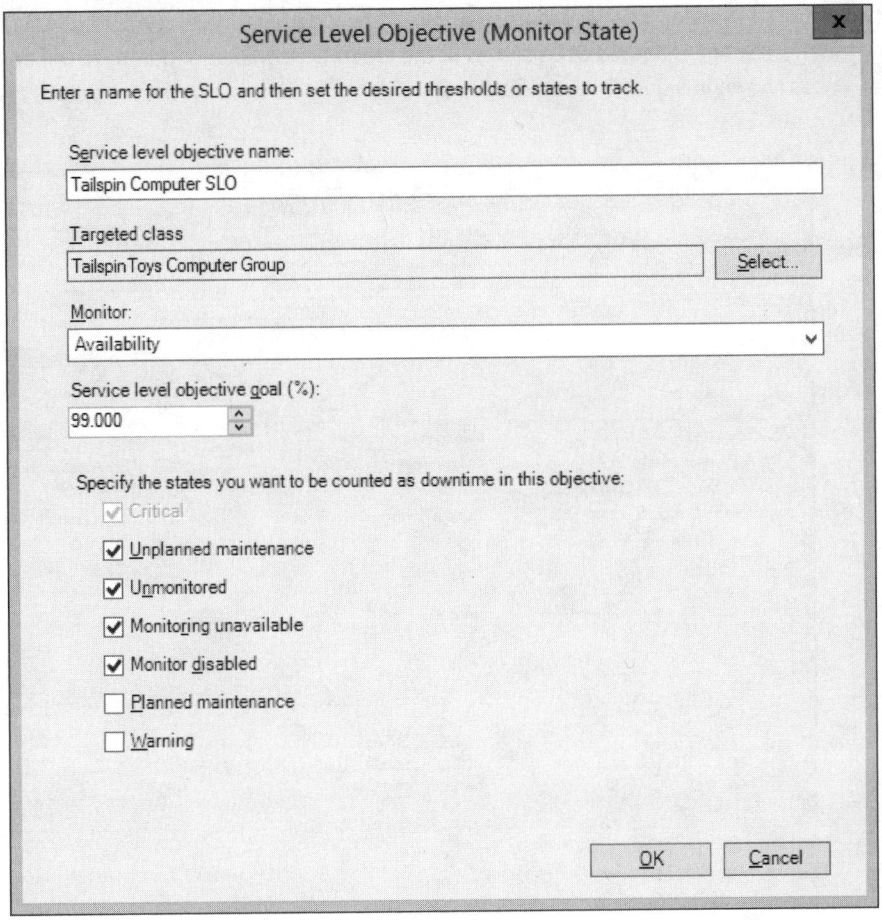

FIGURE 2-69 SLO Monitor State

MORE INFO **GROUP SLOs**

You can learn more about monitoring group related service level objectives using Operations Manager at *http://technet.microsoft.com/en-us/library/hh212877.aspx*.

Service level tracking reports

Running a service level tracking report allows you to view how an application or group is performing in terms of the defined SLO. To create a service level tracking report, perform the following general steps:

1. In the Reporting workspace of the Operations Manager console, click the Microsoft Service Level Report Library under the Reporting node.

2. Click Service Level Tracking Summary Report, and click Open on the taskbar.

3. On the Service Level Tracking Summary Report dialog box, click Add, and click Search. The list of configured SLOs stored in the Operations Manager database will be listed as shown in Figure 2-70. Select the SLOs that you want to run the report on, and click Add.

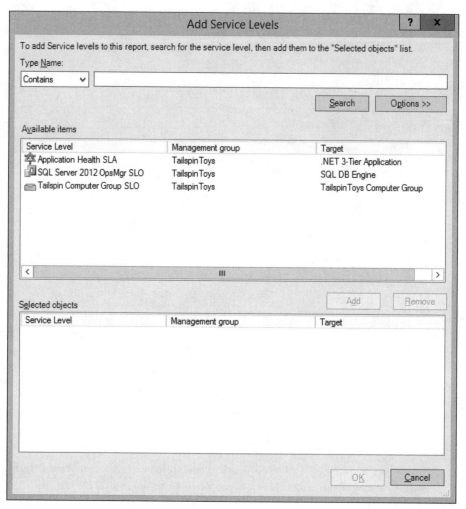

FIGURE 2-70 Add Service Levels

4. On the Service Level Tracking Summary Report dialog box, specify the range that you want the report to encompass and the frequency that you want to use for data aggregation. Figure 2-71 shows a report that will be configured to be run over the last 24 hours using an hourly aggregation.

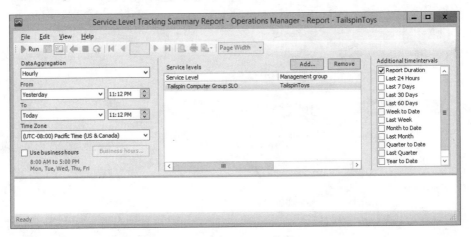

FIGURE 2-71 Report properties

5. Click Run, to run the Service Level Tracking Summary Report.

MORE INFO SERVICE LEVEL TRACKING REPORTS

You can learn more about monitoring service level objectives using Operations Manager at *http://technet.microsoft.com/en-us/library/hh212726.aspx.*

Reports

Operations Manager leverages the functionality of SQL Server Reporting Services to provide comprehensive reporting functionality. Operations Manager ships with a large number of built-in reports. Importing management packs also adds to the available reports. Administrators can also create their own reports. Reports are available in the Reporting node. Figure 2-72 shows the reports in the Generic Report Library.

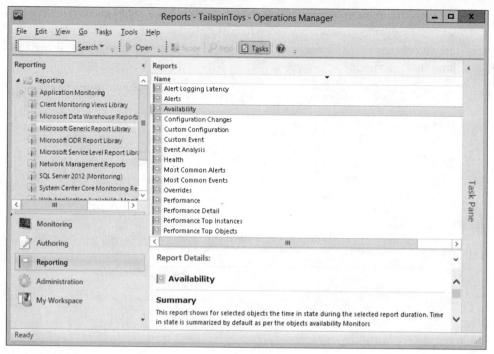

FIGURE 2-72 Generic Reports

The generic report library includes the following reports:

- **Alert Logging Latency**   Displays the logging latency of an alert for monitored objects over time.

- **Alerts**   Lists alerts raised during a specific duration for given filter parameters.

- **Availability**   Availability state for selected monitored objects.

- **Configuration Changes**   Changes in configuration for monitored objects over time.

- **Custom Configuration**   Configuration data filtered by specific parameters.

- **Custom Event**   Event data filtered by specific parameters.

- **Event Analysis**   Events and a count by monitored server filtered by specific parameters.

- **Health**   Health state for monitored objects based on overall entity health. Figure 2-73 shows a health report for three monitored computers over the last 24 hours.

- **Most Common Alerts**   Most common alerts rose during report duration for given parameters.

- **Most Common Events**   Most common events rose during report duration for specific parameters.

- **Overrides**   Overrides applied to specific management packs over time.

- **Performance**   Performance counter values over time.

- **Performance Detail**   Detailed performance information over time.
- **Performance Top Instances**   Top or bottom set of instances for selected objects for a specific performance counter rule.
- **Performance Top Objects**   Top or bottom set of objects for selected objects for a specific performance counter rule.

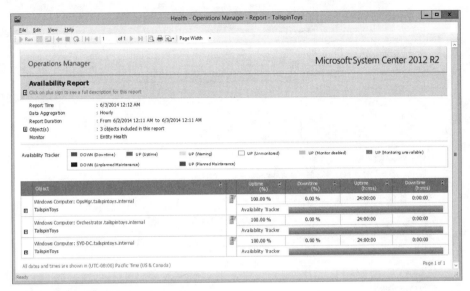

FIGURE 2-73 Availability report

***MORE INFO* OPERATIONS MANAGER REPORTS**

You can learn more about reports in Operations Manager at *http://technet.microsoft.com/en-us/library/hh212786.aspx*.

Running reports

When running a report you'll need to specify the report parameters. This includes specifying the objects you want the report run on, and the period that the report should recover. Other reports will require report specific parameters be configured.

For example, to run the generic Availability report for the last day, perform the following steps:

1. In the Reporting workspace of the Operations Manager console, expand the Reporting pane, click the Microsoft Generic Report Library node, and click the Availability Report.

2. On the ribbon, click Open.

3. On the Availability - Operations Manager - Report dialog box click Today under From, and then click Yesterday.

4. On the Availability - Operations Manager - Report dialog box, click Add Object.

5. On the Add Object dialog box, click Options. On the Options dialog box, click Add.

6. On the Add Class dialog box, type **Computer**, and click Search. Click Computer, and click Add, as shown in Figure 2-74, and click OK.

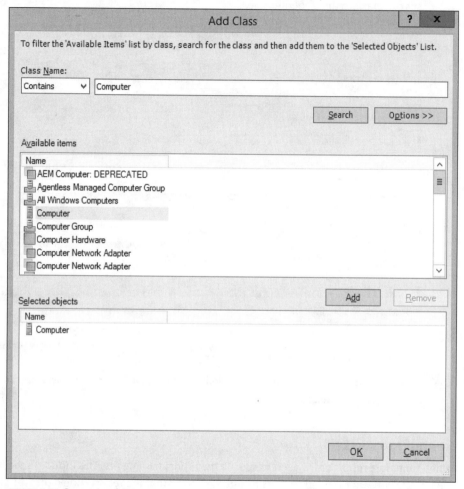

FIGURE 2-74 Computer class

7. On the Options dialog box, click OK, and on the Add Object dialog box, click Search.

8. A list of Computers that are monitored by Operations Manager will be displayed, as shown in Figure 2-75. Select the computers that you wish to generate the Availability Report for, and then click OK.

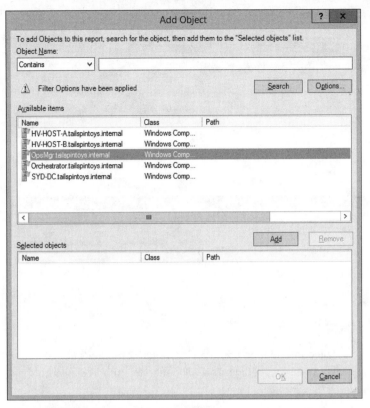

FIGURE 2-75 Add computer objects

9. In the list of Down Time items, select all of the options. Figure 2-76 shows an approximation of what this dialog box would look like if completed using these instructions for computers OpsMgr.tailspintoys.internal, Orchestrator.tailspintoys.internal, and SYD-DC. tailspintoys.internal.

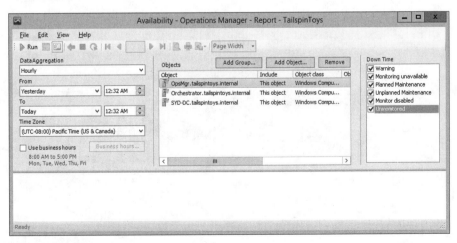

FIGURE 2-76 Report properties

10. Click Run, to run the report. Figure 2-77 shows a sample of the report output.

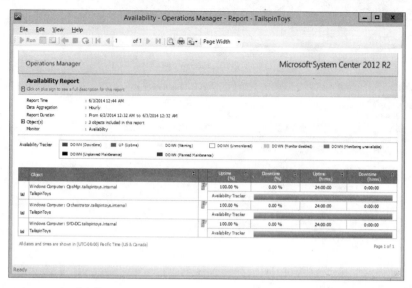

FIGURE 2-77 Availability report

11. To view more detailed information about an individual computer's availability, you can click the Availability Tracker hyperlink. This will generate a report similar to the one shown in Figure 2-78.

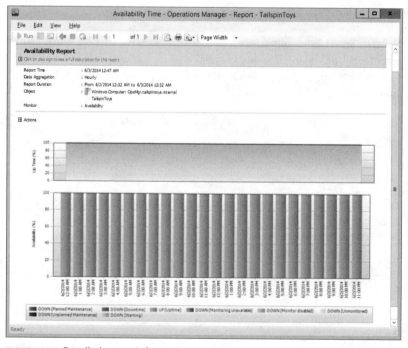

FIGURE 2-78 Detailed report information

12. You can save the report parameters by clicking Save To Favorites on the file menu once the report has run. When you do this, you provide a name for the report. Figure 2-79 shows the Save To Favorites dialog box.

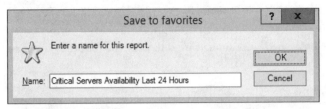

FIGURE 2-79 Save To Favorites

MORE INFO **RUNNING OPERATIONS MANAGER REPORTS**

You can learn more about running reports in Operations Manager at *http://technet. microsoft.com/en-us/library/hh230683.aspx.*

Scheduling reports

By scheduling reports, you can have reports periodically delivered through email or published to a file share. SQL Server's report server also caches scheduled reports, making them quicker to access through the console. Prior to scheduling a report, you should create a template of the report that you wish to schedule and save it as a favorite report. If you want to email reports, you'll need to create an email channel by specifying an SMTP server through the channel's node, under notifications in the Administration workspace.

To create a scheduled report based on a report that has been saved as a favorite report, perform the following steps:

1. In the Reporting workspace of the Operations Manager console, click the Favorite Reports node, and then click the favorite report that you want to configure as a scheduled report.

2. On the Tasks menu, click Report, and then click Schedule.

3. On the Delivery Settings page, shown in Figure 2-80, specify the following information:

   - **Description** A description of the scheduled report.
   - **Delivery Method** How the report will be delivered. By default you can select a file share location, or, if configured, for the report to be emailed.
   - **File Name** The name associated with the report.
   - **Path** When using a network share, this will be the share that will host the report.
   - **Render Format** The format the report will be saved in. Options include Excel, HTML 4.0, Word, Data Feed, TIFF file, RPL Renderer, MHTML, PDF, Excel 2003, CSV, Word 2003, and XML file with report data.

- **Write Mode** This determines whether the name of the report will be updated each time the report is run, whether any existing report will be overwritten, or if no report will be written if one already exists.
- **File Extension** Determines if the appropriate file extension will be appended to the report name.
- **User Name and Password** Credentials used to write the report to the shared folder.

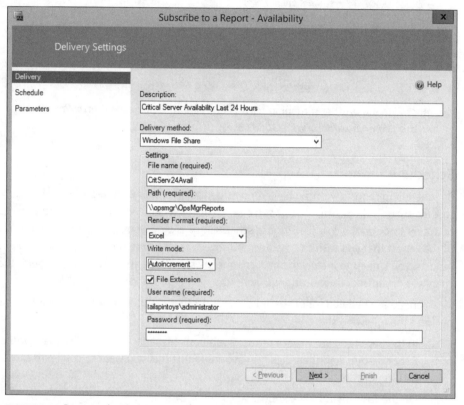

FIGURE 2-80 Report subscription

4. On the Schedule page, shown in Figure 2-81, specify the report schedule. You can configure reports to be run once, hourly, daily, weekly, or monthly, as well as configuring how often each period the reports are generated.

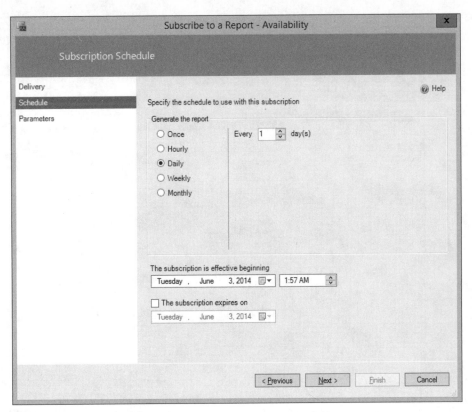

FIGURE 2-81 Report schedule

5. On the Parameters page, you can review or alter the parameters of the report. For example, if you had a favorite report for availability that included four servers, but you wanted the scheduled report to only provide information on three, you could alter the parameters of the report to generate the desired report here. Figure 2-82 shows the parameters page of the Subscribe To A Report Wizard. Click Finish to create the report.

MORE INFO **SCHEDULING OPERATIONS MANAGER REPORTS**

You can learn more about scheduling reports in Operations Manager at *http://technet. microsoft.com/en-us/library/hh230723.aspx.*

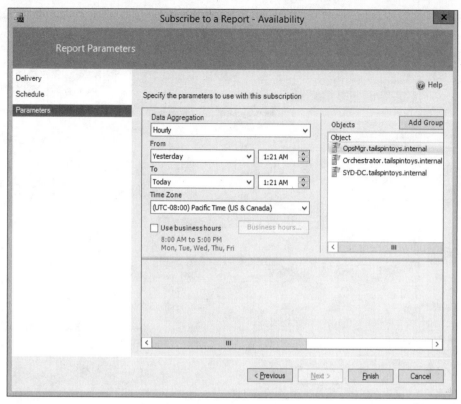

FIGURE 2-82 Report parameters

Dashboards

Dashboards provide a method of quickly displaying relevant Operations Manager information by allowing you to present multiple types of data in a single view. Dashboards can be viewed using the Operations Manager console, or published to SharePoint.

When creating a dashboard, you can choose from one of the following templates, as shown in Figure 2-83:

- Column Layout
- Grid Layout
- Service Level Dashboard
- Summary Dashboard

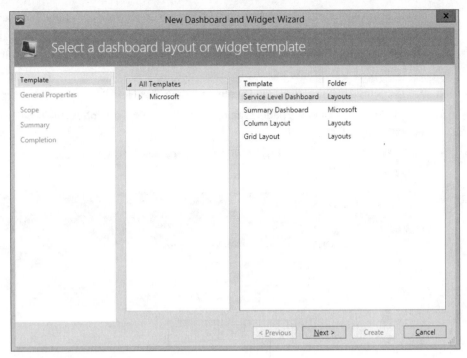

FIGURE 2-83 Dashboard layout

The service level dashboard allows you to display service level tracking information. The summary dashboard will display the top selected number of performance counters for chosen values. Column layouts consist of multiple columns. Grid layouts consist of multiple cells. Once you choose between a flow layout or a grid layout, you add widgets to the dashboard that display information. Operations Manager includes the following widgets:

- **State**   Allows you to view the state of monitored objects.
- **Performance**   Allows you to view performance metrics.
- **Alert**   Allows you to view alert information.
- **Details**   The properties of the item that is highlighted in the dashboard.
- **Instance Details**   Provides details of the instances related to the object.
- **Objects By Performance**   Performance counter data in tabular format for the selected object.

To create a grid layout dashboard view named Domain Controller Availability And Alerts in Operations Manager, perform the following tasks:

1. In the My Workspace view of the Operations Manager console, right-click New View, and then click Dashboard View.

2. On the Template page, click Grid Layout, and then click Next.

3. On the General Properties page, type the name **Domain Controller Availability and Alerts,** and click Next.

4. On the Layout page, click 2 Cells, and then click the layout on the left as shown in Figure 2-84, and click Next.

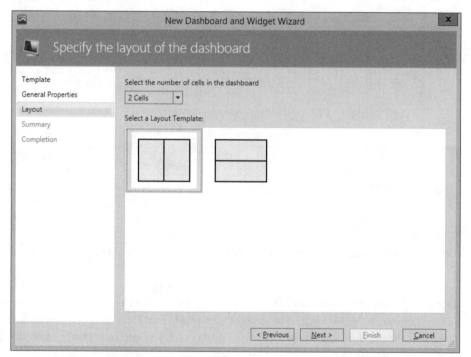

FIGURE 2-84 Dashboard cells

5. On the Summary page, click Create, and then click Close.

6. The new Dashboard will appear under the Favorite Views node. Click the new dashboard, in this case named Domain Controller Availability, and then click the text Click To Add Widget. This will open the New Dashboard And Widget Wizard. Click State Widget as shown in Figure 2-85, and click Next.

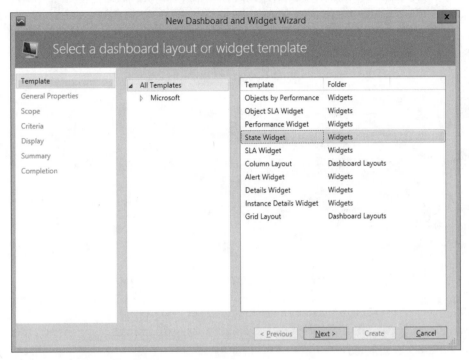

FIGURE 2-85 Dashboard widget

7. On the General Properties page, type **Domain Controller State,** and then click Next.

8. On the Scope page, click Add. On the Add Groups Or Objects dialog box, click Show All Objects And Groups. Type the domain suffix to limit the displayed items, and then navigate to the object that represents one of your organization's domain controllers. Figure 2-86 shows SYD-DC.tailspintoys.internal selected. Click Add, and then click OK.

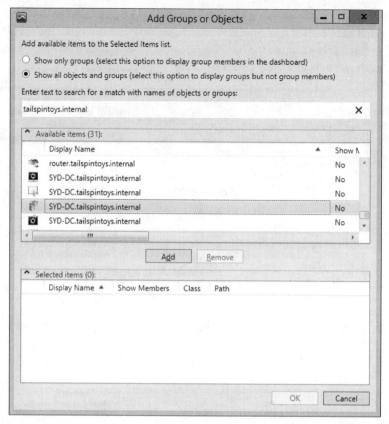

FIGURE 2-86 Add object

9. On the Scope page, verify that the domain controller computer object is listed.

10. On the Criteria page, select all of the available criteria except Display Only Objects In Maintenance Mode, as shown in Figure 2-87.

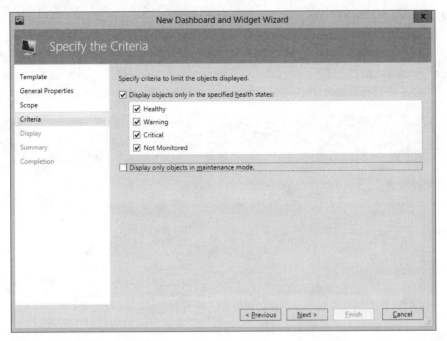

FIGURE 2-87 Dashboard criteria

11. On the Display page, select the Columns To Display, as shown in Figure 2-88, and then click Next.

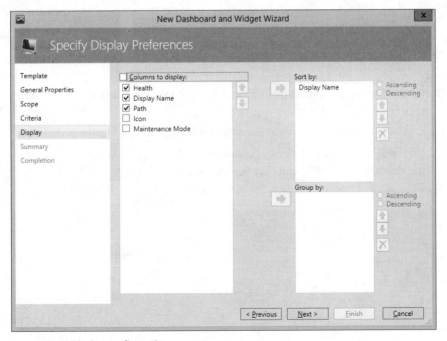

FIGURE 2-88 Display configuration

12. On the Summary page, click Create, and then close.

13. With the Domain Controller Availability And Alerts node selected, click the Click To Add Widget text.

14. On the Select A Dashboard Layout Or Widget template page of the New Dashboard And Widget Wizard, click Alert Widget, as shown in Figure 2-89, and click Next.

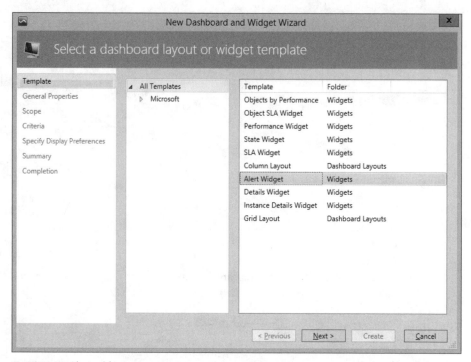

FIGURE 2-89 Alert widget

15. On the General Properties page, type the name, **Domain Controller Host Alerts,** and click Next.

16. On the Select Group Or Object page, click the ellipsis button (...).

17. On the Select A Group Or Object dialog box, click Groups And Objects, and then type the domain name suffix, and click Search. Figure 2-90 shows the SYD-DC.tailspintoys. internal object, and the Health Service Watcher Class is selected. Click OK.

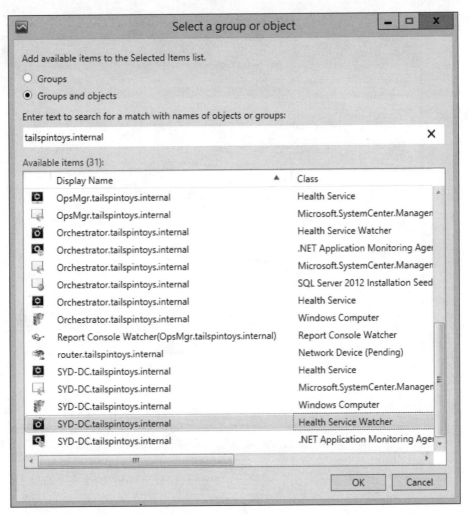

FIGURE 2-90 Health Service Watcher object

18. On the Criteria page, select the following check boxes as shown in Figure 2-91:
   ■ Display Alerts Only With The Specified Severities
   ■ Critical
   ■ Warning

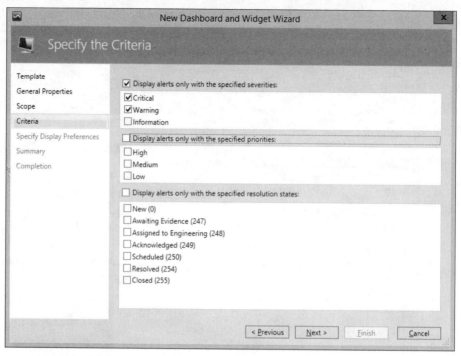

FIGURE 2-91 Criteria selection

19. Review the options on the Display tab, and click Next. Then click Create, and click Close. The resultant dashboard will look similar to Figure 2-92.

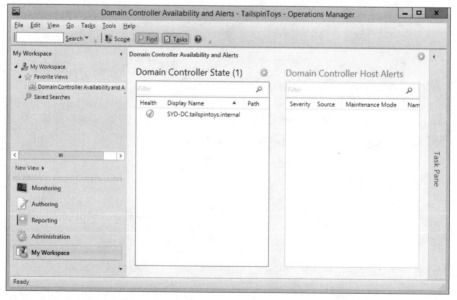

FIGURE 2-92 Dashboard view

To be able to display a dashboard in SharePoint, you need to have installed the Operations Manager SharePoint Web Part on the SharePoint server. A user that has administrative permissions on the SharePoint server must install the Operations Manager SharePoint Web Part.

> **MORE INFO** **OPERATIONS MANAGER DASHBOARDS**
>
> You can learn more about dashboards at *http://blogs.technet.com/b/momteam/archive/2011/09/27/introducing-operations-manager-2012-dashboards.aspx*.

Thought experiment

Performance dashboards at Contoso

You want to provide application administrators with dashboards, published on your organization's SharePoint server that allows them to view performance counter data about services that you monitor in tabular format. With this information in mind, answer the following questions:

1. Which widget would you include in the dashboard to provide the appropriate information?

2. What steps must the SharePoint Administrator take before you can publish the dashboard to SharePoint?

Objective summary

- You can use Operations Manager service level objectives (SLOs) to set availability and performance benchmarks.
- You run service level tracking reports against SLOs to determine whether those availability and performance objectives have been met.
- Operations Manager includes a number of built in reports that allow you to view the data collected by Operations Manager agents. Management packs contain additional reports.
- Dashboards allow you to build "at-a-glance" summaries of important Operations Manager information. Dashboards can be published to SharePoint.

Objective review

Answer the following questions to test your knowledge of the information in this objective. You can find the answers to these questions and explanations of why each answer choice is correct or incorrect in the "Answers" section at the end of the chapter.

1. You want to perform service level tracking to verify the availability of your organization's Exchange 2013 mailbox servers. You want to measure the availability of the

virtual machines that host this role. Which of the following would you configure to accomplish this goal?

A. Windows Service synthetic transaction

B. Group SLO

C. Application SLO

D. Computer Group

2. Which of the following reports would you run to view figures for a group SLO used to measure the availability of a number of critical servers?

A. Availability

B. Service level tracking summary report

C. Overrides

D. Performance

3. You want to create a dashboard that provides performance and alert information for a group of computers. Which of the following widgets should you include when creating the dashboard?

A. State

B. Alert

C. Performance

D. Details

Answers

This section contains the solutions to the thought experiments and answers to the lesson review questions in this chapter.

Objective 2.1: Thought experiment

1. You must remove any management packs that have the management pack that you want to remove as a dependency.

2. An SNMP v3 Run As account includes User name, Context, Authentication Protocol, Authentication key, Privacy protocol, and Privacy key.

3. You use the MOMADAdmin.exe utility to configure automatic agent assignment.

Objective 2.1: Review

1. **Correct answer:** A

   A. **Correct:** You must configure the Run As account with the SNMP v2 community string.

   B. **Incorrect:** You do not have to configure the Run As account with the device name.

   C. **Incorrect:** You do not have to configure the Run As account with the Device IP address.

   D. **Incorrect:** You do not have to configure the Run As account with the Authentication key. This is only necessary with SNMP v3 Run As accounts.

2. **Correct answers:** A, B and D

   A. **Correct:** For a domain joined computer to automatic connect to a management server, Active Directory must be configured.

   B. **Correct:** This option will allow automatic agent installation, as long as Active Directory is configured and the other Global Management Server setting is configured.

   C. **Incorrect:** This option, if configured, would not allow automatic agent installations.

   D. **Correct:** You must configure the Review New Manual Agent Installations In Pending Management View before you can configure the Automatically Approve option.

3. **Correct answer:** A

   A. **Correct:** You use MOMADAdmin.exe to configure Active Directory with management server settings.

   B. **Incorrect:** Cmtrace.exe is a log file viewer usually used with Configuration Manager.

C. **Incorrect:** MOMagent.msi is used to manually install the Operations Manager agent.

D. **Incorrect:** Gpedit.msc is used to configure local Group Policy settings.

Objective 2.2: Thought experiment

1. You would configure Global Service Monitor to verify that the external web application is available to people around the world.

2. You would configure a distributed application model to monitor the disparate segments that make up the external web application.

3. You would configure Application Performance Monitoring to assess and monitor the performance of the web application.

Objective 2.2: Review

1. **Correct answer:** C

   A. **Incorrect:** You use this type of synthetic transaction to verify that a service is running.

   B. **Incorrect:** You use this type of synthetic transaction to verify that a TCP Port is available.

   C. **Correct:** You can use this type of synthetic transaction to verify that an OLE DB compatible database is responding to remote queries.

   D. **Incorrect:** You use this type of synthetic transaction to verify that a web application is responding to requests.

2. **Correct answer:** D

   A. **Incorrect:** You use this type of synthetic transaction to verify that a TCP Port is available. While a TCP Port test would verify that a web server was present, you couldn't use it to test the functionality of an application.

   B. **Incorrect:** You use this type of synthetic transaction to verify that a service is running.

   C. **Incorrect:** You use this type of synthetic transaction to verify that an OLE DB compatible database is responding to remote queries.

   D. **Correct:** You use this type of synthetic transaction to verify that a web application is responding to requests.

3. **Correct answer:** D

   A. **Incorrect:** You use this type of synthetic transaction to verify that an OLE DB compatible database is responding to remote queries.

   B. **Incorrect:** You use this type of synthetic transaction to verify that a service is running.

C. **Incorrect:** You use this type of synthetic transaction to verify that a web application is responding to requests.

D. **Correct:** You use this type of synthetic transaction to verify that a TCP Port, such as port 25 on an SMTP smart host, is available.

Objective 2.3: Thought experiment

1. You would select the Object By Performance as this presents performance counter data in tabular format.

2. To be able to display a dashboard in SharePoint, you need to have installed the Operations Manager SharePoint Web Part on the SharePoint server.

Objective 2.3: Review

1. **Correct answer:** B and D

   A. **Incorrect**: You want to measure the availability of a group of computers.

   B. **Correct**: You should use a group SLO to measure the availability of a group of computers.

   C. **Incorrect:** You use an application SLO to measure the availability of an application or service.

   D. **Correct**: You must add the computers that you want to monitor to an Operations Manager group before you'll be able to configure a group SLO.

2. **Correct answer:** B

   A. **Incorrect**: While an availability report will provide availability information, it won't provide information in terms of a specific service level benchmark.

   B. **Correct**: The service level tracking summary report allows you to view information on an existing SLO.

   C. **Incorrect**: The overrides report provides information on configured overrides.

   D. **Incorrect**: The Performance report provides performance information, but does not measure this data against a specific service level benchmark.

3. **Correct answers:** B and C

   A. **Incorrect**: The State widget allows you to view state information about a monitored object.

   B. **Correct**: The alert object provides Alert information.

   C. **Correct**: The performance widget provides performance information.

   D. **Incorrect**: The details widget provides details of the instances related to an object.

CHAPTER 3

Monitor resources

On a day-to-day basis, an Operations Manager administrator needs to manage and respond to alerts, ensuring that they are notified about particularly important events that have occurred with the items that they are monitoring. They also need to be familiar with the variety of ways that Operations Manager displays collected data, knowing which dashboards and views are going to provide the most meaningful insight into the health and performance of the objects that they are responsible for monitoring.

Objectives in this chapter:

- Objective 3.1: Monitor network devices
- Objective 3.2: Monitor servers
- Objective 3.3: Monitor the virtualization layer
- Objective 3.4: Monitor application health

Objective 3.1: Monitor network devices

Once you have configured Operations Manager to collect data from network data, you need to configure how Operations Manager displays and interprets that data, from configuring notifications and alerts, through to analyzing overall network health. In the previous chapter you learned how to set up synthetic transactions, how to monitor network devices and how to perform device discovery. In this section you'll learn about managing alerts as well as how to view network devices and data.

> **This section covers the following topics:**
> - Managing alerts
> - Configuring alert notifications
> - Analyzing network devices and data

Managing alerts

Rules and monitors generate Operations Manager alerts. You view alerts in the Monitoring workspace shown in Figure 3-1. Rules and monitors can be configured to trigger an alert when certain sets of conditions are encountered. For example, an alert might be generated if a specific event is written to an event log of a monitored device or server, or when a monitored port on a network device surpasses a specific error threshold. Not all rules and monitors generate alerts. Alerts are raised by all types of monitored objects and aren't specific to network devices. However, rather than provide the same coverage across the different sections of this chapter, managing alerts is covered in this first section in a way that is universal to the way alerts are dealt with across all of the different objects you can monitor with Operations Manager.

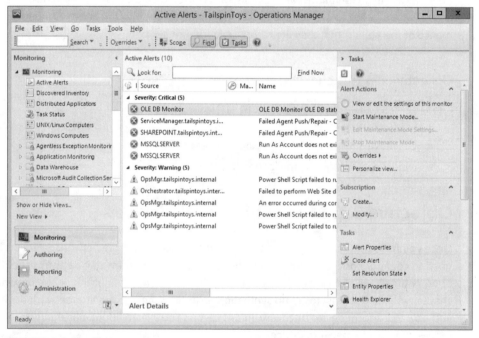

FIGURE 3-1 Active Alerts

You can configure a monitor to create an alert when the monitored item's health state changes from healthy (green) to warning (yellow), or from healthy to critical (red). An alert is only sent if the state changes from warning to critical, if the original alert sent when the monitor changed from healthy to warning has been closed. Alerts are not sent if the health state changes from warning or critical to healthy, but will again be sent if, once returned to healthy, the state changes again to warning or critical.

The majority of alerts generated by monitors automatically resolve when the monitor returns to a healthy state. If an alert does not automatically resolve when a monitor returns to a healthy state, you can ensure that it will in the future by configuring an override on the Auto-Resolve Alert parameter for the monitor. Figure 3-2 shows the configuration of an override for the Auto-Resolve Alert parameter on a monitor named Security.

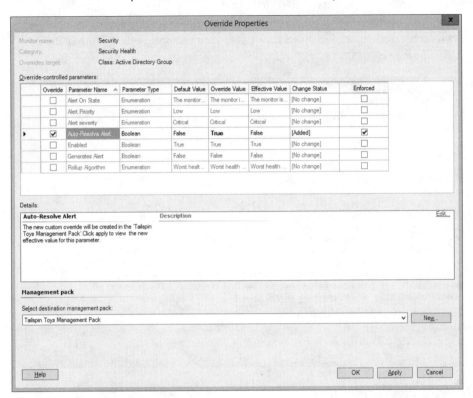

FIGURE 3-2 Override auto-resolve

Just as it is possible to configure a monitor that sends alerts with an override to stop it from sending alerts, it is also possible to configure a monitor that does not send alerts by default with an override so that it does send alerts.

Rules and monitors handle alerts differently. Rules cannot automatically resolve alerts. Unlike a monitor, that will send one alert while the condition that caused the alert is present, rules will continue to send alerts while the condition that caused the alert is present. To deal with the potential flood of alerts, you can configure alert suppression for the rule during rule creation. When you configure alert suppression, only the initial alert will be sent. Further alerts will be suppressed. Operations Manager will only suppress duplicate alerts that have suppression criteria, specified in the rule, that are identical. To be tagged as a duplicate, an alert must be created by the same rule and be in an unresolved state.

EXAM TIP

You can only configure alert suppression during rule creation. You can't configure alert suppression as an override.

To view the number of suppressed alerts for a particular alert, you can add the Repeat Count column to the Active Alerts view. The repeat count will be incremented each time a new alert is suppressed. Figure 3-3 shows the Repeat Count column, with a figure of 307 for the first alert from MSSQLSERVER.

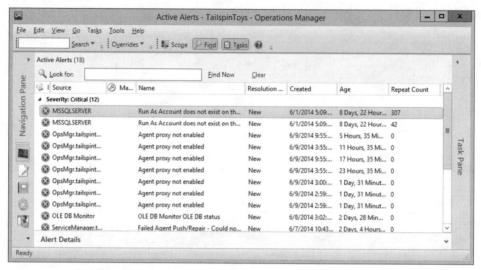

FIGURE 3-3 Repeat count

MORE INFO ALERT CREATION

You can learn more about alert creation at *http://technet.microsoft.com/en-us/library/hh212847.aspx*.

Alert details

Viewing the details of an alert is straightforward. Locate the alert in the Active Alerts node of the Monitoring workspace, and then click Alert Properties. This will bring up the Alert Properties dialog box, an example of which is shown in Figure 3-4. The General tab will provide information about the alert source, severity, priority, and repeat count in the event that the error has occurred more than once.

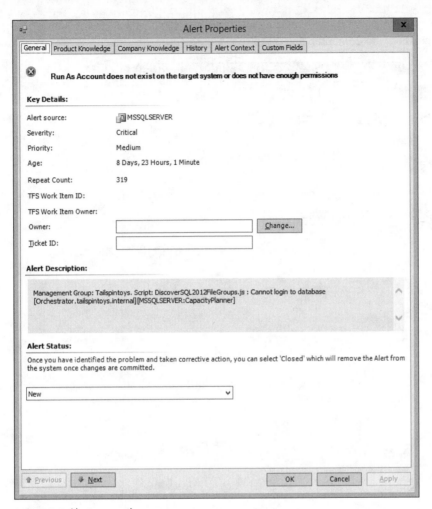

FIGURE 3-4 Alert properties

The Alert Properties dialog box also has the following information:

- The Product Knowledge tab will provide you with a summary of the alert, information about the causes of the alert, and possible resolution steps that you could implement.
- The Company Knowledge tab allows you to edit the rule that triggered the alert, and add extra information about the alert.
- The History tab allows you to enter history information in the form of comments about the alert.

- The Context tab provides further detail, including Log Name, Source, Event Number, Level, and Logging Computer, and is shown in Figure 3-5.

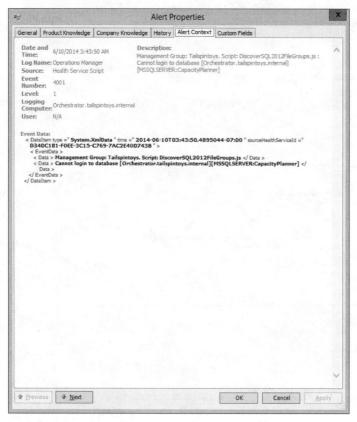

FIGURE 3-5 Alert context

- The Custom Fields tab allows you to enter custom field information.

MORE INFO **VIEWING ALERT DETAILS**

You can learn more about viewing alert details at *http://technet.microsoft.com/en-us/ library/hh212923.aspx*.

Closing alerts

Closing an alert removes it from the list of Active Alerts. In most cases, you'll only close an alert if you can verify that the issue has been resolved. Resolving alerts works differently depending on whether an alert was generated by a monitor, or by a rule. The differences are as follows:

- If you close an alert that was generated by a rule and the issue that generated the alert occurs again, another alert will be sent. You can close an alert generated by a rule as part of the diagnostic process, as new alerts will be sent if you haven't resolved the underlying issue.

- If you close an alert that was generated by a monitor when the issue is not fixed, no additional alerts will be sent because alerts from monitors are generated by changes in state.

Since the alert won't be raised again unless there is a negative change of health state, you have to take care when closing alerts generated by monitors as you may simply hide an issue rather than fix it. For the most part, monitors automatically resolve the alerts that they generate. Having said that, not every monitor will automatically resolve the alerts it generates. Before closing an alert generated by a monitor, check Health Explorer, and verify that the state of the monitored segment has returned to healthy.

You can set multiple resolution states for alerts, and even create your own alert resolution states. Resolution states can have a value between 1 and 254, with the ID of 1 assigned for the New resolution state, and the ID of 255 assigned for the Closed resolution state. Figure 3-6 shows configuring the resolution state for an alert.

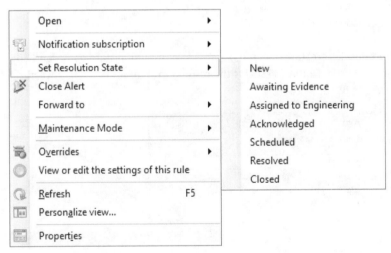

FIGURE 3-6 Resolution states

You configure additional alert resolution states by performing the following steps:

1. In the Administration workspace of the Operations Manager console, click Settings, click Alerts, and then click Properties in the Tasks pane.

2. On the Alert Resolution States dialog box, shown in Figure 3-7, click New.

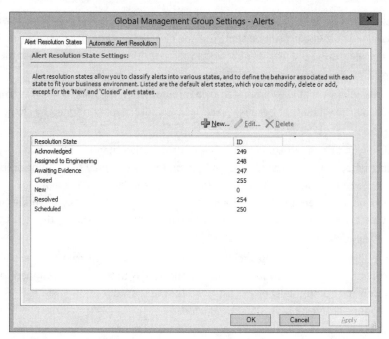

FIGURE 3-7 Alert resolution states

3. On the Add Alert Resolution State dialog box, provide a resolution state name, and an ID that has not been used. Figure 3-8 shows the resolution state set to Under Investigation, and a Unique ID set to 100.

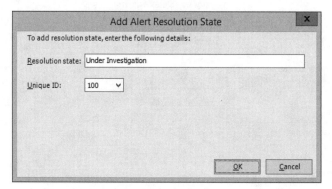

FIGURE 3-8 Add Alert Resolution state

4. The new resolution state will be listed, as shown in Figure 3-9.

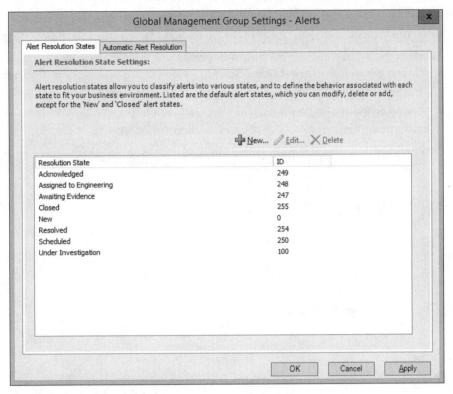

FIGURE 3-9 Review alert resolution states

MORE INFO **CLOSING ALERTS**

You can learn more about closing alerts at *http://technet.microsoft.com/en-us/library/hh212903.aspx*.

Automatic alert resolution

Operations Manager automatically resolves alerts after a certain number of days. The default settings are to automatically resolve all active alerts that are in a new resolution state after 30 days. This automatic resolution only applies to alerts that haven't had their resolution changed to another resolution state. If, for example, the resolution state had been set to Acknowledged or Scheduled, then the alert will not be automatically resolved.

Automatic alert resolution will also occur in the event that the alert source remains in a healthy state after a specified number of days, with the default being 7 days. To configure Automatic Alert Resolution settings, perform the following steps:

1. In the Administration workspace of the Operations Manager console, click Settings, click Alerts, and on the Tasks pane, click Properties.

2. On the Global Management Group Settings - Alerts dialog box, click the Automatic Alert Resolution tab.

3. Configure the appropriate automatic alert resolution settings on the Global Management Group Settings - Alerts dialog box, as shown in Figure 3-10.

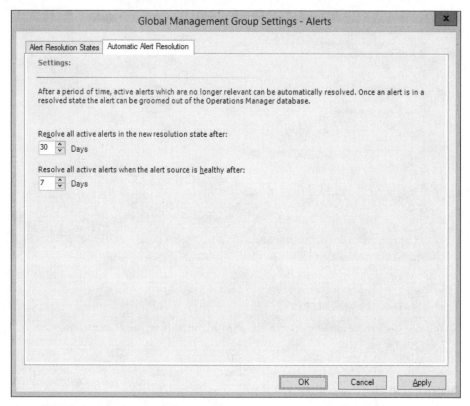

FIGURE 3-10 Automatic alert resolution

MORE INFO AUTOMATIC ALERT RESOLUTION

You can learn more about automatic alert resolution at *http://technet.microsoft.com/en-us/library/hh212897.aspx*.

Configuring alert notifications

You can configure Operations Manager to automatically send an email, instant message, send an SMS, or run a command when an alert is raised. Of course, you learned in Chapter 1 that if you integrate Orchestrator with Operations Manager, you can trigger runbook automation when an Operations Manager alert is raised, however this chapter is focused on Operations Manager.

To configure alert notifications, you must have prepared the following elements:

- Configure the Notification Account Run As Profile with a Run As account.
- Prepare a notification channel. The notification channel defines the notification format and method of transmission.
- Configure notification subscribers. Subscribers define the notification recipients and notification schedule.
- Prepare a notification subscription. This specifies the conditions for sending a notification, which notification is used, and which subscribers receive the notification.

> **MORE INFO** **ALERT NOTIFICATIONS**
>
> You can learn more about alert notifications at *http://technet.microsoft.com/en-us/library/hh212725.aspx*.

Notification action accounts

Operations Manager uses the Notification Account Run As profile to send notifications. The Notification Account Run As profile requires a Run As account that has the necessary credentials for sending notifications. To create a notification action account, perform the following steps:

1. Right-click the Security node in the Administration workspace of the Operations Manager console, and click Create Run As Account.

2. On the General Properties page of the Create Run As Account Wizard, ensure that Windows is selected as the Run As account type. In the Display Name text box, type **Notification Action Account,** as shown in Figure 3-11.

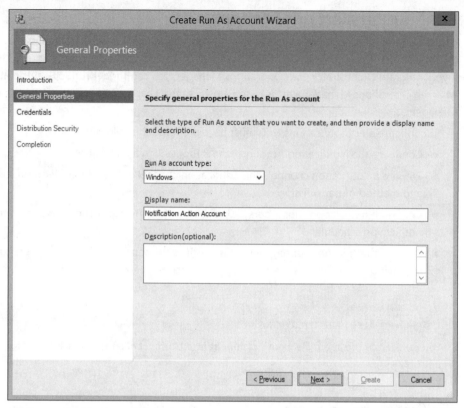

FIGURE 3-11 Notification action account

3. On the Credentials page, provide the username, password, and domain of the user account that will be used to send notifications.

4. On the Distribution Security options page, click More Secure, and then click Create, and then click Close.

5. Under Run As Configuration in the Administration workspace, click Accounts.

6. Double-click Notification Action Account.

7. On the Distribution tab, click Add. On the Computer Search page, click Search. In the list of available items, specify the computers to which you want the Action account distributed, and click Add, as shown in Figure 3-12, and then click OK. Click OK again to close the Run As Account Properties dialog box.

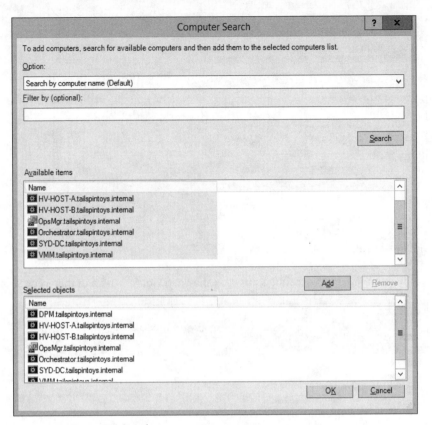

FIGURE 3-12 Computer Search

8. In the Administration workspace of the Operations Manager console, click Profiles under Run As Configuration. Double-click the Notification Account profile.

9. On the Run As Accounts page of the Run As Profile Wizard, click Add.

10. On the Add A Run As Account dialog box, use the drop-down menu to select the Notification Action Account created earlier, as shown in Figure 3-13, and then click OK.

FIGURE 3-13 Add a Run As Account

11. Verify that the Run As account is listed, as shown in Figure 3-14, and then click Save.

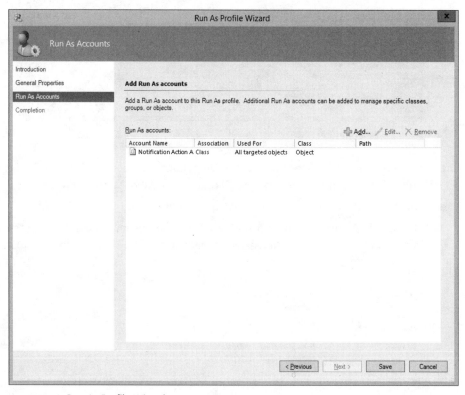

FIGURE 3-14 Run As Profile Wizard

MORE INFO NOTIFICATION ACTION ACCOUNTS

You can learn more about configuring notification action accounts at *http://technet. microsoft.com/en-us/library/hh212835.aspx.*

Email notification channel

The most common method of notification is through email. This is especially true now that smartphones have email capability, and the cost of sending an email to a smartphone is an order of magnitude lower than the cost of sending an SMS. Prior to configuring an email notification channel, you'll need to have access to an SMTP server and have configured a mailbox to be used for return email addresses, should it be necessary to provide an email response to a notification.

To enable an email notification channel, perform the following steps:

1. In the Administration workspace of the Operations Manager console, right-click the Channels node under Notifications, click New Channel, and then click E-Mail (SMTP).

2. On the Settings page of the E-Mail Notification Channel Wizard, click Add.

3. On the Add SMTP Server dialog box, enter the FQDN of the SMTP server. Figure 3-15 shows this set to Smtp.tailspintoys.internal, and click OK.

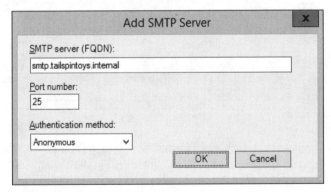

FIGURE 3-15 Add SMTP Server

4. On the Settings page, enter the return address. Figure 3-16 shows this set to alerts@ tailspintoys.internal.

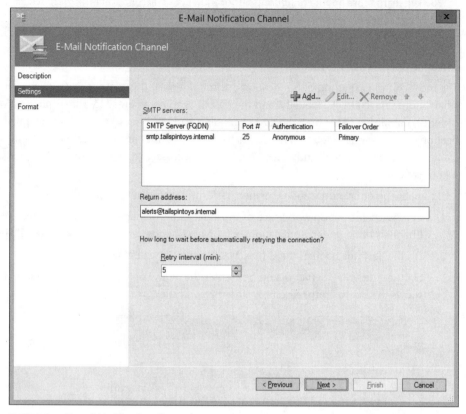

FIGURE 3-16 E-mail Notification Channel

5. On the Format page, review the default email format, as shown in Figure 3-17. You can modify this as necessary for your own environment. Click Finish to complete the wizard.

> **MORE INFO** **EMAIL NOTIFICATION CHANNELS**
>
> You can learn more about configuring email notification channels at *http://technet. microsoft.com/en-us/library/hh212914.aspx*

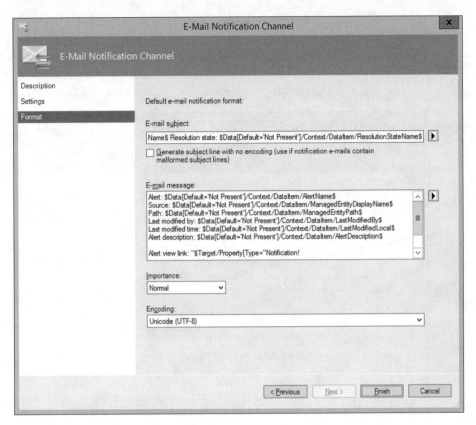

FIGURE 3-17 E-Mail Notification Channel

Notification subscribers

Notification subscribers are the people who you want to receive notifications about an alert. You can only create notification subscribers after you've created a notification channel. To create a notification subscriber, perform the following steps:

1. In the Administration workspace of the Operations Manager console, click Subscribers under the Notifications node. In the Tasks menu, click New.

2. On the Description page of the Notification Subscriber Wizard, specify a name for the subscriber.

3. On the Schedule page, select whether you want to send notifications at any time, or whether subscribers should only receive notifications at specific times. For example, Figure 3-18 shows a configuration where notifications will only be sent between 9:00 A.M. and 5:30 P.M. on weekdays. This is the master schedule. It is possible to configure schedules for individual subscribers when adding those individual subscribers.

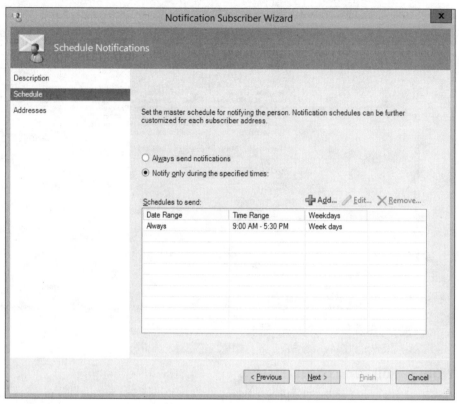

FIGURE 3-18 Notification subscriber schedule

4. On the Addresses page, click Add. This will launch the Subscriber Address Wizard, allowing you to specify the notification.

5. On the General page, specify the name of the address. This does not need to be the email address, but instead needs to be descriptive. For example, Figure 3-19 shows this set as Administrator Email Address.

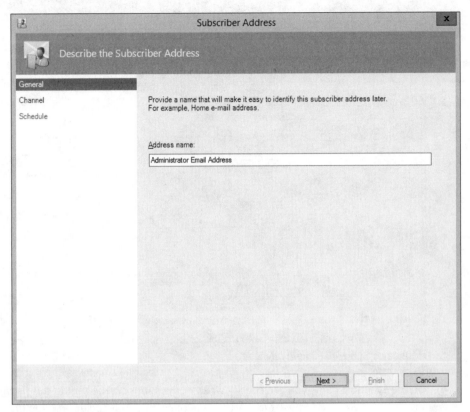

FIGURE 3-19 Subscriber Address

6. On the Channel page, use the drop-down menu to select the E-Mail (SMTP) Channel Type, and then specify the email address that will be used with this channel. Figure 3-20 shows the delivery address set to administrator@tailspintoys.internal.

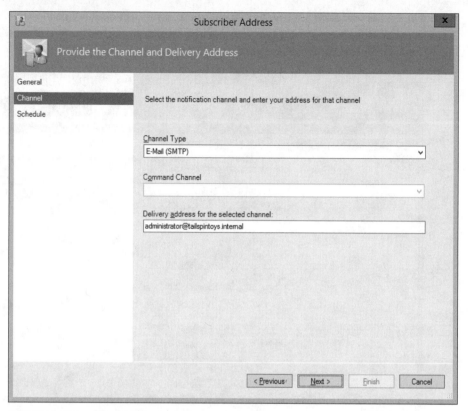

FIGURE 3-20 Subscriber address channel

7. On the Schedule page, you can specify when notifications can be sent to this particular subscriber. If you want to use the master schedule configured earlier, you don't have to configure a schedule here.

> **MORE INFO** **NOTIFICATION SUBSCRIBERS**
>
> You can learn more about configuring notification subscribers at *http://technet.microsoft. com/en-us/library/hh212812.aspx.*

8. On the Addresses page, shown in Figure 3-21, verify that all of the individual subscribers that you want to add are listed, and then click Finish.

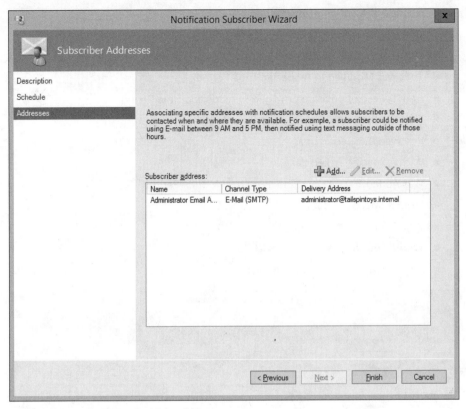

FIGURE 3-21 Notification subscriber addresses

Notification subscriptions

Notification subscriptions allow you to define the criteria for when a notification should be sent, whom it should be sent to, and the method that should be used to send that notification. You can create notification subscriptions based on the following criteria, shown in Figure 3-22:

- Raised By Any Instance In A Specific Group
- Raised By Any Instance Of A Specific Class
- Created By Specific Rules Or Monitors
- Raised By An Instance With A Specific Name
- Of A Specific Severity
- Of A Specific Priority
- With A Specific Resolution State
- With A Specific Name
- With Specific Text In The Description

- Created In A Specific Time Period
- Assigned To A Specific Owner
- Last Modified By A Specific User
- That Was Modified In A Specific Time Period
- Had Its Resolution State Changed In A Specific Time Period
- That Was Resolved In A Specific Time Period
- Resolved By Specific User
- With A Specific Ticked ID
- Was Added To The Database In A Specific Time Period
- From A Specific Site
- With Specific Text In Custom Field (1-10)
- With A Specific TFS Work Item ID
- With A Specific TFS Work Item owner

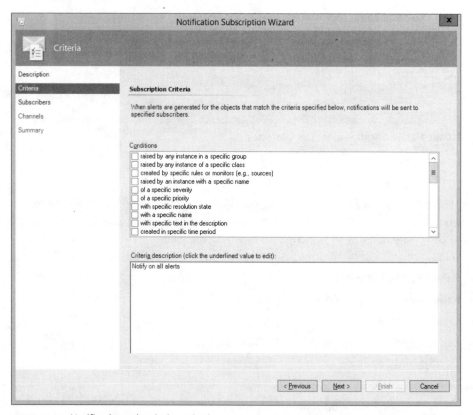

FIGURE 3-22 Notification subscription criteria

To create a notification subscription, perform the following steps:

1. In the Administration workspace of the Operations Manager console, click the Subscriptions node under the Notifications node. In the Tasks pane, click New.

2. On the Description page of the Notification Subscription Wizard, provide a meaningful subscription name.

3. On the Criteria page, specify the criteria that should trigger the notification. For example, Figure 3-23 shows a notification subscription that uses the criteria that an alert must have a critical severity and a high priority.

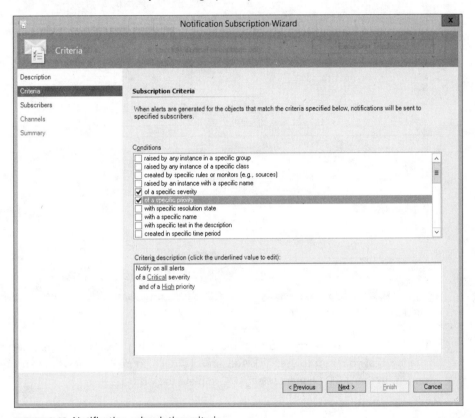

FIGURE 3-23 Notification subscription criteria

4. On the Subscribers page, click Add. On the Subscriber Search page, click Search. The list of subscribers that you have configured will be displayed. Select the ones that you wish to add to the notification subscription, and click OK. Figure 3-24 shows the subscriber named TAILSPINTOYS\Administrator being added as a selected subscriber.

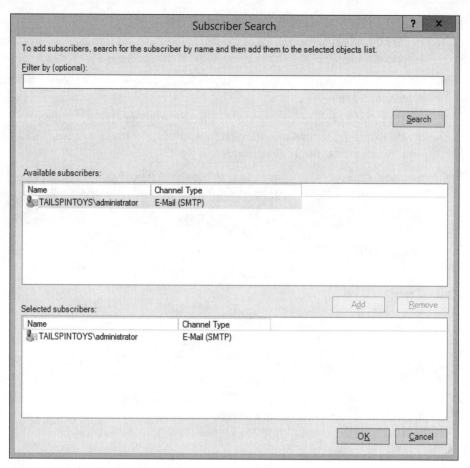

FIGURE 3-24 Subscriber Search

5. On the Channels page, click Add. On the Channel Search page, click Search. Select the channel that you want to use, click Add, and click OK. Figure 3-25 shows the Channels page with the SMTP Channel selected. Complete the wizard.

MORE INFO **NOTIFICATION SUBSCRIPTIONS**

You can learn more about creating notification subscriptions at *http://technet.microsoft. com/en-us/library/hh212789.aspx.*

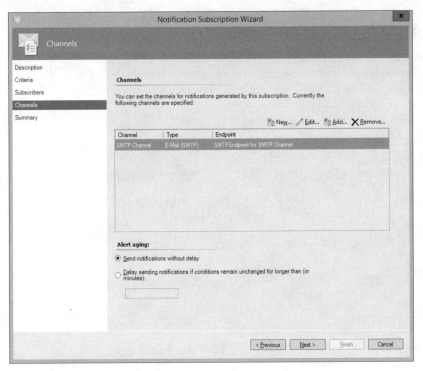

FIGURE 3-25 Notification subscription channels

Subscribe to an alert notification

While you can configure a notification subscription by setting up the conditions under which you should be notified, you can also use the Alerts view in the Monitoring workspace to locate a specific alert and use that as the basis of creating a new notification subscription.

To create a notification subscription from an existing alert, perform the following steps:

1. In the Monitoring workspace of the Operations Manager console, select the alert for which you want to create the notification subscription.

2. In the Tasks pane, under Subscription, click Create. This will launch the Notification Subscription Wizard. The Description and Criteria pages of this wizard will already be populated with description and criteria information about the alert from which you are creating the notification subscription.

3. On the Subscribers page, click Add to select the subscriber who will be notified by the notification subscription.

4. On the Channels page, click Add to specify the method through which the subscriber will be notified. Figure 3-26 shows that the SMTP Channel is selected.

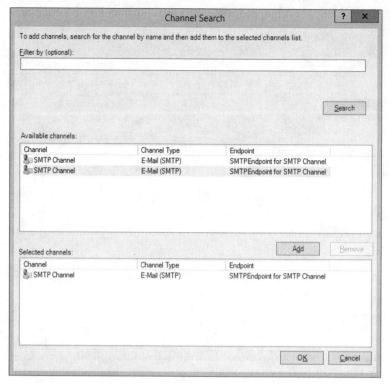

FIGURE 3-26 Channel Search

5. Complete the wizard to create the notification subscription based off of the alert.

> *MORE INFO* **SUBSCRIBE TO NOTIFICATIONS FROM AN ALERT**
>
> You can learn more about subscribing to notifications from an alert at *http://technet.micro-soft.com/en-us/library/hh212895.aspx*.

Analyzing network devices and data

The Network Monitoring node of the Monitoring workspace of the Operations Manager console allows you to view network-related monitoring information. These views include:

- Active Alerts
- Hosts
- HSRP Groups

- Legacy Network Devices
- Network Devices
- Network Summary Dashboard
- Routers
- Switches
- VLANS
- Performance

Network Summary Dashboard view

The Network Summary Dashboard view provides you with the following information about network devices, termed nodes that Operations Manager monitors:

- Nodes With Slowest Response (ICMP Ping)
- Nodes With Highest CPU Usage
- Interfaces With Highest Utilization
- Interfaces With Most Send Errors
- Interfaces With Most Receive Errors
- Notes With The Most Alerts
- Interfaces With The Most Alerts

Network Node Dashboard view

The Network Node Dashboard view is a network device specific dashboard view. You can access this view by selecting the network device you wish to view information for, and then in the Tasks pane, clicking Network Node Dashboard. This view allows you to view the following information about a specific device:

- Vicinity view of the node
- Availability statistics of the node over the last 24 hours / 48 hours / 7 days / 30 days
- Node properties
- Average response time
- Processor usage over the last 24 hours
- Current node interface health
- Alerts generated by the node
- Alert details

Network Interface Dashboard view

Operations Manager monitors network interfaces, such as the ports on monitored switches, as long as they are connected to other devices that Operations Manager also monitors. For example, a port on a monitored switch will be monitored if it also connects to a computer that is monitored by Operations Manager. The Network Interface Dashboard view allows you to view information about a specific interface on a monitored network device. This dashboard is accessible through the Network Node Dashboard view by clicking on Network Interface Dashboard in the Health Of Interfaces on this node area. The Network Interface Dashboard view provides the following information:

- Bytes sent and received over the past 24 hours
- Packets sent and received over the past 24 hours
- Interface properties
- Send and receive errors and discards over the past 24 hours
- Network interface usage percentage
- Alerts generated by this interface
- Alert details

EXAM TIP

Remember what is visible through the Network Interface Dashboard view.

Network Vicinity Dashboard

The Network Vicinity Dashboard allows you to view a diagram of a device and all of the monitored devices and computers that connect directly to that device. You can configure the Network Vicinity Dashboard to go beyond direct connection, expanding out to five levels of connection. The Network Vicinity Dashboard provides a graphical representation of each monitored object and the health of the connections between those objects.

> *MORE INFO* **NETWORK DEVICES AND DATA**
>
> You can learn more about network devices and data at *http://technet.microsoft.com/en-us/library/hh212706.aspx*.

Thought experiment

Network device monitoring at Contoso

You are in the process of deploying Operations Manager as a network monitoring device solution at Contoso. As part of this deployment, you are training the existing network monitoring team on the features of Operations Manager's network monitoring dashboards. With this in mind, answer the following questions:

1. Which dashboard would you use to view the list of network device interfaces in the organization that had the most send errors?

2. Which dashboard would you use to view the availability statistics of a particular network device over the last seven days?

3. Which dashboard would you use to view the number of bytes sent on a specific router interface where Operations Manager monitors the router?

Objective summary

- Automatic alert resolution allows you to specify how long it will be before an alert is in a new resolution state.

- Closing an alert generated by a monitor will mean no new alerts will be generated unless a state change occurs from healthy to warning, healthy to critical, or warning to critical.

- Closing an alert generated by a rule will close the current alert, but new alerts generated by the rule will still be displayed.

- To subscribe to an alert notification, you need to configure a notification action account, notification channel, notification subscriber, and a notification subscription.

- The Network Summary Dashboard provides information about monitored network devices.

- The Network Node Dashboard provides information about a specific monitored network device.

- The Network Interface Dashboard provides information about a specific monitored device interface.

- The Network Vicinity Dashboard provides information about monitored objects connected to a monitored device.

Objective review

Answer the following questions to test your knowledge of the information in this objective. You can find the answers to these questions and explanations of why each answer choice is correct or incorrect in the "Answers" section at the end of this chapter.

1. A monitor is configured for a network device. In which of the following situations will an alert be generated?

   A. Monitor state changes from healthy to critical

   B. Monitor state changes from critical to healthy

   C. Monitor state changes from warning to healthy

   D. Monitor state changes from healthy to warning

2. You have imported a management pack for a network device that includes a monitor that raises an alert related to network connectivity. While you find this alert useful, you have noticed that the alert does not automatically resolve itself when the monitor returns to a healthy state. Which of the following parameters would you configure an override for on the monitor to ensure that the alert was automatically resolved when the monitor returned to a healthy state?

   A. Alert On State

   B. Alert Priority

   C. Alert Severity

   D. Auto-Resolve Alert

3. Which of the following statements about closing alerts generated by rules and monitors is true?

   A. If you close an alert generated by a monitor without resolving the issue that generated the alert, the monitor will generate another alert.

   B. If you close an alert generated by a rule without resolving the issue that generated the alert, the rule will generate another alert.

   C. If you close an alert generated by a monitor without resolving the issue that generated the alert, the monitor will not generate another alert.

   D. If you close an alert generated by a rule without resolving the issue that generated the alert, the rule will not generate another alert.

4. Which of the following Operations Manager network dashboards would you use to determine the monitored servers connected to a specific monitored switch?

   A. Network Summary Dashboard

   B. Network Node Dashboard view

   C. Network Interface Dashboard view

   D. Network Vicinity Dashboard

5. Which of the following Operations Manager network dashboards would you use to determine the statistics of a switch uplink port that connected two network switches monitored by Operations Manager?

   A. Network Vicinity Dashboard

   B. Network Interface Dashboard view

   C. Network Node Dashboard view

   D. Network Summary Dashboard

Objective 3.2: Monitor servers

Once you have configured Operations Manager to collect data from the servers in your environment, you will need to configure how Operations Manager displays and interprets that data, including configuring notifications and alerts about important items that should be brought to the attention of the people responsible for monitoring these computers. Managing servers also involves following up on agents that are reporting problems, being able to put monitored objects into maintenance mode, understanding how heartbeat alerts work, as well as configuring health explorer, and audit collection services.

> **This section covers the following topics:**
> - Understanding not monitored and gray agents
> - Using maintenance mode
> - Understanding heartbeat alerts
> - Using Health Explorer
> - Configuring Audit Collection Services (ACS)

Understanding not monitored and gray agents

In some scenarios, you'll find computers that you've just deployed the Operations Manager agent to, listed as having a healthy agent status, also shown to be in a not monitored state. Figure 3-27 shows several computers with this status. A computer is in a state where the Operations Manager agent is shown to be in a healthy state and the computer is not monitored when the management pack for the computer's operating system is not installed. For example, the computers shown below are in this state because it was only after I took this screenshot that I installed the Windows Server 2012 R2 related management packs.

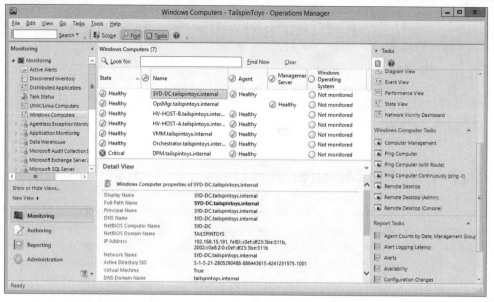

FIGURE 3-27 Not monitored

Another reason why the status of a server might show as not monitored is because you have uninstalled and then reinstalled it. The default configuration of Operations Manager has the grooming of deleted agents occur after 48 hours. If the previous agent information is still in the database, the newly installed agent won't be recognized.

If the Operations Manager agent is shown as healthy, but is dimmed, it means that the health service on the monitored computer is not receiving heartbeat data from the Operations Manager agent. The healthy status is shown in gray because everything was functioning properly at some point in the recent past. Common causes for a gray state include:

- Heartbeat failure
- Nonfunctioning health service
- Improper configuration
- System workflows failure
- Poor Operations Manager or data warehouse database performance
- Network problems
- Authentication issues

When diagnosing the cause of gray agents, you can run the Show Gray Agent Connectivity Data task. This will provide the following information:

- The last time a management server received a heartbeat from the agent.
- The status of the System Center Management Health service.

- Whether the agent responds to ping requests.
- The last time the agent's configuration was updated.
- The management server to which the agent reports.

> **MORE INFO** NOT MONITORED AND GRAY AGENTS
>
> You can learn more about not monitored and gray agents at *http://technet.microsoft.com/en-us/library/hh212870.aspx*.

Using maintenance mode

You use maintenance mode to apply a special status to a monitored object to stop errors and alerts occurring when you are performing maintenance tasks on that object. For example, you want to restart a server to apply software updates or shut it down temporarily to change the hardware configuration. Prior to performing these maintenance tasks, you would use the Operations Manager console to place the server into maintenance mode so that the server restarting or going offline does not trigger a host of alerts and notifications. Enabling maintenance mode suspends the following features:

- Rules and monitors
- Notifications
- Automatic responses
- State changes
- New alerts

To put a computer into maintenance mode, perform the following steps:

1. In the Operations Manager console, click the Windows Computers node under the Monitoring node. This node is shown with the computer SYD-DC.tailspintoys.internal selected in Figure 3-28.

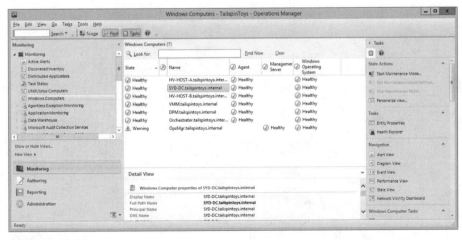

FIGURE 3-28 Windows Computers node

2. With the computer that you want to put into maintenance mode selected, click Start Maintenance mode on the Tasks menu.

3. In the Maintenance Mode Settings dialog box, shown in Figure 3-29, configure the following settings:

- **Apply To** You can select between the selected object, and the selected object and all contained object.

- **Category** You can use this to specify the reason for the object being put into maintenance mode. You can select whether the maintenance mode is planned, and can specify one of the following reasons:

  - Other (Planned/Unplanned)

  - Hardware: Maintenance (Planned/Unplanned)

  - Hardware: Installation (Planned/Unplanned)

  - Operating System: Reconfiguration (Planned/Unplanned)

  - Application: Maintenance (Planned/Unplanned)

  - Application: Installation (Planned/Unplanned)

  - Security Issue

- **Duration** You can specify the number of minutes, or a specific end time for the maintenance mode status.

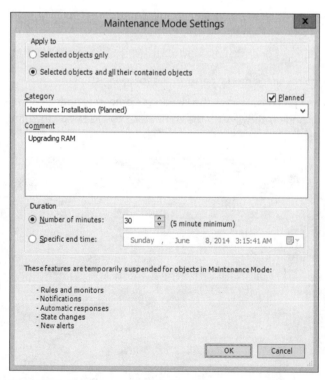

FIGURE 3-29 Maintenance Mode Settings

4. Once in maintenance mode, a maintenance mode icon, like the one shown in Figure 3-30, will appear next to the computer until the maintenance period expires.

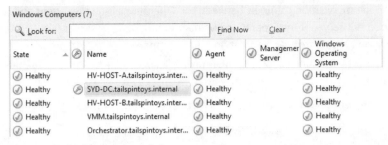

FIGURE 3-30 Maintenance mode icon

You can edit maintenance mode, for example to increase the amount of time that the maintenance period lasts, by right-clicking the object, and clicking Maintenance Mode, and then clicking Edit Maintenance Mode settings. This will return you to the Maintenance Mode Settings dialog box that you can use to change the maintenance mode settings.

EXAM TIP

Remember how to extend maintenance mode.

You can stop maintenance mode on a computer by clicking the computer in the Windows Computers node of the Monitoring workspace, and clicking Stop Maintenance Mode. You will then be prompted to confirm that you want to stop maintenance mode, as shown in Figure 3-31.

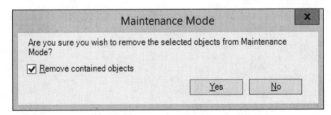

FIGURE 3-31 Maintenance Mode

MORE INFO **MAINTENANCE MODE**

You can learn more about maintenance mode at *http://technet.microsoft.com/en-us/library/hh212870.aspx*.

Understanding heartbeat alerts

A heartbeat is a UDP packet sent on port 5723 every 60 seconds that Operations Manager uses to monitor communication channels between the Operations Manager agent and its primary management server. If the Operations Manager management server fails to receive four consecutive heartbeats from an agent, two things happen:

- Operations Manager will generate a Health Service Heartbeat Failure alert, as shown in Figure 3-32.
- The management server will attempt to ping the computer that hosts the agent.

FIGURE 3-32 Alert properties

If the computer that hosts the agent does not respond to the ping request, Operations Manager will generate a Failed To Connect To Computer alert. If you see the Health Service Heartbeat Failure alert, but not the Failed To Connect To Computer alert, you can deduce that there is a problem with the Operations Manager agent, as the computer itself remains contactable. Both of these alerts will be closed automatically once heartbeat traffic resumes.

You can change the heartbeat settings for all management servers by performing the following steps:

1. In the Settings node of the Administration workspace of the Operations Manager console, click Heartbeat under Agent, and then click Properties.

2. On the Global Agent Settings dialog box, shown in Figure 3-33, adjust the heartbeat interval to the desired figure.

FIGURE 3-33 Global heartbeat settings

3. Under Server, click Heartbeat, and then click Properties in the Tasks pane.

4. On the Global Management Server Settings - Heartbeat dialog box, set the Number Of Missed Heartbeats Allowed, as shown in Figure 3-34.

FIGURE 3-34 Heartbeat settings

You can change the heartbeat settings for an individual computer by performing the following steps:

1. In the Agent Managed node of the Administration workspace of the Operations Manager console, click the computer for which you want to change the heartbeat settings, and then click Properties in the Tasks pane.

2. On the Heartbeat tab of the Agent Properties dialog box, select the Override Global Agent Settings check box, and specify the new Heartbeat settings. Figure 3-35 shows the heartbeat interval for computer Orchestrator.tailspintoys.internal set to 90 seconds.

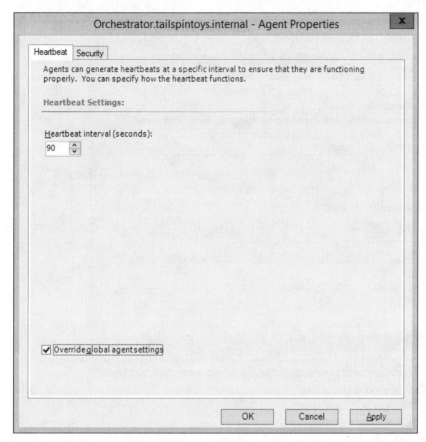

FIGURE 3-35 Individual server heartbeat settings

You can trigger a Health Service Heartbeat Failure alert for testing purposes by stopping the Microsoft monitoring agent (formerly System Center Management service) on a computer with an agent installed, as shown in Figure 3-36.

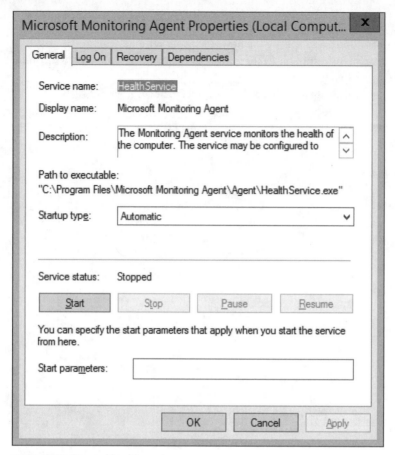

FIGURE 3-36 Stopped health service

MORE INFO **HEARTBEAT ALERTS**

You can learn more about heartbeat alerts at *http://technet.microsoft.com/en-us/library/hh212798.aspx*.

Using Health Explorer

The Health Explorer tool allows you to view the health of an entity, for example the health of a monitored computer. Health Explorer also allows you to view the history of state changes for that object. For example, Figure 3-37 shows the Health Explorer for the computer Orchestrator.tailspintoys.com. You can see in the figure where the health state of the computer has changed between healthy to warning, and then from warning back to healthy.

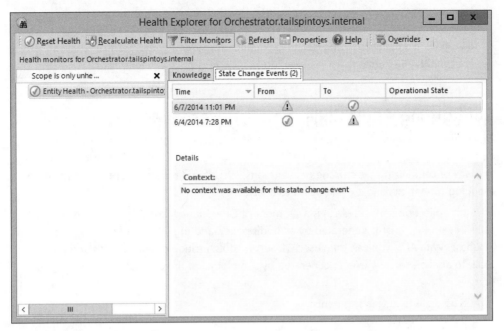

FIGURE 3-37 State change events

Through Health Explorer, you can view the alerts that are present on a particular entity. Figure 3-38 shows the alerts that are relevant to the monitored computer Orchestrator. tailspintoys.internal. You can use Health Explorer to locate all of the monitors that are in a state that requires attention. This allows you to quickly assess and diagnose the issues with a particular computer, which might be responsible for a multitude of separate alerts.

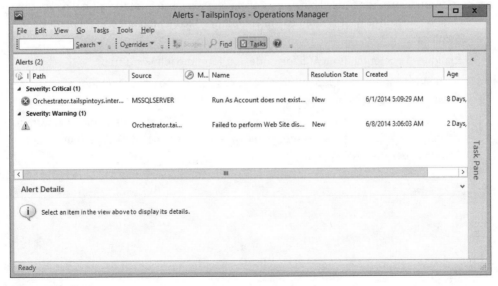

FIGURE 3-38 Alerts

Configuring Audit Collection Services

One of the challenges of using the built-in auditing capabilities of Windows computers is that each computer stores event logs locally. While it is possible to configure event log forwarding as a way of centralizing the storage of event logs, event log data is still kept in the standard event log format, making it challenging to analyze.

Audit Collection Services (ACS) is a segment of Operations Manager that allows you to collect event log records generated by an audit policy, and to place them in a SQL Server database. With ACS, you can then use SQL Server tools, including data analysis and reporting tools, to analyze security events generated by some or all of the computers in your organization.

ACS uses the following segments:

- ACS forwarders
- ACS collectors
- ACS database

ACS forwarders

ACS forwarders forward security event log information to ACS collectors. The ACS forwarder is part of the Operations Manger agent. While the service is installed, the ACS forwarder will not be active until you run the Enable Audit Collection task. Once this task has been run, all events that would normally be written to the computer's Security log are also forwarded to the ACS collector.

To configure a computer as an ACS forwarder, perform the following steps:

1. In the Monitoring workspace of the Operations console, expand Operations Manager, expand Agent Details, and then select Agent Health State.

2. Two panes are displayed. In the right pane, select all of the computers that you want to configure as ACS forwarder, as shown in Figure 3-39, and then click Enable Audit Collection under Health Service Tasks.

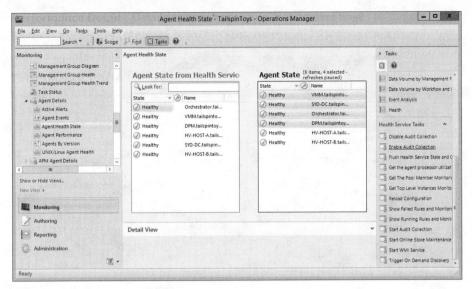

FIGURE 3-39 Enable audit collection

3. On the Run Task - Enable Audit Collection, click Override under Task Parameters.

4. On the Override Task Parameters dialog box, enter the FQDN of the ACS collector, as shown in Figure 3-40, and click Override.

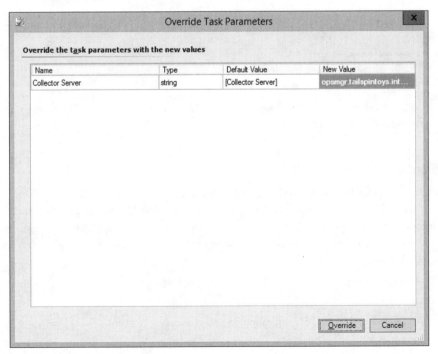

FIGURE 3-40 Set collector server

5. Verify that the Collector Server is listed properly under Task Parameters, as shown in Figure 3-41, and click Run.

FIGURE 3-41 Enable audit collection

ACS collectors

A computer that functions as an ACS collector processes security event information forwarded by ACS forwarders, and then forwards this data to the ACS database. Microsoft recommends that you don't install the ACS collector on an Operations Manager management server. This is because the ACS collector role can place an undue performance burden on the management server.

It is possible to deploy multiple ACS collectors. Each ACS collector requires an individual ACS database. ACS collectors require the following:

- An Operations Manager management server must be present.
- The server that hosts the ACS collector role must be a member of an Active Directory domain that is in the same forest as the Operations Manager management server.

- The server that hosts the ACS collector role has a minimum of 1 GB of RAM, with 2GB or more recommended, and 10 GB of free space to store the ACS database.

ACS database

The ACS database hosts all of the security event log items forwarded to the ACS collectors by the ACS forwarders. System Center 2012 Operations Manager SP1 and System Center 2012 R2 Operations Manager support using SQL Server 2008 R2 SP1 and later, and SQL Server 2012 and later to host the ACS database. Microsoft recommends using the Enterprise rather than Standard edition of SQL Server because of the performance requirements involved in processing traffic from the ACS forwarder.

To install the ACS collector and ACS database role, perform the following steps:

1. On the Operations Manager installation screen, shown in Figure 3-42, click Audit Collection Services in the list of Optional Installations. This will start the Audit Collection Services Collector Setup Wizard.

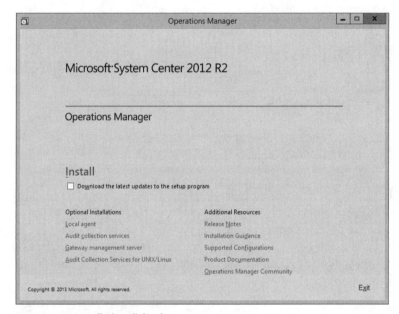

FIGURE 3-42 Installation dialog box

2. After accepting the license terms, select Create A New Database, and enter the data source name and the database instance details.

3. On the Database Authentication page, select whether Windows or SQL authentication is being used, and the folders that will store the database and log files.

4. On the Event Retention Schedule page, shown in Figure 3-43, specify how long events will be retained in the database.

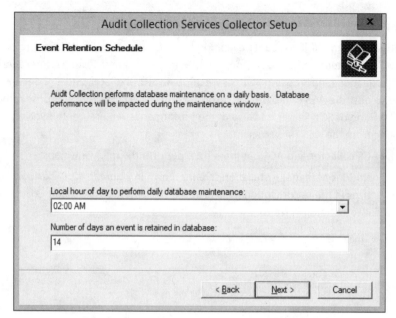

FIGURE 3-43 ACS collector setup

5. On the ACS Stored Timestamp Format page, choose between Local Time or Universal Coordinated Time, and then complete the Setup Wizard.

ACS and Dynamic Access Control

System Center 2012 SP1 Operations Manager and later supports integration with Dynamic Access Control. Dynamic Access Control allows audit policies based on user, resource, environmental claims, and properties. Operations Manager doesn't require additional configuration to support integration with Dynamic Access Control. Interaction with this feature is through additional reports that become available when you install ACS Reporting

> **MORE INFO** **AUDIT COLLECTION SERVICES**
>
> You can learn more about using Audit Collection Services at *http://technet.microsoft.com/en-us/library/hh212908.aspx.*

Thought experiment

Server monitoring at Margie's Travel

You are working on some issues related to the monitoring of server operating systems at Margie's travel. Specifically:

- You have deployed the Operations Manager agent to 10 new servers running the Windows Server 2012 R2 operating system. Each of these servers is shown in the Monitoring console as having a healthy agent, but is also listed as not monitored.

- In the last day, two servers have switched from having their health statuses displayed in green in the Monitoring workspace of the Server Manager console, to having their health statuses displayed in gray.

With this information in mind, answer the following questions:

1. What steps can you take to ensure that all of the computers with the Windows Server 2012 R2 operating system are no longer listed as not monitored?

2. Which service should you check first, on the two servers with a gray health status?

Objective summary

- An agent may show a server to be in a not monitored state because the management pack of the host operating it is not installed on the Operations Manager management server.

- Maintenance mode suspends rules and monitors, notifications, automatic responses, state changes, and new alerts.

- An Health Service Heartbeat Failure alert will be triggered if the Operations Manager server fails to receive four consecutive heartbeats from an agent.

- When a Health Service Heartbeat Failure alert is triggered, the Operations Manager server attempts to ping the computer. If the computer does not respond to the ping request, a Failed To Connect To Computer alert will be raised.

- An ACS forwarder is installed on a computer that will forward security event logs to an ACS collector.

- An ACS collector processes data forwarded from an ACS forwarder, and sends it to the ACS database.

Objective review

Answer the following questions to test your knowledge of the information in this objective. You can find the answers to these questions and explanations of why each answer choice is correct or incorrect in the "Answers" section at the end of this chapter.

1. A Health Service Heartbeat Failure alert for computer SYD-FS1 is present in alerts view. You look for a Failed To Connect To Computer alert in alerts view, but one is not present. Which of the following diagnoses is probable given this state of affairs?

   A. SYD-FS1 is in a healthy state.

   B. There is a problem with the Operations Manager agent on SYD-FS1.

   C. The Operations Manager management server is unable to ping SYD-FS1.

   D. SYD-FS1 has been assigned a new IP address.

2. You have five domain controllers that audit user logon activity. You want to deploy Operations Manager Audit Collection Services on a new server named ACS1. ACS1 will host the ACS database. Which of the following answers best describes how you should deploy ACS roles in this scenario?

   A. Enable the ACS forwarder role on each domain controller

   B. Install the ACS collector role on each domain controller

   C. Enable the ACS forwarder role on ACS1.

   D. Enable the ACS collector role on ACS1.

3. Which of the following is disabled or suspended when you put a monitored server into maintenance mode using the Operations Manager console?

   A. Microsoft monitoring agent service on the monitored server.

   B. Rules and monitors related to the monitored server.

   C. New alerts from the monitored server.

   D. Message queuing service on the monitored server.

Objective 3.3: Monitor the virtualization layer

Once you have configured Operations Manager to collect data from virtualization hosts and virtual machines, you need to configure how Operations Manager displays and interprets that data. This means configuring notifications and alerts through to analyzing overall virtualization layer health. When integrated with Virtual Machine Manager, Operations Manager provides a number of dashboards and views that allow you to monitor the functionality and performance of your organization's fabric.

Integrating Operations Manager with Virtual Machine Manager

To be able to monitor your organization's virtualization layer when you are using a System Center 2012 and System Center 2012 R2 managed private cloud, you need to integrate Operations Manager with Virtual Machine Manager.

Integrating Operations Manager with Virtual Machine Manager provides you with the following dashboards and views as shown in Figure 3-44:

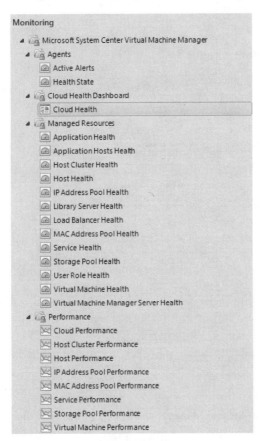

FIGURE 3-44 Virtualization dashboards and views

- Cloud Health
- Application Health
- Application Hosts Health
- Host Cluster Health
- Host Health
- IP Address Pool Health
- Library Server Health
- Load Balancer Health
- MAC Address Pool Health
- Service Health
- Storage Pool Health
- User Role Health
- Virtual Machine Health
- Virtual Machine Manager Server Health

The Virtual Machine Health dashboard is shown in Figure 3-45.

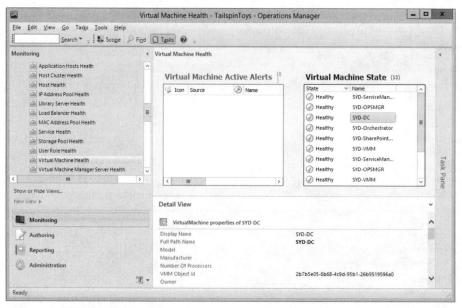

FIGURE 3-45 Virtual Machine Health

Integrating Operations Manager and Virtual Machine Manager also allows you to view the following performance information:

- Cloud Performance
- Host Cluster Performance
- Host Performance

- IP Address Pool Performance
- MAC Address Pool Performance
- Service Performance
- Storage Pool Performance
- Virtual Machine Performance

Figure 3-46 shows the Virtual Machine Performance view.

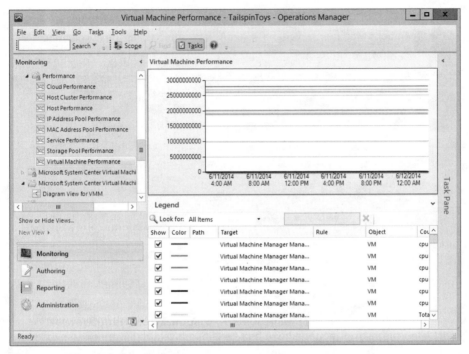

FIGURE 3-46 Virtual Machine Performance

To integrate Operations Manager with Virtual Machine Manager, you need to configure the connector between VMM and Operations Manager. Prior to configuring the connection between VMM and Operations Manager, you need to ensure you perform the following prerequisite configuration tasks:

- Install the Operations Manager console on the VMM server.
- Install the following Operations Manager management packs on the Operations Manager server:
  - SQL Server Core Library version 6.0.5000.0 or later
  - Windows Server Internet Information Services Library version 6.0.5000.0 or later
  - Windows Server Internet Information Services 2003 version 6.0.5000.0 or later
  - Windows Server 2008 Internet Information Services 7 version 6.0.6539.0 or later

To link VMM and Operations Manager, you need the credentials of an account that is a member of the Operations Manager Administrators user role, and the credentials of an account that is a member of the VMM Administrator user role. These can be separate accounts or the same accounts. To configure a connection between VMM and Operations Manager, perform the following steps:

1. In the Settings workspace of the VMM console, click System Center Settings, and then click Operations Manager Server.

2. On the ribbon, click Properties.

3. On the Connection To.. page of the Add Operations Manager Wizard, type the name of the Operations Manager server and a Run As account that has the appropriate permissions, as shown in Figure 3-47.

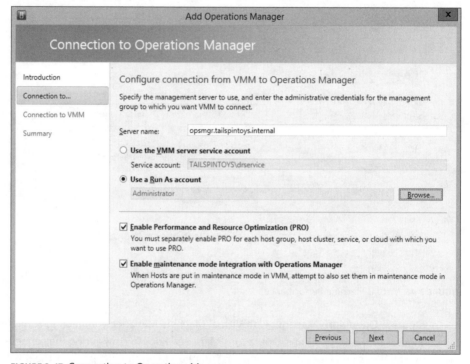

FIGURE 3-47 Connection to Operations Manager

4. On the Connection To VMM page, specify the credentials of the account that will be used by Operations Manger to connect to the VMM server.

5. Complete the wizard.

Configuring the connection between Operations Manager and VMM automatically loads the Management Packs, shown in Figure 3-48, which allow you to monitor the health and performance of your private cloud's virtualization layer.

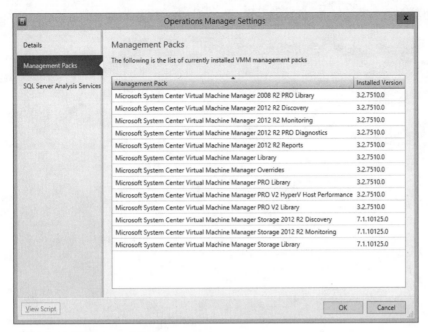

FIGURE 3-48 Management Packs

MORE INFO **OPERATIONS MANAGER INTEGRATION WITH VMM**

You can learn more about configuring Operations Manager integration with VMM at *http://technet.microsoft.com/library/hh427287.aspx*.

Using the Fabric Health Dashboard

You use the Fabric Health Dashboard to view detailed information about the health of VMM private clouds and the infrastructure, sometimes termed fabric, which supports them. Fabric Health Dashboard is available from the Cloud Health node and provides you with information about:

- Host State
- Storage Pools State
- File Share and LUN State
- Network Node State
- Instance Details
- Activity Alerts

Figure 3-49 shows the Fabric Health Dashboard scoped to the TailspinToys cloud.

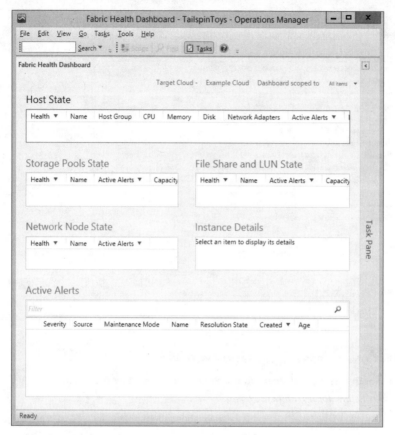

FIGURE 3-49 Fabric Health Dashboard

MORE INFO **FABRIC HEALTH DASHBOARD**

You can learn more about the Fabric Health Dashboard at *http://technet.microsoft.com/en-us/library/dn458591.aspx*.

EXAM TIP

Remember what information you can view through the Fabric Health Dashboard.

Understanding the Fabric Monitoring Diagram view

The Fabric Monitoring Diagram view provides you with a diagram view of the entire infrastructure that VMM manages, and provides you with the health state of each segment that makes up the virtualization fabric. The view is located within the Monitoring workspace of the Operations Manger console when VMM is integrated with Operations Manager. Each node is presented as a roll-up that can be expanded. If a node is displayed as healthy, you can assume that all of the nodes it comprises are also believed by Operations Manager to be healthy. Figure 3-50 shows the Fabric Monitoring Diagram view.

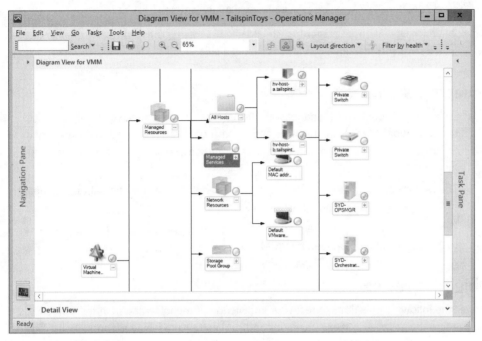

FIGURE 3-50 Diagram View

Where a node shows is displayed as unhealthy, you are able to expand it until you locate the monitored segment that is causing the unhealthy state.

MORE INFO FABRIC DIAGRAM VIEW

You can learn more about Fabric Diagram view at *http://technet.microsoft.com/en-us/ library/dn458593.aspx.*

Objective summary

- To integrate Operations Manager with Virtual Machine Manager, you need to install the Operations Manager console on the VMM server. You also need to ensure that the appropriate SQL Server and Internet Information Services management packs are installed.

- The Fabric Health Dashboard allows you to view detailed information about the health of VMM private clouds and infrastructure.

- The Fabric Monitoring Diagram view allows you to view the health state of the entire virtualization fabric managed by VMM.

Objective review

Answer the following questions to test your knowledge of the information in this objective. You can find the answers to these questions and explanations of why each answer choice is correct or incorrect in the "Answers" section at the end of this chapter.

1. Which of the following Operations Manager dashboards would you use to determine the health state of virtual machines hosted on virtualization hosts managed by VMM?

    A. User Role Health

    B. Storage Pool Health

    C. Virtual Machine Manager Server Health

    D. Virtual Machine Health

2. You are setting up integration between Operations Manager and Virtual Machine Manager. Which of the following credentials do you need, to configure this integration?

    A. An account that is a member of the Operations Manager Administrators user role.

    B. An account that is a member of the VMM Administrator user role.

    C.   An account that is a member of the Domain Admins security group.

    D.   An account that is a member of the Local Administrators group on the Operations Manager server.

3.   Which of the following is displayed in the Fabric Health Dashboard?

    A.   VMM Server Health

    B.   Storage Pools State

    C.   File Share and LUN State

    D.   Domain Controller State

Objective 3.4: Monitor application health

Once you have configured Operations Manager to collect data from applications, you need to configure how Operations Manager displays and interprets that data. This involves configuring appropriate notifications and alerts.

> **This section covers the following topics:**
> - Monitoring .NET applications
> - Monitoring Java applications

Monitoring .NET applications

Operations Manager allows you to monitor .NET web applications either from the perspective of the server, or from the client. This allows you to collect information about application reliability and performance. Collecting this data allows you to generate reliable information about how frequently a particular application problem is occurring, the performance of the host server when the issue occurred, and any related events. Two of the most important tools that you use to monitor .NET applications are the Application Diagnostics console, and Application Advisor.

> **MORE INFO** **MONITORING .NET APPLICATIONS**
>
> You can learn more about monitoring .NET applications at *http://technet.microsoft.com/en-us/library/hh212856.aspx*

Application Diagnostics console

The Application Diagnostics console allows you to monitor .NET applications for failures, faults, and slowdowns. To use the Application Diagnostics console, the Operations Manager web console must be installed on the Operations Manager management server. The Application Diagnostics console is available at the address *http://hostname/AppDiagnostics*, and is shown in Figure 3-51.

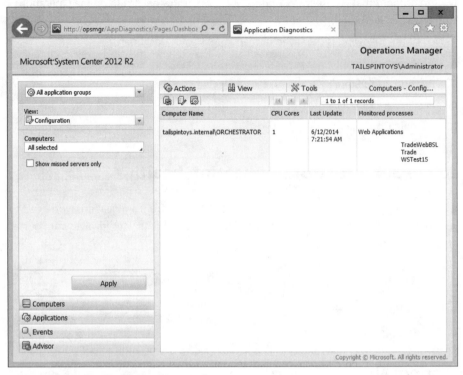

FIGURE 3-51 Application Diagnostics console

The Application Diagnostics console allows you to view events related to application performance and events related to application failures and errors. Application failures and errors can be displayed based on connectivity, security, and failure issues.

> **MORE INFO APPLICATION DIAGNOSTIC CONSOLE**
>
> You can learn more about the Application Diagnostics console at *http://technet.microsoft.com/en-us/library/hh530058.aspx*.

Application Advisor

Application Advisor is a tool that you use with .NET APM to manage and prioritize application related alerts. Application Advisor allows you to run reports that allow you to determine which applications are triggering the most alerts. Application Advisor is a web application that you can use if you have installed the Operations Manager web console. The address of the Application Advisor is *http://hostname/AppAdvisor*. The Application Advisor console is shown in Figure 3-52.

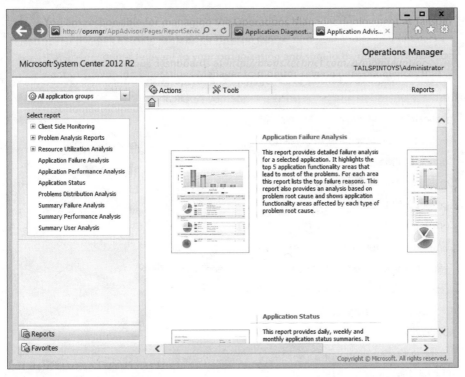

FIGURE 3-52 Application Advisor

Application Advisor provides client side monitoring, problem analysis, and resource utilization analysis reports. The client side monitoring reports are as follows:

- Application AJAX Calls Analysis
- Application Analysis
- Application Status
- Client Latency Distribution
- Load Time Analysis Based On Subnet
- Summary Performance Analysis
- Summary Size Analysis
- Summary User Analysis

The problem analysis reports provided by Application Advisor are as follows:

- Application Activity Breakdown
- Application Daily Activity
- Application Failure Breakdown By Functionality

- Application Failure Breakdown By Resources
- Application Heavy Resources Analysis
- Application Slow Request Analysis
- Day Of Week Utilization
- Hour Of Day Utilization
- Utilization Trend

The resource utilization analysis reports provided by Application Advisor are as follows:

- Application CPU Utilization Analysis
- Application IO Utilization Analysis
- Application Memory Utilization Analysis
- Computer Application Load Analysis
- Computer CPU Utilization Analysis
- Computer IO Utilization Analysis
- Computer Memory Utilization Analysis

Application Advisor also provides the following general reports:

- Application Failure Analysis
- Application Performance Analysis
- Application Status
- Problems Distribution Analysis
- Summary Failure Analysis
- Summary Performance Analysis
- Summary User Analysis

> **MORE INFO** **APPLICATION ADVISOR**
>
> You can learn more about the Application Advisor at *http://technet.microsoft.com/en-us/library/hh322034.aspx*

Monitoring Java applications

Operations Manager 2012 R2 supports Java Application Performance Monitoring (APM). Java APM allows you to monitor Java applications, providing you with information about the application's performance and details of exception events that allow you, or the application owners, to determine the root cause of application issues. You do this by using Operations Manager Application Advisor.

Operations Manager Application Advisor allows you to perform the following tasks:

- Investigate method and resource timing for performance events

- Perform stack traces for exception events
- Monitor Java specific counters for events (including Average Request Time, Requests Per Second, JVM Memory, and Class Loader)

Java APM supports the following configurations:

- Tomcat 5, Tomcat 6, Tomcat 7
  - Windows
  - Linux
- Java JDK 5, Java JDK 6
- Web Technologies
  - GenericServlet
  - Struts
  - Struts2
  - Axis2

EXAM TIP

Remember which configurations are supported for .NET and Java APM.

The Java APM management pack requires the management pack for Java Enterprise Edition, which you must configure for deep monitoring. You use Application Advisor reports, for example the Application Performance Analysis report, to view the performance of Java applications in the same way that you monitor .NET applications.

MORE INFO **MONITORING JAVA APPLICATIONS**

You can learn more about monitoring Java applications at *http://technet.microsoft.com/ en-us/library/dn440936.aspx.*

Thought experiment
Application Performance Monitoring at Contoso

You are in the process of writing documentation to support the monitoring of .NET application performance at Contoso using System Center 2012 R2 operations monitor. As part of the process, you need to answer the following questions:

1. Which tool would you use to view events related to application performance and events related to application failures and errors?

2. Which tool do you use to manage and prioritize application related alerts?

Objective summary

- The Application Diagnostics console allows you to monitor .NET applications for failures, faults, and slowdowns.
- To use the Application Diagnostics console, the Operations Manager web console must be installed on the Operations Manager management server.
- Application Advisor is a tool that you use with .NET APM to manage and prioritize application related alerts.
- Application Advisor is a web application that you can use if you have installed the Operations Manager web console.

Objective review

Answer the following questions to test your knowledge of the information in this objective. You can find the answers to these questions and explanations of why each answer choice is correct or incorrect in the "Answers" section at the end of this chapter.

1. Which of the following must be installed before you can access the Application Advisor functionality of Operations Manager?

   A. Operations Manager web console

   B. Orchestrator connector for Service Manager

   C. SQL Server Analysis Services

   D. Operations Manager connector for Service Manager

2. Which of the following tools would you use to view an application performance monitoring report that provided client application load time analysis on a per-subnet basis?

   A. Application Advisor

   B. Application Diagnostics Console

   C. Operations Manager Web Console

   D. Operations Manager Console

3. Which of the following tools can you use with Operations Manager application performance monitoring to view events related to application errors?

   A. Application Advisor

   B. Application Diagnostics Console

   C. Operations Manager Web Console

   D. Operations Manager Console

Answers

This section contains the solutions to the thought experiments and answers to the lesson review questions in this chapter.

Objective 3.1: Thought experiment

1. You would use the Network Summary dashboard to view the list of network device interfaces in the organization that had the most send errors.

2. You would use the Network Node Dashboard View to view the availability statistics of a particular network device over the last seven days.

3. You would use the Network Interface Dashboard view, to view the number of bytes sent on a specific router interface.

Objective 3.1: Review

1. **Correct answers:** A and D

   A. **Correct**: Alerts will be generated when the health state changes from healthy to critical.

   B. **Incorrect:** Alerts are not generated when the health state changes from critical to healthy.

   C. **Incorrect:** Alerts are not generated when the health state changes from warning to healthy.

   D. **Correct:** Alerts are generated when the health state changes from healthy to warning.

2. **Correct answer:** D

   A. **Incorrect:** You need to configure an override for the Auto-Resolve Alert parameter to ensure that the alert was automatically resolved.

   B. **Incorrect**: You need to configure an override for the Auto-Resolve Alert parameter to ensure that the alert was automatically resolved.

   C. **Incorrect**: You need to configure an override for the Auto-Resolve Alert parameter to ensure that the alert was automatically resolved.

   D. **Correct**: You need to configure an override for the Auto-Resolve Alert parameter to ensure that the alert was automatically resolved.

3. **Correct answers:** B and C

   A. **Incorrect**: A monitor only sends an alert when a state change occurs, from either healthy to warning, healthy to critical, or warning to critical.

   B. **Correct**: A rule will continue to generate alerts as long as the condition that triggers the alert persists.

C. **Correct**: A monitor only sends an alert when a state change occurs, from either healthy to warning, healthy to critical, or warning to critical.

D. **Incorrect**: A rule will continue to generate alerts as long as the condition that triggers the alert persists.

4. **Correct answer:** D

A. **Incorrect**: The Network Summary Dashboard will show information about all monitored network devices.

B. **Incorrect**: The Network Node Dashboard view will display information, including performance information, about a specific monitored device.

C. **Incorrect**: The Network Interface Dashboard view will show information about a specific network device interface.

D. **Correct**: The Network Vicinity Dashboard view will show monitored devices and computers that are connected to a monitored network device.

5. **Correct answer:** B

A. **Incorrect**: The Network Vicinity Dashboard view will show monitored devices and computers that are connected to a monitored network device.

B. **Correct:** The Network Interface Dashboard view will show information about a specific network device interface.

C. **Incorrect:** The Network Node Dashboard view will display information, including performance information about a specific monitored device.

D. **Incorrect**: The Network Summary Dashboard will show information about all monitored network devices.

Objective 3.2: Thought experiment

1. You need to install the Windows Server 2012 R2 management packs to change the status from not monitored.

2. You should check the status of the Microsoft monitoring agent service as a failure of this service can cause a server to be shown with a gray agent status.

Objective 3.2: Review

1. **Correct answer:** B

A. **Incorrect:** A Health Service Heartbeat Failure alert that doesn't have a corresponding Failed To Connect To Computer alert indicates that the computer can be pinged by the Operations Manager management server, but that heartbeat traffic is not occurring. A likely cause is that there is a problem with the Operations Manager agent.

B. **Correct**: A Health Service Heartbeat Failure alert that doesn't have a corresponding Failed To Connect To Computer alert indicates that the computer can be pinged by the Operations Manager management server, but that heartbeat traffic is not occurring. A likely cause is that there is a problem with the Operations Manager agent.

  C. **Incorrect**: A Health Service Heartbeat Failure alert that doesn't have a corresponding Failed To Connect To Computer alert indicates that the computer can be pinged by the Operations Manager management server, but that heartbeat traffic is not occurring. A likely cause is that there is a problem with the Operations Manager agent.

  D. **Incorrect**: A Health Service Heartbeat Failure alert that doesn't have a corresponding Failed To Connect To Computer alert indicates that the computer can be pinged by the Operations Manager management server, but that heartbeat traffic is not occurring.

2. **Correct answers:** A and D

  A. **Correct:** ACS forwarders send security event log data to the ACS collector.

  B. **Incorrect**: The domain controllers should be configured as ACS forwarders.

  C. **Incorrect**: As ACS1 is not generating the initial security log events, it should not function as an ACS forwarder.

  D. **Correct**: ACS1 should function as the ACS collector.

3. **Correct answers:** B and C

  A. **Incorrect**: No services on the monitored service will be disabled when the server is placed into monitoring mode on the Operations Manager server.

  B. **Correct:** Rules and monitors related to the monitored server will be suspended while the server is in maintenance mode.

  C. **Correct**: New alerts from the monitored server will be suspended while the server is in maintenance mode.

  D. **Incorrect**: No services on the monitored service will be disabled when the server is placed into monitoring mode on the Operations Manager server.

Objective 3.3: Thought experiment

1. You must in stall the Operations Manager console on the VMM server.

2. The Fabric Monitoring Diagram view allows you to view the health state of all of the segments managed by VMM as part of a diagram.

Objective 3.3: Review

1. **Correct answer:** D

   A. **Incorrect**: User Role Health will display the health of user roles.

   B. **Incorrect**: Storage Pool Health will display the health of storage managed by VMM.

   C. **Incorrect**: Virtual Machine Manager Server Health will show the health status of VMM servers.

   D. **Correct**: Virtual Machine Health allows you to view the health status of virtual machines hosted on virtualization hosts managed by VMM.

2. **Correct answer:** A and B

   A. **Correct**: You need access to an account that is a member of the Operations Manager Administrator user role and an account that is a member of the VMM Administrator role.

   B. **Correct**: You need access to an account that is a member of the Operations Manager Administrator user role and an account that is a member of the VMM Administrator role.

   C. **Incorrect:** You need access to an account that is a member of the Operations Manager Administrator user role and an account that is a member of the VMM Administrator role.

   D. **Incorrect**: You need access to an account that is a member of the Operations Manager Administrator user role and an account that is a member of the VMM Administrator role.

3. **Correct answers:** B and C

   A. **Incorrect**: The Fabric Health Dashboard does not display VMM Server Health.

   B. **Correct**: The Fabric Health Dashboard does display Storage Pools State.

   C. **Correct**: The Fabric Health Dashboard does display File Share and LUN State.

   D. **Incorrect:** The Fabric Health Dashboard does not display Domain Controller Health.

Objective 3.4: Thought experiment

1. The Application Diagnostics console allows you to view events related to application performance and events related to application failures and errors.

2. Application Advisor is a tool that you can use to manage and prioritize application related alerts.

Objective 3.4: Review

1.   **Correct answer:** A

     A.   **Correct:** The Operations Manager web console must be installed before you can access the Application Advisor functionality of Operations Manager.

     B.   **Incorrect:** You do not have to have the Orchestrator connector for Service Manager, or Service Manager, installed to access the Application Advisor.

     C.   **Incorrect:** You do not have to have SQL Server Analysis Services installed to access the Application Advisor.

     D.   **Incorrect:** You do not have to have the Operations Manager connector for Service Manager, or Service Manager, installed to access the Application Advisor.

2.   **Correct answer:** A

     A.   **Correct:** You can use the application diagnostics console to view a load time analysis based on subnet report.

     B.   **Incorrect:** You cannot use the application diagnostics console to view a load time analysis based on subnet report.

     C.   **Incorrect:** You cannot use the Operations Manager Web console to view a load time analysis based on subnet report.

     D.   **Incorrect:** You cannot use the Operations Manager console to view a load time analysis based on subnet report.

3.   **Correct answer:** B

     A.   **Incorrect:** You can use the application diagnostics console to view events related to application errors.

     B.   **Correct:** You can use the application diagnostics console to view events related to application errors.

     C.   **Incorrect:** You can use the application diagnostics console to view events related to application errors.

     D.   **Incorrect:** You can use the application diagnostics console to view events related to application errors.

CHAPTER 4

Configure and maintain service management

IT professionals are responsible for providing specific services to the organization for which they work. Service Manager provides the ability to measure the performance of IT professionals in providing these services by tracking the speed at which incidents and problems are resolved. This chapter includes information on configuring Service Manager to track performance against service level objectives. You'll learn how to configure and manage Service Manager incidents, problems, and knowledge articles. You'll also learn about managing cloud resources through VMM by configuring available profiles and templates.

Objectives in this chapter:

- Objective 4.1: Implement service level management
- Objective 4.2: Manage problems and incidents
- Objective 4.3: Manage cloud resources

Objective 4.1: Implement service level management

This objective deals with how you implement service level management with Service Manager. This includes the steps that you need to take to allow Service Manager to measure and track whether service level objectives are being breached by configuring calendars, metrics, and service level objectives.

> **This section covers the following topics:**
> - Understanding service level management
> - Creating calendar items
> - Creating metrics
> - Creating queues
> - Creating service level objectives
> - Sending notifications
> - SLA reporting

Understanding service level management

Service level management is a term used to describe measuring incident and service request lifecycle. The lifecycle of an incident and service request starts when the incident or service request is created and concludes when the incident or service request is resolved.

A service level item comprises:

- Queues for specific service levels
- Time metrics for those queues

As a part of service level management, you can also configure notifications to be sent to users prior to and after service levels defined by those queue metrics is exceeded. You use the Calendar, Metric, and Service Level Objectives node of the Administration workspace of the Service Manager console, shown in Figure 4-1, to configure service level management.

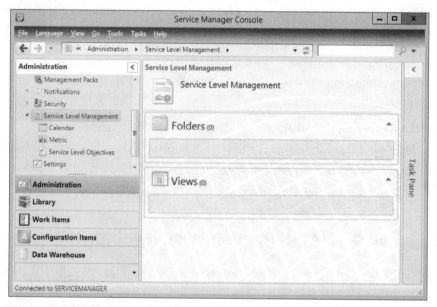

FIGURE 4-1 Administration workspace

MORE INFO SERVICE LEVEL MANAGEMENT

You can learn more about service level management at *http://technet.microsoft.com/en-US/library/hh519775.aspx*.

Creating calendar items

You use the Calendar node to define operational periods, such as which days are workdays, which hours are work hours, and which days, such as holidays, count as exceptions. Calendar items are separate work schedules that constitute time that is available and which is measured where IT professionals resolve Service Manager incidents and service requests.

To create a calendar item, perform the following steps:

1. In the Administration workspace of the Service Manager console, click Calendar, under Service Level Management.

2. In the Tasks menu, click Calendar, and then click Create Calendar.

3. On the General page of the Create/Edit Calendar dialog box, provide the following information (Figure 4-2 shows an example calendar):

   - **Title** A name for the calendar.
   - **Time Zone** The time zone in which the calendar will be used.
   - **Working Days And Hours** Select which days of the week and which hours of each day will make up the period over which IT professionals are expected to resolve incidents and service requests.
   - **Holidays** Specify any holidays that will function as exemptions to the calendar when it comes to calculating incident and service request metrics.

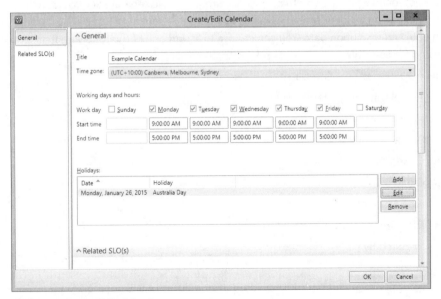

FIGURE 4-2 Create/Edit Calendar

4. Click OK to create the calendar.

MORE INFO CALENDAR ITEMS

You can learn more about calendar items at *http://technet.microsoft.com/en-us/library/ hh519740.aspx.*

Creating metrics

You use the Metric node to create time metrics using calendar items that correspond to service objectives. A Service Manager time metric is the amount of time that occurs between a start time and an end time. Service Manager terminology specifies both of these as "date," but it is important for you to note that a Service Manager "date" includes the hour, minute, and second information, and is not simply the calendar day.

Service Manager includes the following predefined metrics:

- **Resolution Time**   This is the maximum allowed time for incident resolution. Service Manager calculates resolution time using an incident's creation time and resolution date.

- **Completion Time**   This is the maximum allowed time for service request completion. Service Manager calculates completion time, a service request's creation time, and completion date.

Metrics for incidents and metrics for service requests use separate Service Manager classes. When creating an incident or metric for service requests, you don't just have to choose creation date and resolution date. You can choose to assign one of the following items for Start Date and for End Date:

- Actual Downtime End Date
- Actual Downtime Start Date
- Actual End Date
- Actual Start Date
- Closed Date
- Created Date
- First Assigned Date
- First Response Date
- Required By
- Resolve By
- Resolved Date

- Scheduled Downtime End Date
- Scheduled Downtime Start Date
- Scheduled End Date
- Scheduled Start Date

To create a metric for incidents, perform the following steps:

1. In the Administration workspace of the Service Manager console, click Metric, under Service Level Management.

2. In the Tasks menu, click Metric, and then click Create Metric.

3. In the Create/Edit Metric dialog box, click Browse.

4. In the Select A Class dialog box, click Incident, as shown in Figure 4-3, and click OK.

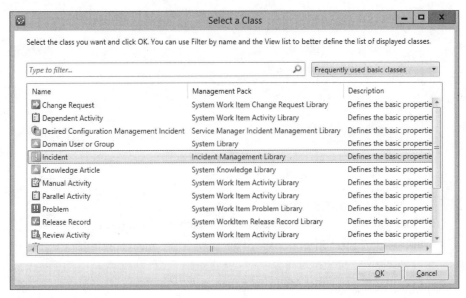

FIGURE 4-3 Select a class

5. Provide a name for the metric. On the Start Date drop-down list, select the event that you will use to start measuring the time taken to resolve the incident. For example, you might choose First Assigned Date. On the End Date drop-down list, select the event that will be used to conclude measuring the time taken to resolve the incident. For example, you might choose Resolved Date. Figure 4-4 shows an example of the Create/Edit Metric dialog box for an incident.

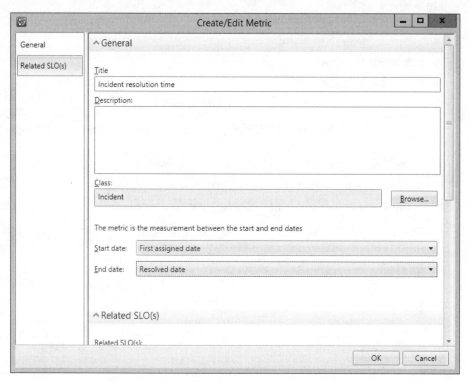

FIGURE 4-4 Create/Edit Metric

6. Click OK to create the metric.

To create a metric for service requests, perform the following steps:

1. In the Administration workspace of the Service Manager console, click Metric, under Service Level Management.

2. In the Tasks menu, click Metric, and then click Create Metric.

3. In the Create/Edit Metric dialog box, click Browse.

4. In the Select A Class dialog box, click Service Request, as shown in Figure 4-5, and click OK.

5. Provide a name for the metric. On the Start Date drop-down list, select the event that you will use to start measuring the time taken to resolve the service request. For example, you might choose Created Date. On the End Date drop-down list, select the event that will be used to conclude measuring the time taken to resolve the service request. For example, you might choose Completed Date. Figure 4-6 shows an example of the Create/Edit Metric dialog box for a service request.

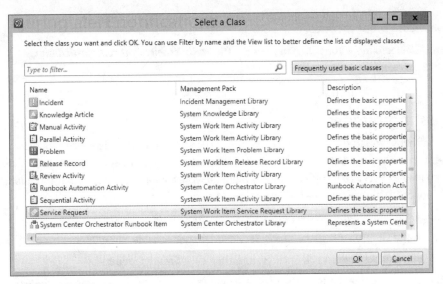

FIGURE 4-5 Select a Class

6. Click OK to close the Create/Edit Metric dialog box.

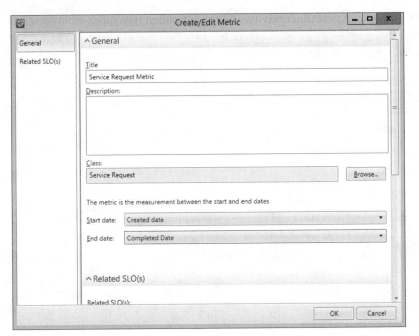

FIGURE 4-6 Create/Edit Metric

MORE INFO **SLA METRICS**

You can learn more about SLA metrics at *http://technet.microsoft.com/en-us/library/hh519571.aspx.*

Creating queues

Queues allow you to group related work items, such as incidents and service requests. You need to already have a queue, or create a queue, when creating a service level objective. When linking a service level objective to a queue, you will need to ensure that the queue and the service level objective are the same type of class.

To create an incident queue, perform the following steps:

1. In the Library workspace of the Service Manager console, click Queues, under Library.

2. In the Tasks menu, click Queues, and then click Create Queue.

3. On the General page of the Create A Queue Wizard, specify a name, set the work item type to Incident (or Service Request if creating a queue for service requests), and specify a management pack in which to save the queue. Figure 4-7 shows the General page.

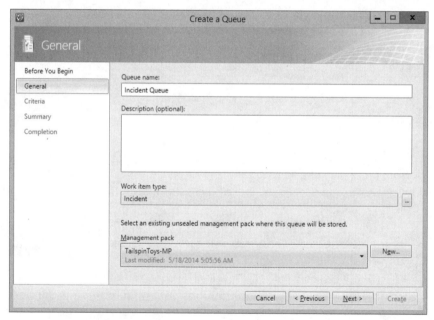

FIGURE 4-7 Create A Queue

4. On the Criteria page, select the work items that you want to use to filter the queue. For example, you might only want to allow the queue to contain items with a specific minimum priority, so you'd choose the Priority filter, and set it to a value, as shown in Figure 4-8.

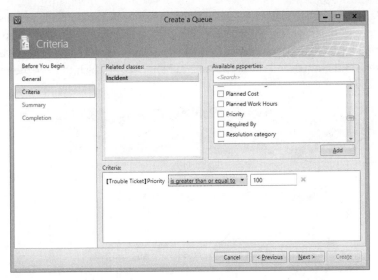

FIGURE 4-8 Create a queue criteria

5. Complete the wizard to create the queue.

MORE INFO **QUEUES**

You can learn more about queues at *http://technet.microsoft.com/en-us/library/hh519613. aspx.*

Creating service level objectives

A service level objective (SLO) is a relationship that you define using Service Manager be-tween: a calendar item and a time metric, a queue and a service level, and actions occurring before or after a service level is exceeded. For example, you could configure a service level objective so that a notification is sent if a service request is not completed within a desig-nated amount of time.

Although it is possible to create the metric, calendar items, and queues that the service level objective will use while creating the service level objective, best practice is to create these separately as detailed earlier before creating the service level objective.

To create a service level objective for incidents where a calendar item and time metric already exist, perform the following steps:

1. In the Administration workspace of the Service Manager console, click Service Level Objectives, under Service Level Management.

2. On the Tasks menu, click Service Level Objectives, and then click Create Service Level Objective.

3. On the General page of the Create Service Level Objective Wizard, provide a name for the service level objective, ensure that the class is set to Incident, as shown in Figure 4-9, (you would set the class to Service Request if creating a service level objective related to service requests), and specify a management pack in which to store the service level objective.

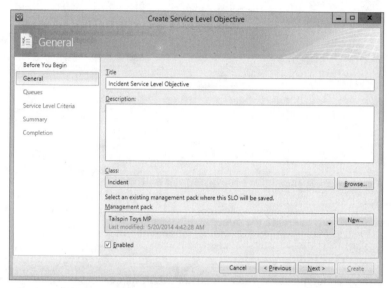

FIGURE 4-9 Create a service level objective

4. On the Queues page, select or create a queue that is configured for the same type of work item as the service level objective. Figure 4-10 shows the selection of a queue named Incident Queue.

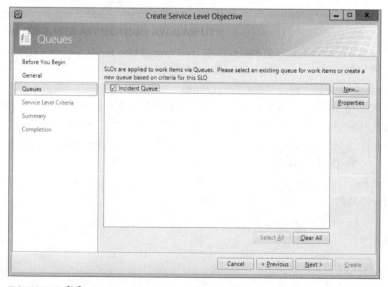

FIGURE 4-10 SLO queue

5. On the Service Level Criteria page, specify the following, as shown in Figure 4-11:

- **Calendar** The calendar that will be used to track which times count as work hours.

- **Metric** The metric that will be used to define the start and end date of the incident.

- **Target** The service level objective target that will be used to specify how much time can be spent on the incident or service request before being in breach of the service agreement.

- **Warning Threshold** The amount of time before the target is reached to send a warning notification.

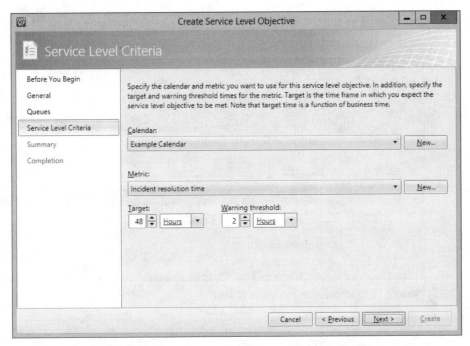

FIGURE 4-11 Service Level Criteria

6. Complete the wizard to create the service level objective.

To view incidents with SLA (Service Level Agreement) information, perform the following steps:

1. In the Work Items workspace, expand the Incident Management node.

2. Select either the Incidents with Service Level Breached node or the Incidents with Service Level Warning node, as shown in Figure 4-12.

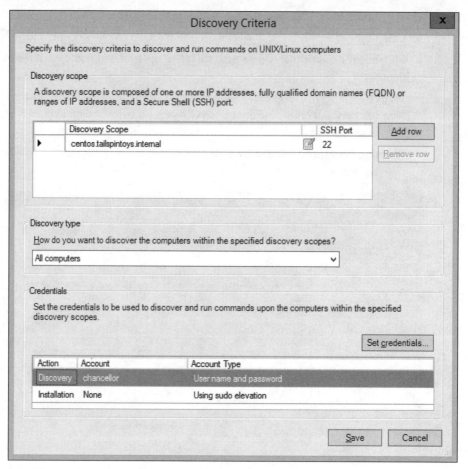

FIGURE 4-12 Incidents With Service Level Warning

MORE INFO SERVICE LEVEL OBJECTIVES

You can learn more about service level objectives at *http://technet.microsoft.com/en-US/ library/hh519603.aspx*.

Sending notifications

You can configure Service Manager to send notifications to the responsible IT professional when a service level objective reaches certain states, such as the warning or breach state. For example, to configure the responsible IT professional to be notified when an incident enters the warning state prior to breaching a SLO, perform the following steps:

1. In the Administration workspace of the Service Manager console, click Subscriptions, under Notifications.

2. In the Tasks menu, click Subscriptions, and then click Create Subscription.

3. On the General page of the Create E-Mail Notification Subscription Wizard, provide a name of the notification, select a management pack in which to store the notification, and configure the following settings, as shown in Figure 4-13:

   - **When To Notify**   When An Object Of The Selected Class Is Updated
   - **Targeted Class**   Service Level Instance Time Information

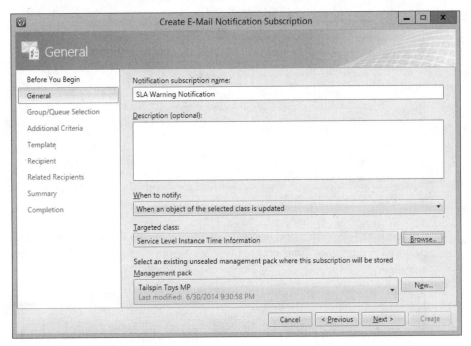

FIGURE 4-13 SLA Warning Notification

4. On the Group/Queue Selection page, click Next.

5. On the Additional Criteria page, configure the following settings:

   - On the Changed From tab, set [Service Level Instance Time Information] Status Does Not Equal Warning.

   - On the Changed To tab, set [Service Level Instance Time Information] Status Equals Warning. This setting is shown in Figure 4-14.

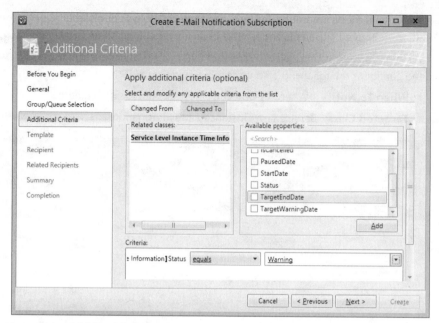

FIGURE 4-14 Additional Criteria

6. On the Template page, select or create an email template that is targeted at the Service Level Instance Time Information class. Figure 4-15 shows the creation of this template.

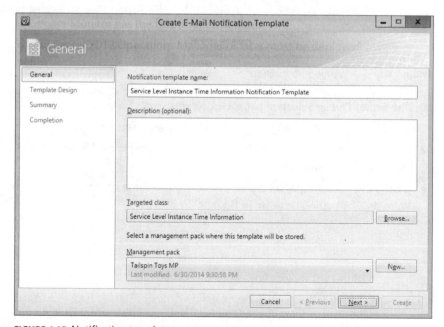

FIGURE 4-15 Notification template

7. On the Recipient page, click Add to select the groups and users to which the notification should be sent.

8. On the Related Recipient page, click Add. On the Select Related Recipient dialog box, click [Work Item] Work Item has Service Level Instance Information, and select Primary Owner, as shown in Figure 4-16, and Assigned To User.

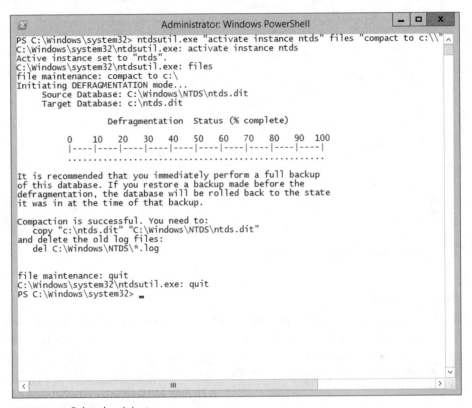

```
Administrator: Windows PowerShell

PS C:\Windows\system32> ntdsutil.exe "activate instance ntds" files "compact to c:\\"
C:\Windows\system32\ntdsutil.exe: activate instance ntds
Active instance set to "ntds".
C:\Windows\system32\ntdsutil.exe: files
file maintenance: compact to c:\
Initiating DEFRAGMENTATION mode...
    Source Database: C:\Windows\NTDS\ntds.dit
    Target Database: c:\ntds.dit

            Defragmentation  Status (% complete)

    0    10   20   30   40   50   60   70   80   90  100
    |----|----|----|----|----|----|----|----|----|----|
    ..................................................

It is recommended that you immediately perform a full backup
of this database. If you restore a backup made before the
defragmentation, the database will be rolled back to the state
it was in at the time of that backup.

Compaction is successful. You need to:
    copy "c:\ntds.dit" "C:\Windows\NTDS\ntds.dit"
and delete the old log files:
    del C:\Windows\NTDS\*.log


file maintenance: quit
C:\Windows\system32\ntdsutil.exe: quit
PS C:\Windows\system32> _
```

FIGURE 4-16 Related recipient

9. Verify that the Related Recipients page matches Figure 4-17, and then complete the wizard.

> **MORE INFO   SLA NOTIFICATIONS**
>
> You can learn more about SLA notifications at *http://technet.microsoft.com/en-US/library/hh519605.aspx*

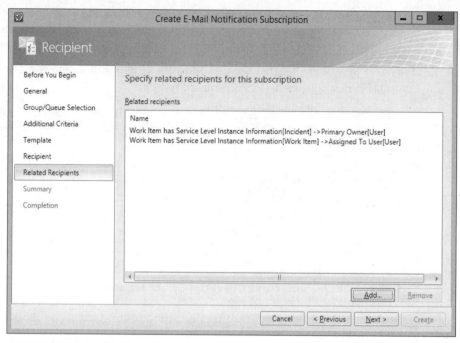

FIGURE 4-17 Email notification subscription

SLO escalation

You can use the Change To Warning Of Incident or a service request's Service Level Instance
Time Information as the trigger point for a custom workflow that automatically escalates
incidents, or service requests that are in danger of breaching. You can also create and use an
Orchestrator runbook to escalate an incident or service request when it enters a warning or
breached state.

EXAM TIP

**Remember which methods you can use to configure automatic escalation of incidents that
are in danger of breaching SLO.**

SLA reporting

Service Manager has a number of reports available through the Reporting workspace that
you can use to analyze performance against service level agreements. Reports that can be
used to analyze SLA performance include:

- **Incident KPI Trend**   This report provides the number of incidents, the number of
  incidents past their target resolution time, the number of escalated incidents, average
  resolution time, labor minutes per incident, and the size of the incident backlog.

- **Incident Resolution**   This report provides the number of incidents, including number of incidents that have exceeded targeted resolution time, and average resolution time.
- **Service KPI Trend**   This report provides metrics across services, groups, and collections for Service Manager, as well as for Operations Manager and Configuration Manager.

MORE INFO **SERVICE MANAGER REPORTS**

You can learn more about Service Manager reports at *http://technet.microsoft.com/en-us/library/hh519764.aspx.*

Thought experiment

Service level management at Tailspin Toys

Tailspin Toys is going through a restructuring. As part of the restructuring until business picks up, the office will be closed every third Monday of each month. The service desk at Tailspin Toys has strict service level agreements, and incidents must be resolved in a timely manner. As part of ensuring that the service desk meets its obligations, the service desk manager needs to be made aware if any incidents are in danger of breaching SLO metrics. With this information in mind, answer the following questions:

1. How can you ensure that the Mondays that the office is closed are not measured when calculating SLOs?

2. How can you ensure that the service desk manager is made aware when incidents are in danger of breaching SLO metrics?

Objective summary

- A calendar allows you to specify which times and days constitute work hours when determining the basis of measuring time for service level objectives.
- A Service Manager time metric is the amount of time that occurs between a start time and an end time, and is used to measure whether service objectives have been achieved.
- Queues allow you to group related work items, such as incidents and service requests.
- A Service Level Objective (SLO) is a relationship defined in Service Manager between a calendar item and a time metric, a queue and a service level, and actions, that occur preceding or after a service level is exceeded.

- Service Manager can send notifications when a service level objective reaches certain states, such as the warning or breach state.

- You can use the Change To Warning Of Incident or a service request's Service Level Instance Time Information as the trigger point for a custom workflow that automatically escalates incidents, or service requests that are in danger of breaching.

Objective review

Answer the following questions to test your knowledge of the information in this objective. You can find the answers to these questions and explanations of why each answer choice is correct or incorrect in the "Answers" section at the end of this chapter.

1. Which of the following must be present to complete the configuration of a Service Manager SLO?

   A. Calendar

   B. Metric

   C. Queues

   D. Subscriptions

2. You are configuring Service Manager to send notifications in the event that a service level objective reaches a warning or breach state. Which of the following targeted classes would you use when configuring this notification?

   A. Service Level Instance Time Information

   B. Change Request

   C. Review Activity

   D. Problem

3. You want to automatically have an incident be escalated when it is in danger of breaching the SLO. Which of the following could you configure to accomplish this goal?

   A. A custom workflow

   B. Orchestrator runbook

   C. Scheduled task

   D. Review activity

4. You are configuring a metric that should involve measuring the time between incident creation and the first response made to the incident. Which of the following should you choose for Start Date and End Date?

   A. Required By

   B. First Assigned Date

   C. First Response Date

   D. Created Date

Objective 4.2: Manage problems and incidents

This objective deals with Service Manager incidents, problems, and knowledge articles. This includes how to configure priorities for incidents and problems, how priority relates to resolution time, how to create incidents manually, how to have incidents automatically created using email messages sent to the service desk, and how to resolve incidents by resolving problems.

> **This section covers the following topics:**
> - Understanding problems and incidents
> - Managing incidents
> - Managing problems
> - Creating knowledge articles

Understanding problems and incidents

A problem in Service Manager is a record that groups incidents that share a common cause. Addressing the cause and solving the problem means that the incidents that are associated with the problem also are resolved. For example, different users contact the service desk to lodge the following tickets:

- Oksana is unable to sign on to her computer.
- Rooslan is unable to browse the Internet.
- Kasia is unable to print.

These separate issues may have a common cause; such as the failure of the hardware switch that each user's computer uses to connect to the network. Replacing the failed switch will resolve each of these separate incident tickets.

Managing incidents

IT professionals that work on the help desk constantly create and resolve Service Manager incidents as a way of tracking their daily activity. Someone in the accounting department may ring the service desk, reporting an issue that they are having. The IT professional on the service desk instructs the caller to restart their computer, and the issue is resolved. During this process the IT professional creates an incident related to the issue, and if the issue is resolved by the restart, closes the incident. Incident templates allow you to pre-populate certain fields for a specific type of incident.

Incident priority

Service Manager determines incident priority using the settings you configure related to incident impact and incident urgency. You configure incident priority using the Incident Settings dialog box. You can configure priority values from 1 to 9 in a table where urgency is measured on one axis, and impact is measured on the other.

In almost all cases, organizations will assign a priority of 1 to high impact/high urgency incidents, and a priority of 9 to low impact/low urgency incidents. Priority values determine the assigned incident target resolution time. You configure incident target resolution time on another page of the same dialog box. To configure incident priority calculation settings, perform the following steps:

1. Select the Settings node of the Administration workspace of the Service Manager console.

2. Double-click Incident Settings in the details pane. This opens the Incident Settings dialog box.

3. In the Priority Calculation section of the Incident Settings dialog box, shown in Figure 4-18, configure priority settings from 1 through 9 based on the combination of impact and urgency.

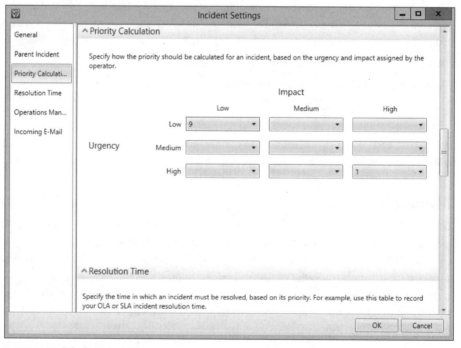

FIGURE 4-18 Priority calculation

MORE INFO PRIORITY CALCULATION

You can learn more about priority calculation at *http://technet.microsoft.com/en-us/library/hh524340.aspx*.

Incident resolution time

You configure incident resolution time based on priority. The values that you assign for each incident priority will depend on the SLA you are working with, and with different organizations using different values for each priority. To configure default incident resolution time, perform the following steps:

1. Select the Settings node of the Administration workspace of the Service Manager console.

2. Double-click Incident Settings in the details pane. This opens the Incident Settings dialog box.

3. In the Resolution Time section of the Incident Settings dialog box, shown in Figure 4-19, specify the target resolution time for each priority.

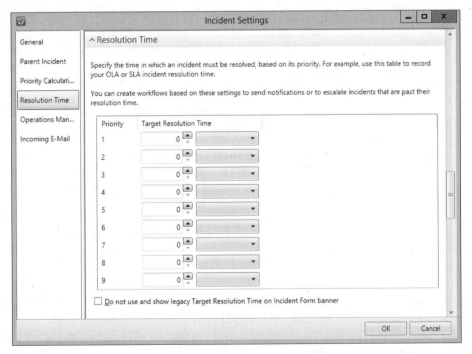

FIGURE 4-19 Resolution time

MORE INFO **INCIDENT RESOLUTION TIME**

You can learn more about incident resolution time at *http://technet.microsoft.com/en-us/library/hh495593.aspx*.

Incident prefix

Service Manager incidents are automatically prefixed with the letters IR (Incident Record) by default. You can modify this prefix by performing the following steps:

1. Select the Settings node of the Administration workspace of the Service Manager console.

2. Double-click Incident Settings in the details pane. This opens the Incident Settings dialog box.

3. Change the Prefix setting, shown in Figure 4-20, to the desired prefix for your organization.

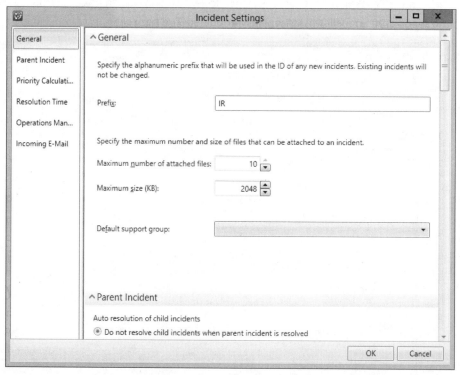

FIGURE 4-20 Incident prefix

Manually creating incidents

To manually create an incident using the Service Manager console, perform the following steps:

1. Determine what configuration item will serve as the basis for the incident. You can choose between the following categories:

    - Builds
    - Business Services
    - Computers
    - Environments
    - Printers
    - Software
    - Software Updates
    - Users

2. Select the item for which you want to create the incident. For example, if there is a problem with a specific computer, you should select the computer under the Computers node, and on the Tasks menu, select the name of the computer, and then click Create Related Incident. This will load the Incident form.

3. In the Tasks pane of the Incident form, click Apply Template. This will open the Apply Template dialog box, shown in Figure 4-21. You can use this to apply an existing template that will automatically apply existing settings to the form. As a method of simplifying the process of incident creation, you can create incident templates for common incident profiles.

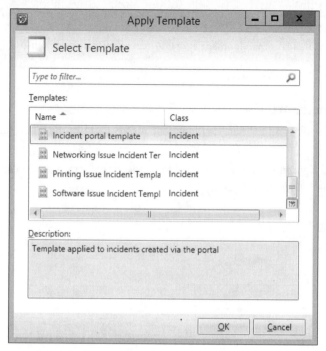

FIGURE 4-21 Apply template

4. Using the Incident form, shown in Figure 4-22, you can then configure the following additional settings:

- **Affected User** Which user is affected by the incident.
- **Alternate Contact Method** Alternate method of contacting the affected user, such as telephone number.
- **Title** Name for the incident.
- **Description** Description of the incident.
- **Classification Category** Allows you to classify the problem. Service Manager supports the creation of custom categories.
- **Source** Shows how the incident was entered into Service Manager. Manual incident creation is usually through the Service Manager console.
- **Impact** Incident impact rating.
- **Urgency** Incident urgency rating.
- **Support Group** Shows which support group is responsible for the incident.
- **Assigned To** IT Professional who the incident has been assigned to.
- **Primary Owner** Primary incident owner.
- **Escalated** Allows you to specify if the incident is escalated.

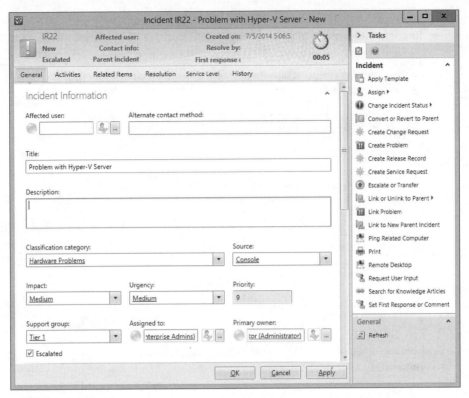

FIGURE 4-22 Incident form

Once the Incident has been created, it will be visible in the Work Items workspace of the Service Manager console, under the Incident Management node, as shown in Figure 4-23.

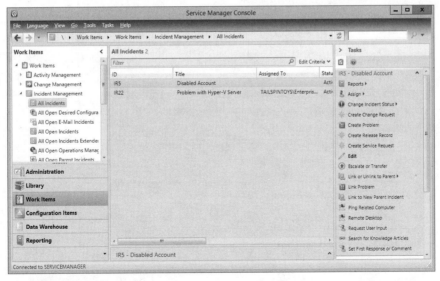

FIGURE 4-23 All incidents

From here, you can use the Tasks pane for the following:

- **Reports** Allows you to run an Incident KPI Trend, Incident Analyst, Incident Details, Incident Resolution, or List Of Incidents report based on the properties of the incident.

- **Assign** Allows you to assign the incident using the Select Objects dialog box, as shown in Figure 4-24.

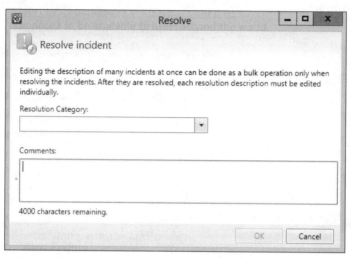

FIGURE 4-24 Select objects

- **Change Incident Status** Allows you to activate, close, resolve, or set another status using the Other option. When you resolve an incident, you provide a resolution category and comments, as shown in Figure 4-25.

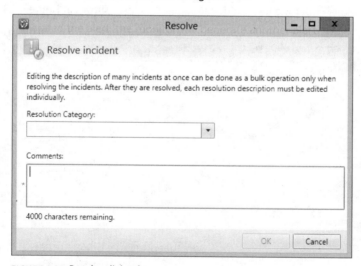

FIGURE 4-25 Resolve dialog box

Remember that you can resolve an incident using the Change Incident Status task from the Work Items workspace of the Service Manager console.

- **Create Change Request**   Allows you to create a change request. The incident will be configured as a related item.
- **Create Problem**   Allows you to create a Problem. The incident will be configured as a related item.
- **Create Service Request**   Allows you to create a Service Request. The incident will be configured as a related item.
- **Edit**   Allows you to edit the incident.
- **Escalate Or Transfer**   Allows you to escalate or transfer the incident. Figure 4-26 shows the Escalate Or Transfer dialog box. You use this dialog box to specify the support group to which the incident should be escalated or transferred.

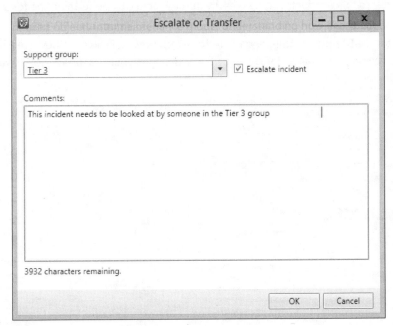

FIGURE 4-26 Escalate Or Transfer

- **Link Or Unlink To Parent**   Allows you to link to a parent incident, or unlink the incident from a parent incident.
- **Link Problem**   Allows you to link to a Problem. You'll learn about managing Service Manager problems later in this chapter.
- **Link To New Parent Incident**   Allows you to create a new parent incident and link the incident to that parent.

- **Ping Related Computer**   Allows you to send an ICMP request to the affected computer.

- **Remote Desktop**   Allows you to make a remote desktop connection to the affected computer.

- **Request User Input**   Sends a message from Service Manager to the user, requesting more information.

- **Search For Knowledge Articles**   Allows you to search for related knowledge articles.

- **Set First Response Or Comment**   Allows you to add comments to incidents.

Configuring email incidents

You can configure Service Manager to automatically create incidents based on email requests from users. If the user who sent the email is recognized by Service Manager as a user, Service Manager will automatically create a new incident.

If you have deployed Exchange in your organizational environment, you can configure Service Manager so that incidents can be created through email, by performing the following steps:

1.   Install the SMTP server feature and related administrative consoles, as shown in Figure 4-27, on a computer that is not currently participating in your organization's Exchange deployment.

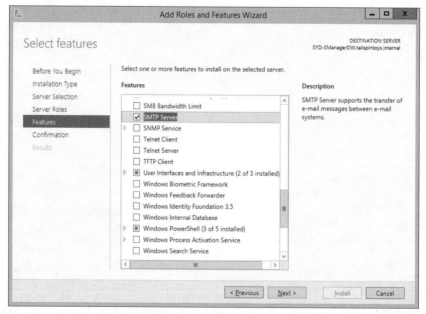

FIGURE 4-27 SMTP server feature

2.   Rename the server from SMTP Virtual Server #1, or the name it had been automatically assigned, to the FQDN of the server hosting this service.

3. In the list of domains, rename the domain to the FQDN of the server hosting this service.

4. Edit the properties of the SMTP server. On the Access tab, click Relay, click All Except The List Below, and ensure that Allow All Computers Which Successfully Authenticate To Relay Regardless Of The List Above, as shown in Figure 4-28, is enabled, and click OK.

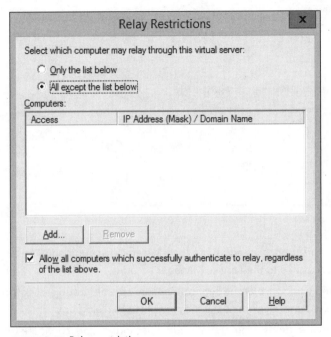

FIGURE 4-28 Relay restrictions

5. On the Delivery tab, click Advanced. In the Advanced Delivery dialog box, type the following, as shown in Figure 4-29, and click OK:

- **Masquerade Domain** The root domain of the domain in which the server is a member.

- **Fully Qualified Domain Name** The name of an Exchange mailbox server (Exchange 2013), or server that hosts the Hub Transport role (Exchange 2010).

- **Smart Host** The name of an Exchange mailbox server (Exchange 2013) or server that hosts the Hub Transport role (Exchange 2010).

FIGURE 4-29 Advanced delivery

6. Close the SMTP server's properties and share the <SystemDrive>:\Inetpub\Mailroot folder so that it is accessible to the Service Manager account.

7. In the Administration workspace of the Service Manager console, double-click Incident Settings in the details pane. This opens the Incident Settings dialog box.

8. In the Incoming E-mail settings page of the Incident Settings dialog, configure the following settings, as shown in Figure 4-30, and then click OK:

   ■ **SMTP Service Drop Folder Location**   This will be the UNC path of the Drop folder under the Mailroot folder that you shared in step 6.

   ■ **SMTP Service Bad Folder Location**   This will be the UNC path of the Badmail folder under the Mailroot folder that you shared in step 6.

   ■ **Maximum Number Of E-mail Messages To Process At A Time**   This is the number of email messages that you want Server Manager to import at a time.

   ■ **Turn On Incoming E-mail Processing**   Enable this setting.

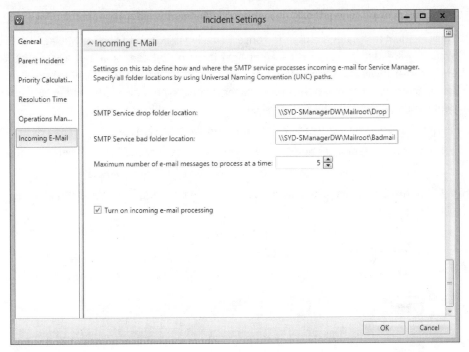

FIGURE 4-30 Incident settings

9. In Exchange:

- Configure *.servername.domain.name (where servername.domain.name is the FQDN of the SMTP server configured earlier) as an accepted domain.

- Configure a receive connector to accept anonymous inbound traffic from the SMTP server configured earlier.

- Configure a send connector to route email to the SMTP server when addressed to the *@servername.domain.name email domain.

- Configure a mail contact in Exchange that will be used as the address for messages that should be converted as incidents. For example helpdesk@SYD-SmanagerDW. tailspintoys.internal.

MORE INFO **EMAIL INCIDENT SMTP CONFIGURATION**

You can learn more about incident SMTP configuration at *http://technet.microsoft.com/ en-us/library/jj900204.aspx.*

Email incident templates

Email incident templates are used to convert email messages into Service Manager incidents. When Service Manager detects new messages in the drop folder on a specially configured SMTP server, it will take information from the email message and use it with an email incident template, to populate a new Service Manager incident. The process of creating an email incident template is very similar to that of creating any other type of incident template.

To create an email incident template, perform the following steps:

1. Select the Templates node in the Library workspace of the Service Manager console.

2. On the Tasks menu, click Templates, and then click Create Template.

3. In the Create Template dialog box, fill out the following settings, as shown in Figure 4-31:

    -   Name: E-mail incident template

    -   Class: Incident

    -   Management Pack: Service Manager Incident Management Configuration Library

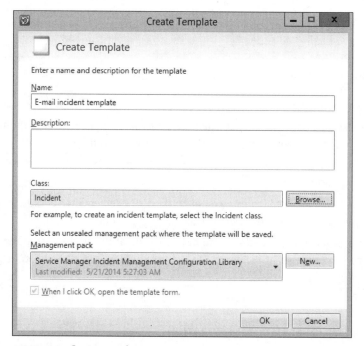

FIGURE 4-31 Create template

4. Clicking OK on the Create Template dialog box will open the Incident Template form. In the form, configure the following settings, as shown in Figure 4-32:

    -   Title: E-mail Template Form

    -   Classification Category: E-Mail Problems

- Impact: Select the initial impact to assign to incidents submitted through email.
- Urgency: Select the initial urgency to assign to incidents submitted through email.
- Support Group: Select the support group that will be initially assigned incidents sent through email.

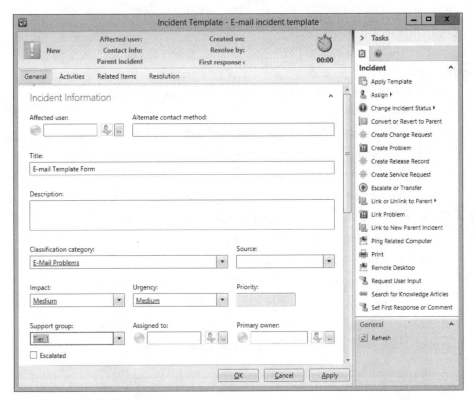

FIGURE 4-32 Incident template

5. Click OK to close the incident template.

MORE INFO CREATING INCIDENT TEMPLATES

You can learn more about email incident templates and creating incident templates at *http://technet.microsoft.com/en-us/library/hh495665.aspx*.

Managing problems

A problem is a Service Manager record that you create to minimize the chance that similar problems, or related incidents, will occur in the future, or to minimize the impact of an issue that you cannot prevent. Service Manager allows related incidents to be closed when a problem that they are related to is resolved.

MORE INFO **MANAGING PROBLEMS**

You can learn more about managing problems at *http://technet.microsoft.com/en-us/library/hh519581.aspx.*

Creating problem records

You can create problem records manually from the Service Manager console by performing the following steps:

1. Select the Problem Management node in the Work Items workspace of the Service Manager console.

2. In the Tasks menu, click Problem Management, and then click Create Problem.

3. On the Problem form, shown in Figure 4-33, provide the following information:

   - **Title** A name for the problem.
   - **Description** A description for the problem.
   - **Assigned To** The person responsible for resolving the problem.
   - **Source** Source of the problem request.
   - **Category** Problem category.
   - **Impact** Impact of the problem. This is used to calculate priority.
   - **Urgency** Problem urgency. This is used to calculate priority.

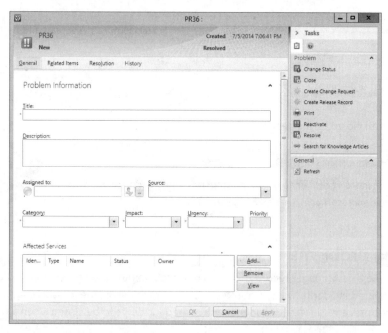

FIGURE 4-33 Problem form

Linking incidents to problems

Service Manager allows you to link incidents to problems. For example, a number of incidents reported to the help desk may have the same root cause, such as users contacting the help desk because they are unable to sign on to their computers. In this scenario, the root cause might be the failure of the DHCP service on the organization's DHCP server. By fixing the DHCP service, the separate sign on failure incidents will also be resolved.

To link incidents to an existing problem, perform the following steps:

1. Select the Active Problems node under Problems in the Work Items workspace of the Service Manager console.

2. Select a problem, and then click Edit in the Tasks pane.

3. On the Related Items tab of the problem dialog box, click Add next to Work Items.

4. On the Select Objects dialog box, add the incidents you want to relate to the problem, as shown in Figure 4-34.

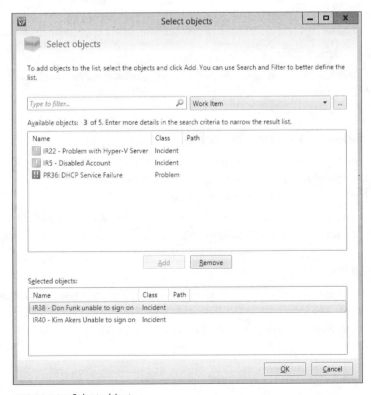

FIGURE 4-34 Select objects

5. Verify that the incidents are listed under work items, as shown in Figure 4-35.

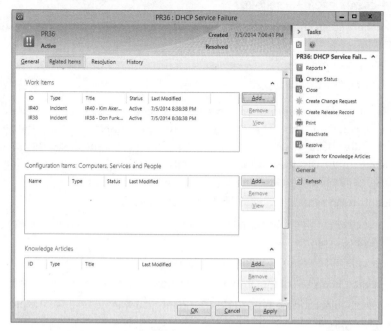

FIGURE 4-35 Related incidents

MORE INFO **LINKING INCIDENTS TO PROBLEMS**

You can learn more about linking incidents to problems at *http://technet.microsoft.com/ en-us/library/hh519687.aspx*.

Resolving problems and related incidents

An advantage to linking incidents with problems is that you are able to resolve all incidents that are linked to a problem automatically when you resolve that problem. To resolve a problem and its related incidents, perform the following steps:

1. In the Work Items workspace of the Service Manager console, locate the problem that you want to resolve in the Active Problems node, under the Problem Management node.

2. Select the problem, and click Edit in the Tasks pane.

3. Select the Resolution tab. In the Tasks pane, click Resolve, and then select Auto-Resolve All Incidents Associated With This Problem under Resolution Details, as shown in Figure 4-36. Also select a resolution category and an appropriate resolution description.

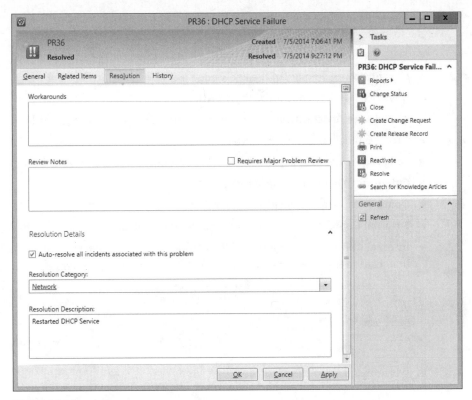

FIGURE 4-36 Resolution

4. Click OK to resolve the problems and the associated incidents.

> **MORE INFO RESOLVING PROBLEMS**
>
> You can learn more about resolving problems at *http://technet.microsoft.com/en-us/library/hh495498.aspx.*

Creating knowledge articles

Knowledge articles are documents, created by people inside the organization that allow the organization's IT professionals and users to understand and remediate problems. To create a knowledge article, perform the following steps:

1. In the Library workspace of the Service Manager console, click the Knowledge node.

2. In the Tasks menu, click Knowledge, and then click Create Knowledge Article.

3. On the General tab of the Knowledge Article dialog box, shown in Figure 4-37, provide the following information:

- **Title**   Name of the knowledge article.
- **Description**   Summary of the knowledge article.
- **Keywords**   Knowledge article keywords.
- **Knowledge Article Owner**   Person responsible for the knowledge article.
- **Tag**   Metadata tags for the article.
- **Language**   The language in which the knowledge article is written.
- **Category**   Knowledge article category.
- **Comments**   Any comments on the article.
- **External Content**   Any links to external documentation hosted on the Internet.
- **Internal Content**   The content of the knowledge article, containing the information that the IT Professional or the user will use to resolve a problem.

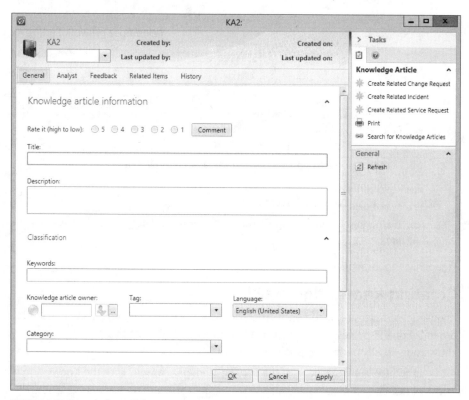

FIGURE 4-37 Knowledge articles

MORE INFO **KNOWLEDGE ARTICLES**

You can learn more about knowledge articles at *http://technet.microsoft.com/en-us/library/hh495650.aspx.*

Thought experiment

Incident management at Fabrikam

The service desk at Fabrikam uses Service Manager to manage user incidents and problems. At present, service desk hours are 9 A.M. to 5 P.M., Monday to Friday. Some users, however, are complaining that they want to be able to forward incidents to the service desk at any time during the day. You are planning on deploying a self-service portal to allow users to submit incident and service requests, but this project will not be completed for several months. In the meantime, you want to provide users with documentation allowing them to remediate their own issues, based on the incidents most commonly encountered by the users at Fabrikam. With this information in mind, answer the following questions:

1. What steps can you take to allow users to attempt to resolve their own incidents before contacting the service desk?

2. Until the self-service portal is deployed, what other method can users use to submit incidents to the service desk staff during the hours when the hotline is not answered?

Objective summary

- Incident templates allow you to pre-populate certain fields for a specific type of incident.
- Service Manager determines incident priority using the settings you configure related to incident impact and incident urgency.
- You configure incident resolution time based on priority. The values that you assign for each incident priority will depend on the SLA.
- Service Manager can be configured to automatically create incidents based on email requests from users.
- Service Manager allows you to link incidents to problems. You do this when incidents have the same root cause.
- Service Manager allows related incidents to be closed when a problem that they are related to is resolved.
- Knowledge articles are documents that allow the organization's IT professionals and users to understand and remediate problems.

Objective review

Answer the following questions to test your knowledge of the information in this objective. You can find the answers to these questions and explanations of why each answer choice is correct or incorrect in the "Answers" section at the end of this chapter.

1. You have three incidents that you want to link to a problem. Which of the following methods can you use to accomplish this goal?

    A. Add the problem to the list of work items on the Related Items tab of each incident's properties.

    B. Add the incidents to the list of work items on the Related Items tab of the problem's properties.

    C. Add each incident's identification numbers to the description field on the General tab of the problem's properties.

    D. Add the problem's identification number to the description field on the General tab of each incident's properties.

2. You have three incidents related to a problem. Which of the following steps should you take to resolve both the problems and the incidents?

    A. Resolve each incident manually.

    B. Resolve the problem and select the option to auto-resolve all incidents associated with the problem.

    C. Resolve an incident and select the option to auto-resolve all problems associated with the incident.

    D. Close the problem and then manually resolve each incident.

3. Which of the following settings should you configure when configuring incident priority?

    A. Low/Low: 9

    B. Low/Low: 1

    C. High/High: 1

    D. High/High: 9

4. Which of the following fields in an incident form are used to calculate priority?

    A. Impact

    B. Source

    C. Urgency

    D. Support Group

Objective 4.3: Manage cloud resources

This objective deals with managing cloud resources through different types of VMM profiles. A VMM profile allows you to configure settings used for the configuration of simulated virtual machine hardware, guest operating systems, applications, SQL Server instances, and multi-tier services that include all of these segments.

> **This section covers the following topics:**
> - Creating hardware profiles
> - Creating guest operating system profiles
> - Creating application profiles
> - Configuring SQL Server profiles
> - Configuring virtual machine templates
> - Creating service templates

Creating hardware profiles

A VMM hardware profile allows you to create templates for virtual machine hardware. This includes configuring the number of processors, the amount of RAM available to the virtual machine, as well as the IDE and SCSI configuration that the VM will use. You can also use a VMM hardware profile configuration, whether a virtual machine will use Generation 1 or Generation 2 hardware. While you can configure virtual machine hardware settings each time you use VMM to create a virtual machine, a VMM hardware profile allows you to create VMs that have a standardized virtual hardware configuration.

To create a hardware profile, perform the following steps:

1. In the Library workspace of the VMM console, right-click the Profiles node, and click Create Hardware Profile.

2. On the General page of the New Hardware Profile dialog box, shown in Figure 4-38, provide a name for the profile and select which VM generation you want to use. This can be Generation 1 or Generation 2. Remember that Generation 2 VMs can only be used with virtualization hosts running Windows Server 2012 R2 or later.

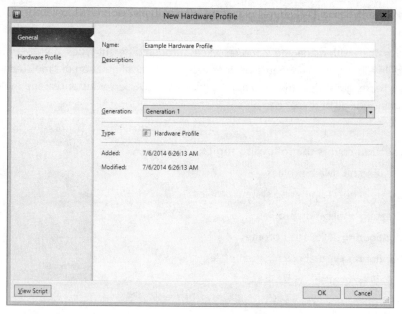

FIGURE 4-38 New Hardware Profile

3. On the Hardware Profile page, you can configure the following settings:

- **Cloud Capability Profiles** Specify which capability profile to use with the hardware profile. You can choose between XenServer, ESX Server, and Hyper-V. Figure 4-39 shows the selection of the Hyper-V profile.

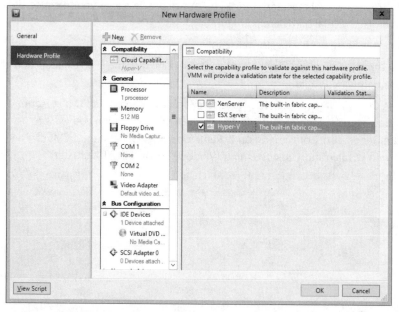

FIGURE 4-39 Cloud compatibility

- **Processor** Allows you to configure the number of processors to be used by the VM. This also allows you to configure whether migration can occur to a virtual machine host running a different processor version.

- **Memory** Allows you to configure the amount of memory that will be allocated to the VM. You can choose to statically assign memory, or to allow the use of dynamic memory. Figure 4-40 shows the memory settings.

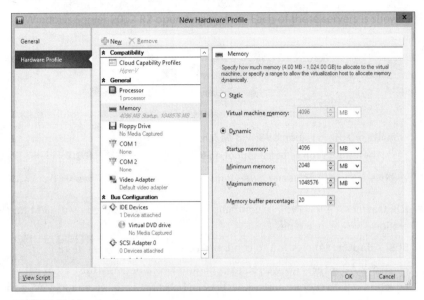

FIGURE 4-40 Memory

- **Floppy Drive** Allows you to configure a virtual floppy drive for Generation 1 virtual machines.

- **COM 1** Allows you to configure Com Port 1 settings for Generation 1 virtual machines.

- **COM 2** Allows you to configure Com Port 2 settings for Generation 1 virtual machines.

- **Video Adapter** Allows you to configure whether a standard video adapter will be used, or a RemoteFX 3D video adapter will be available to virtual machines. You can also configure the maximum number of monitors and the maximum monitor resolution when choosing the RemoteFX 3D video adapter. Figure 4-41 shows this setting.

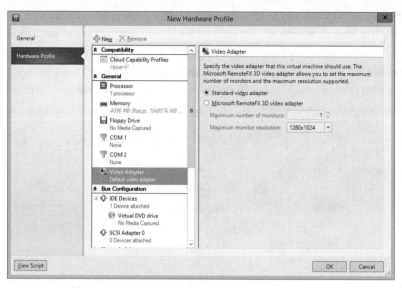

FIGURE 4-41 Video adapter

- **IDE Devices**   Allows you to configure virtual IDE devices used by the VM for Generation 1 virtual machines.
- **SCSI Adapter**   Allows you to configure virtual SCSI adapter settings.
- **Network Adapter**   Allows you to configure which network the virtual network adapters will be connected to, how they will obtain IP addresses and MAC addresses, as well as any virtual network port profiles. Figure 4-42 shows these options.

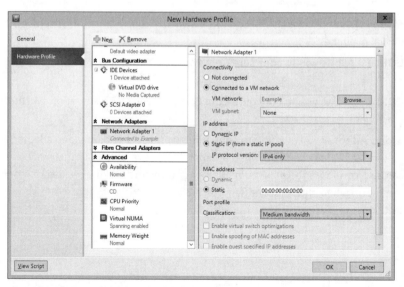

FIGURE 4-42 Network adapter settings

- **Availability**   This option is for virtual machines that should be placed on highly available host clusters.
- **Firmware**   Allows you to configure VM startup order as shown in Figure 4-43.

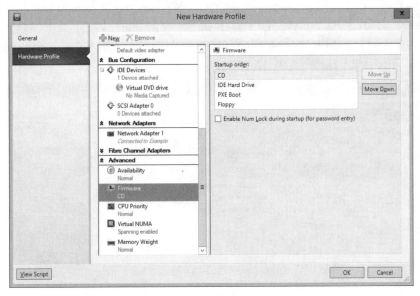

FIGURE 4-43 Firmware

- **CPU Priority**   Allows you to configure the priority for the VM when the host is allocating CPU resources.
- **Virtual NUMA**   Allows you to configure the VM to span hardware NUMA nodes.
- **Memory Weight**   Allows you to configure how the VM is allocated memory when memory utilization on the virtualization host is high.

> *MORE INFO* **HARDWARE PROFILES**
>
> You can learn more about hardware profiles at *http://technet.microsoft.com/en-us/library/ hh427289.aspx.*

Creating guest operating system profiles

Guest operating system profiles allow you to configure guest operating system settings that will automatically be applied to the virtual machine. Depending on the guest OS you are configuring the profile for, this can include the local administrator account password, what roles and features are installed, domain join information, and computer name. You can configure a guest OS profile for Windows or Linux operating systems. Using a guest OS profile saves you having to perform these setup steps manually when deploying a virtual machine.

To create a guest OS profile for a Windows operating system, perform the following steps:

1. In the Library workspace of the VMM console, right-click the Profiles node, and click Create Guest OS Profile.

2. On the General page of the New Guest OS Profile dialog box, provide a name, and select which operating system the guest OS profile will apply to. Figure 4-44 shows a guest OS profile named Example Windows Server 2012 R2 for use with Microsoft Windows operating systems.

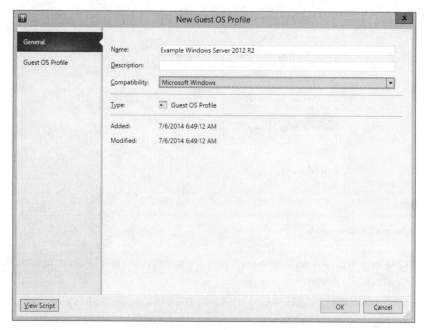

FIGURE 4-44 Guest OS profile

3. On the Guest OS Profile page, specify the following settings:

   - **Operating System** Allows you to select which operating system the guest OS profile applies to. Figure 4-45 shows some of the options that can be selected using the drop-down menu.

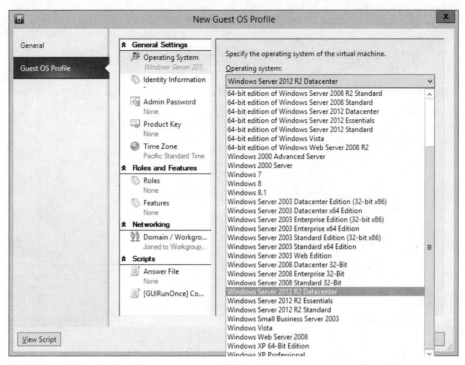

FIGURE 4-45 Operating system

- **Identity Information** Allows you to configure how the VM will be named.

- **Admin Password** Allows you to configure the password of the built-in administrator account.

- **Product Key** Allows you to specify a product key.

- **Time Zone** Allows you to configure which time zone the virtual machine will be configured to use.

- **Roles** Allows you to configure which roles and role services will automatically be installed on the virtual machine. Figure 4-46 shows the Web Server role selected.

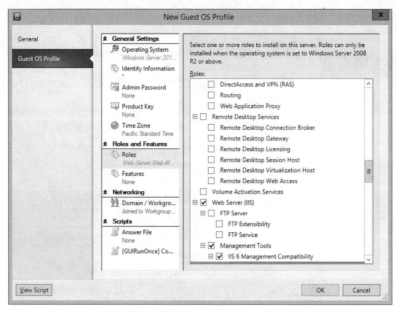

FIGURE 4-46 Roles

- **Features** Allows you to configure which features will be installed on the virtual machine.
- **Domain / Workgroup** Allows you to configure domain or workgroup settings. If specifying that the virtual machine be domain joined, you can provide credentials that allow this to occur. These options are shown in Figure 4-47.

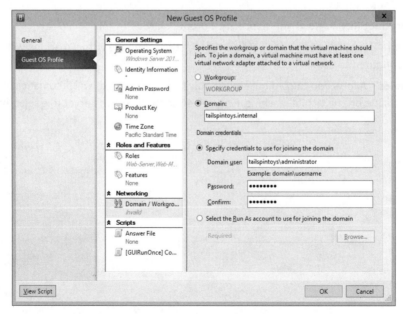

FIGURE 4-47 Domain information

- **Answer File**   Allows you to specify an answer file to automatically configure the virtual machine.
- **[GUIRunOnce] Command**   Allows you to specify a set of commands that will be run automatically the first time a user logs on to the virtual machine.

> **MORE INFO** **GUEST OPERATING SYSTEM PROFILES**
>
> You can learn more about guest operating system profiles at *http://technet.microsoft.com/en-us/library/hh427296.aspx*.

Creating application profiles

Application profiles include information that VMM can use for installing Microsoft Web Deploy applications, SQL Server data-tier applications, Microsoft Server App-V applications, and instructions for running scripts when you deploy a VM as part of a service. You only use application profiles if you are going to deploy a VM as part of a service, and don't use them when deploying standalone VMs. You can add multiple applications of the same type, or applications of different types to the same profile.

Before creating an application profile, you should ensure that all packages and scripts that the profile will use are already present in a VMM library share. To create an application profile, perform the following steps:

1. In the Library workspace of the VMM console, right-click the Profiles node, and click Create Application Profile.

2. On the General page, shown in Figure 4-48, provide a name for the application profile and choose between one of the following compatibility options:

   - **SQL Server Application Host**   Select this option if you will use the profile to deploy SQL Server DAC packages or SQL Server scripts to an existing SQL Server instance.
   - **Web Application Host**   Select this option if you will use the profile to deploy Web Deploy packages to IIS.
   - **General**   Select this option if you are deploying a combination of application types or Server-App-V applications.

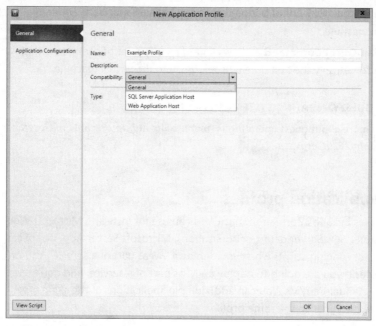

FIGURE 4-48 Application profile

3. On the Application Configuration page, select the operating system compatibility, as shown in Figure 4-49.

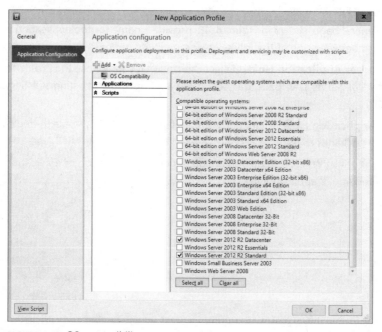

FIGURE 4-49 OS compatibility

4. Click Add, as shown in Figure 4-50, to add one of the following:

- Script Application
- SQL Server Data-Tier Application
- Virtual Application
- Web Application
- Script To Application Profile

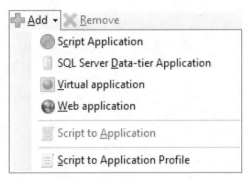

FIGURE 4-50 Add application

MORE INFO **APPLICATION PROFILES**

You can learn more about application profiles at *http://technet.microsoft.com/en-us/library/hh427291.aspx*.

Configuring SQL Server profiles

A SQL Server profile allows you to configure a sysprepped instance of SQL Server 2008 R2, SQL Server 2012, or SQL Server 2014 for deployment through VMM. You use SQL Server profiles when deploying VMs that are part of a service. The SQL Server profile configures SQL Server according to the profile settings.

To configure a SQL Server profile, perform the following steps:

1. In the Library workspace of the VMM console, right-click the Profiles node, and click Create SQL Server Profile.

2. On the General page of the New SQL Server Profile dialog box, provide a name for the SQL Server profile.

3. On the SQL Server Configuration page, click Add SQL Server Deployment, and provide the following information, as shown in Figure 4-51.

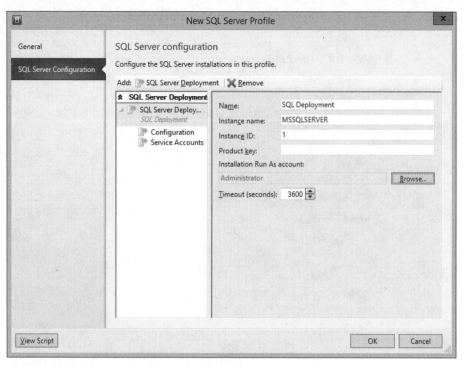

FIGURE 4-51 SQL Deployment

- **Name**   Name for the SQL Server deployment.

- **Instance Name**   The instance name. If left blank, it will use the default name MS-SQLSERVER.

- **Instance ID**   The instance ID used when you sysprepped the SQL instance.

- **Installation Run As Account**   Account with the permission to deploy SQL Server.

- **Media Source**   Location of the SQL Server installation media, such as a VMM Library share.

- **SQL Server Administrators**   Users or groups that will be configured as SQL Server Administrators. You must specify at least one account.

- **Security Mode**   Select Windows or SQL Server authentication.

- **Service accounts**   Configuration for the SQL Server service, SQL Server agent, and Reporting Services service accounts. You must select a Run As account for all three services.

> **MORE INFO** **SQL SERVER PROFILES**
>
> You can learn more about SQL Server profiles at *http://technet.microsoft.com/en-us/library/hh427294.aspx*.

Configuring virtual machine templates

A Virtual Machine Manager VM template allows you to deploy a single virtual machine with a consistent set of settings. A VMM VM template is an XML object that is stored with a VMM library, and includes one or more of the following segments:

- **Guest Operating System Profile** A guest OS profile that includes operating system settings.
- **Hardware Profile** A hardware profile that includes VM hardware settings.
- **Virtual Hard Disk** This can be a blank hard disk, or a virtual hard disk that hosts a specially prepared, sysprepped in the case of Windows based operating systems, version of an operating system.

You can create VM templates based on existing virtual machines deployed on a virtualization host managed by VMM, based on virtual hard disks stored in a VMM library, or by using an existing VM template.

VM templates have the following limitations:

- A VM template allows you to customize IP address settings, but you can only configure a static IP address for a specific VM when deploying that VM from the template.
- Application and SQL Server deployment are only used when you deploy a VM as part of a service.
- When creating a template from an existing VM, ensure that the VM is a member of a workgroup and is not joined to a domain.
- You should create a separate local administrator account on a VM before using it as the basis of a template. Using the built-in administrator account will cause the sysprep operation to fail.
- You cannot create a virtual machine template for a Linux virtual machine based on an existing Linux VM deployed to a virtualization host.

To create a VM template based on an existing virtual hard disk (which can include a blank hard disk), or existing VM template, perform the following steps:

1. In the Library workspace of the VMM console, click Create VM Template on the ribbon.
2. On the Select Source page, click Browse next to Use An Existing VM Template For A Virtual Hard Disk Stored In The Library.
3. On the Select VM Template Source dialog box, select the hard disk that will serve as the basis for the VM template.
4. On the VM Template Identity page, provide a name for the VM template and choose between a Generation 1 and a Generation 2 VM. This page is shown in Figure 4-52.

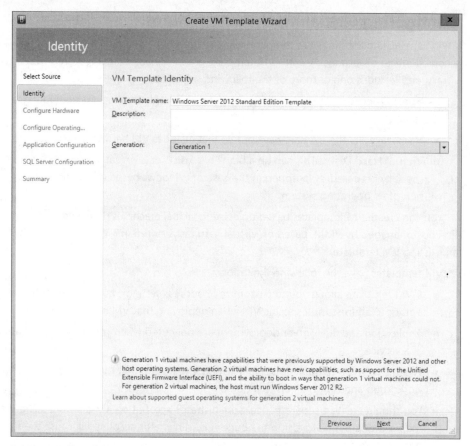

FIGURE 4-52 Template name

5. On the Configure Hardware page, you can select an existing hardware profile, or create a new hardware profile using the steps outlined earlier in this chapter. If you choose to create a new hardware profile, you can save this profile for use in the future. Figure 4-53 shows the selection of the Example Hardware Profile.

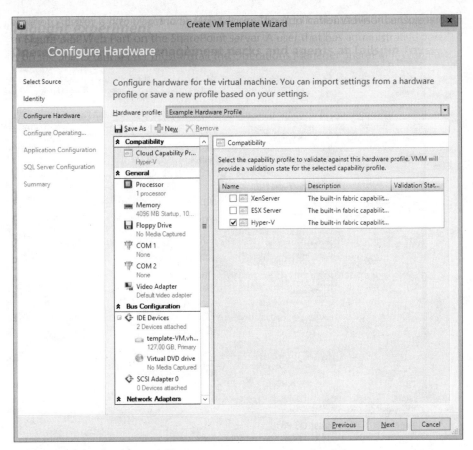

FIGURE 4-53 Select hardware profile

6. On the Configure Operating System page, select a guest OS profile or configure a new Guest OS Profile using the steps outlined earlier. If you choose to create a new guest OS profile, you can save it for use again later. Figure 4-54 shows the Example Windows Server 2012 R2 profile selected.

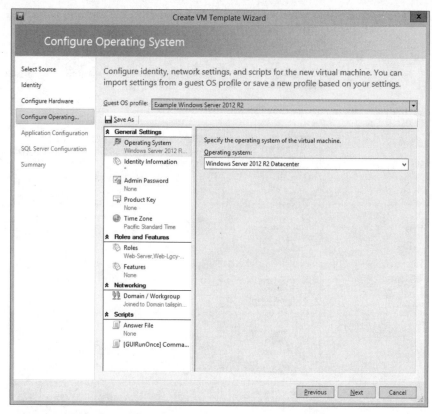

FIGURE 4-54 Select Guest OS Profile

7. On the Application Configuration page, you can select an existing application profile. This will only be used if the VM is deployed as a service, and you don't have to select an application profile when configuring a VM template.

8. On the SQL Server Configuration page, you can select an existing SQL Server profile. This will only be used if the VM is deployed as a service and you don't have to select SQL Server profile when configuring a VM template.

9. Complete the wizard, which creates the profile.

When creating a VM template from a VM that is already deployed, you'll be asked to select an existing VM from a list of those that are deployed on a virtualization host managed by VMM.

MORE INFO **VIRTUAL MACHINE TEMPLATES**

You can learn more about virtual machine templates at *http://technet.microsoft.com/en-us/library/hh427282.aspx.*

Creating service templates

Service templates differ from virtual machine templates in the following ways:

- Service templates allow you to deploy multiple virtual machines rather than a single virtual machine.
- Service templates can include settings for Windows Server roles and features. If a VM template includes role and feature settings, they will only be used if the VM is deployed as part of a service.
- Service templates can include application profiles and SQL server profiles. These profiles are not available when deploying a VM from a VM template.

To create a service template, perform the following steps:

1. In the Library workspace of the VMM console, click the Create Service Template item on the ribbon.

2. In the New Service Template dialog box, specify a Name, a Release version, and select between a Blank, Single Machine, Two Tier Application, or Three Tier Application pattern. Figure 4-55 shows the selection of a Two Tier Application.

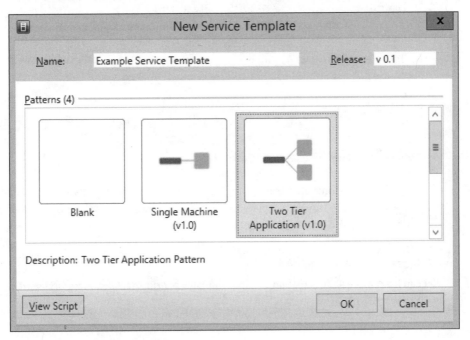

FIGURE 4-55 New Service Template

3. In the Virtual Machine Manager Service Template Designer, shown in Figure 4-56, use the drag and drop interface to add applications and configure which VM templates will be used with the multiple tier application. You can also add VM networks and load balancers, as well as adding additional machine tiers using the designer.

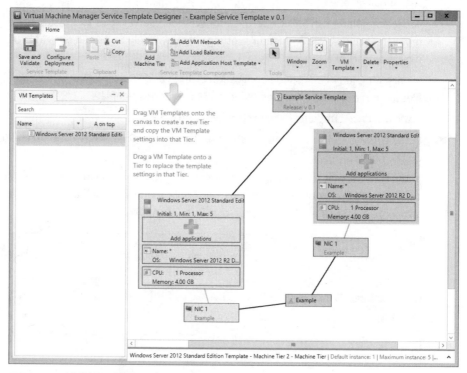

FIGURE 4-56 VMM Service Template Designer

4. When you have competed configuring the service template, click Save And Validate. This will check the service template for errors which must be resolved before the template can be saved and used for deployment.

MORE INFO **SERVICE TEMPLATES**

You can learn more about creating service templates at *http://technet.microsoft.com/en-us/library/gg675105.aspx.*

> ## Thought experiment
>
> ### VMM service deployment at Contoso
>
> You are in the process of configuring service deployment using VMM at Contoso. You want to automate the deployment of VMs, applications, and multi-tier services using VMM profiles and templates. With this in mind, answer the following questions:
>
> 1. What should you configure to automate the deployment of Microsoft Server App-V applications to a virtual service in VMM?
>
> 2. What should you configure so that you can simplify the deployment of a multi-tier application using VMM?

Objective Summary

- Hardware profiles allow you to configure virtual machine hardware settings.
- Guest operating system profiles allow you to configure operating system settings, including settings for local administrator accounts, computer name, and domain join information.
- Application profiles allow you to configure Server App-V, SQL DAC, and Web Deploy settings for when you deploy services.
- SQL Server profiles allow you to configure SQL Server settings for when you deploy services.
- Virtual machine templates allow you to create templates that serve as the basis for virtual machine deployment. These include hardware and guest operating system settings. You can create VM templates based on an existing virtual hard disk, virtual machine, or existing VM template.
- Service templates allow you to deploy multiple virtual machines and applications in multi-tier configurations.

Objective review

Answer the following questions to test your knowledge of the information in this objective. You can find the answers to these questions and explanations of why each answer choice is correct or incorrect in the "Answers" section at the end of this chapter.

1. Which of the following do you use to configure the service account used by a SQL Server instance's SQL Server service?

    A. SQL Server profile

    B. Hardware profile

    C. Guest operating system profile

    D. Application profile

2. Which of the following do you use to configure a virtual machine's memory configuration?

    A. Application profile

    B. Guest operating system profile

    C. Hardware profile

    D. SQL Server profile

3. Which of the following do you use to configure the local administrator account password on a virtual machine?

    A. SQL Server profile

    B. Hardware profile

    C. Guest operating system profile

    D. Application profile

4. Which of the following can you use as the basis for creating a virtual machine template?

    A. Deployed virtual machine

    B. VMM VM template

    C. Virtual hard disk

    D. Guest OS profile

Answers

This section contains the solutions to the thought experiments and answers to the lesson review questions in this chapter

Objective 4.1: Thought experiment

1. You need to configure the Mondays that the office is closed as holidays in the Service Manager calendar used to calculate metrics.

2. You should configure notifications that send an email to the service desk manager when an incident enters a warning state.

Objective 4.1: Review

1. **Correct answers:** A, B, and C

   A. **Correct**: You need a calendar prior to completing the configuration of a Service Manager SLO.

   B. **Correct**: You need a metric prior to completing the configuration of a Service Manager SLO.

   C. **Correct**: You need a queue prior to completing the configuration of a Service Manager SLO.

   D. **Incorrect**: Subscriptions are necessary for notifications, but not necessary for configuring Service Manager SLOs.

2. **Correct answer:** A

   A. **Correct**: You should target the Service Level Instance Time Information class when configuring this notification.

   B. **Incorrect**: You should target the Service Level Instance Time Information class rather than the Change Request class.

   C. **Incorrect**: You should target the Service Level Instance Time Information class rather than the Review Activity class.

   D. **Incorrect**: You should target the Service Level Instance Time Information class rather than the Problem class.

3. **Correct answers:** A and B

   A. **Correct**: You can use a custom workflow or an Orchestrator runbook to automatically escalate an incident in the event that it is likely to breach an SLO.

   B. **Correct**: You can use a custom workflow or an Orchestrator runbook to automatically escalate an incident in the event that it is likely to breach an SLO.

   C. **Incorrect**: You can use a custom workflow or an Orchestrator runbook to automatically escalate an incident in the event that it is likely to breach an SLO.

D. Incorrect: You can use a custom workflow or an Orchestrator runbook to automatically escalate an incident in the event that it is likely to breach an SLO.

4. **Correct answers:** C and D

A. Incorrect: Required By does not measure the incident creation date or when the incident is first responded to.

B. Incorrect: First Assigned Date is when the incident or service request is first assigned.

C. Correct: The First Response Date should be configured as the End Date for the metric.

D. Correct: The Created Date is when the incident is created. This should form the Start Date for the metric.

Objective 4.2: Thought experiment

1. You can configure and make knowledge articles available that detail procedures that users can use to attempt to self-remediate incidents before contacting the service desk.

2. You can configure Service Manager so that incidents can be submitted using email.

Objective 4.2: Review

1. **Correct answers:** A and B

A. Correct: You need to add the problem as a related work item to each incident, or the incidents as related work items to the problem.

B. Correct: You need to add the problem as a related work item to each incident, or the incidents as related work items to the problem.

C. Incorrect: You need to add the problem as a related work item to each incident, or the incidents as related work items to the problem.

D. Incorrect: You need to add the problem as a related work item to each incident, or the incidents as related work items to the problem.

2. **Correct answer:** B

A. Incorrect: You should resolve the problem. When doing so, you should select the option to auto-resolve all incidents associated with the problem.

B. Correct: You should resolve the problem. When doing so, you should select the option to auto-resolve all incidents associated with the problem.

C. Incorrect: You should resolve the problem. When doing so, you should select the option to auto-resolve all incidents associated with the problem.

D. Incorrect: You should resolve the problem. When doing so, you should select the option to auto-resolve all incidents associated with the problem.

3. **Correct answers:** B and C

    A. **Incorrect**: You should assign the highest priority, which is the lowest number, to incidents that are high impact and high urgency.

    B. **Correct**: You should assign the lowest priority, which is the highest number, to incidents that are of low impact and low urgency.

    C. **Correct**: You should assign the highest priority, which is the lowest number, to incidents that are high impact and high urgency.

    D. **Incorrect**: You should assign the lowest priority, which is the highest number, to incidents that are of low impact and low urgency.

4. **Correct answers:** A and C

    A. **Correct**: Priority is calculated using impact and urgency.

    B. **Incorrect**: Priority is calculated using impact and urgency.

    C. **Correct**: Priority is calculated using impact and urgency.

    D. **Incorrect**: Priority is calculated using impact and urgency.

Objective 4.3: Thought experiment

1. You should configure an Application Profile to automate the deployment to Microsoft Server App-V applications to virtual services.

2. You should configure a service template so that you can automate the deployment of multi-tier applications. Service templates include VM templates, application, and SQL Server profiles.

Objective 4.3: Review

1. **Correct answer:** A

    A. **Correct**: You use a SQL Server profile to configure a SQL Server instance's service accounts.

    B. **Incorrect**: You use a hardware profile to configure a virtual machine's hardware settings.

    C. **Incorrect**: You use a guest operating system profile to configure guest operating system settings.

    D. **Incorrect**: You use an application profile to configure application installation settings.

2. **Correct answer:** C

    A. **Incorrect**: You use an application profile to configure application installation settings.

    B. **Incorrect**: You use a guest operating system profile to configure guest operating system settings.

C. **Correct**: You use a hardware profile to configure a virtual machine's hardware settings.

D. **Incorrect**: You use a SQL Server profile to configure a SQL Server instance's service accounts.

3. **Correct answer:** C

A. **Incorrect**: You use a SQL Server profile to configure a SQL Server instance's service accounts.

B. **Incorrect**: You use a hardware profile to configure a virtual machine's hardware settings.

C. **Correct**: You use a guest operating system profile to configure guest operating system settings.

D. **Incorrect:** You use an application profile to configure application installation settings.

4. **Correct answers:** A, B, and C

A. **Correct**: You can use a deployed virtual machine, an existing VMM template, or a virtual hard disk as the basis for a VMM VM template.

B. **Correct**: You can use a deployed virtual machine, an existing VMM template, or a virtual hard disk as the basis for a VMM VM template.

C. **Correct**: You can use a deployed virtual machine, an existing VMM template, or a virtual hard disk as the basis for a VMM VM template.

D. **Incorrect**: You can use a deployed virtual machine, an existing VMM template, or a virtual hard disk as the basis for a VMM VM template.

CHAPTER 5

Manage configuration and protection

There is more to managing a private cloud than just deployment and monitoring. You often times need to ensure that the configuration of the servers that host private cloud resources, as well as the workloads running within the private cloud, do not deviate too far from their appropriate configuration. You need to ensure that the servers that host private cloud resources, as well as the workloads running within the private cloud, are kept current with software updates. You also need to ensure that the workloads and the servers that they run on are regularly backed up and able to be recovered, both for business continuity purposes and to accomplish data retention objectives.

Objectives in this chapter:

- Objective 5.1: Manage compliance and configuration
- Objective 5.2: Manage updates
- Objective 5.3: Implement backup and recovery

Objective 5.1: Manage compliance and configuration

The practice of server administration increasingly involves not just ensuring that a workload functions in a reliable manner, but that servers themselves are configured in a way that meets legislative requirements. In many industries, computers must meet configuration standards dictated by legislation. The compliance functionality of the system center suite allows you to assess whether workloads in a private cloud are configured in a manner that meets the organization's legal responsibilities.

> **This section covers the following topics:**
> - Implementing System Center Process Pack for IT GRC
> - Understanding compliance settings
> - Using Desired State Configuration
> - Understanding System Center Advisor

Implementing System Center Process Pack for IT GRC

GRC is an acronym for governance, risk management, and compliance. The IT GRC Process Pack allows you to provide automated compliance management through the System Center suite. The System Center Process Pack for IT GRC allows you to manage IT operations and information management; it does not include other governance, risk management, and compliance functionality for other areas such as organizational accounting and business operations.

A control objective is a desired state result that has been met through risk assessment. For example, a control objective might be that user accounts of contract workers have an expiry date. This objective might have been selected after risk analysis found that some contractors had network access after their contract term finished. Control activities allow control objectives to be accomplished.

The System Center Process Pack for IT GRC uses the following System Center segments:

- **Service Manager** This hosts the System Center Process Pack for IT GRC and allows you to run the controls and activities that are necessary to meet control objectives. The System Center Process Pack for IT GRC requires that Service Manager be configured with the Active Directory, Operations Manager, and Configuration Manager connectors.

- **Service Manager data warehouse** This allows you to generate compliance and risk reports to audit and review compliance information. It is required for System Center Process Pack for IT GRC reporting.

- **Configuration Manager site server** Configuration Manager provides configuration drift reporting. Configuration drift occurs when a computer's configuration changes from those specified in a desired configuration baseline. It requires the deployment of Configuration Manager agents on monitored computers.

- **Operations Manager** This manages alerts generated when computers drift from the desired configuration baseline. It requires the deployment of the Operations Manager agent on to monitored computers.

You install the System Center Process Pack for IT GRC on to the Service Manager server. After you have the Process Pack, run the MpSyncJob to synchronize Service Manager with the data warehouse. Then import the IT Compliance Management Libraries into Service Manager and the desired Configuration Management configuration items and baselines into Configuration Manager.

> **MORE INFO** **SYSTEM CENTER PROCESS PACK FOR IT GRC**
>
> You can learn more about the System Center Process Pack for IT GRC at *http://technet. microsoft.com/en-us/library/dd206732.aspx.*

When implementing a compliance program, it is occasionally necessary to configure program exceptions. You create exceptions for services or servers that cannot be made compliant with control objectives. You can create the following exception types:

- **Control activity scope exceptions** This type of exception allows you to exclude specific control activities when checking compliance.
- **IT GRC program exceptions** This type of exception allows you to exclude a specific computer from an IT GRC program.
- **IT GRC policy exceptions** This type of exception allows you to exclude control activities that are not applicable to your organization.

EXAM TIP

Remember the different exception types that you can create when implementing a compliance program.

Understanding compliance settings

Compliance settings, which in previous versions of System Center Configuration Manager was termed Desired Configuration Management, allows you to monitor and remediate the configuration of computers.

Configuration Manager's compliance settings functionality uses configuration items and configuration baselines. A configuration item includes one or more settings that you want to assess to determine the compliance state of a computer. The configuration item includes compliance rules to evaluate the settings, as well as providing severity ratings for noncompliance. Some configuration items can be configured for remediation, which allows you to alter a non-compliant setting so that it is compliant. Configuration baselines are collections of software updates, configuration items, and other configuration baselines.

MORE INFO **INTRODUCTION TO COMPLIANCE SETTINGS**

You can learn more about compliance settings in Configuration Manager at *http://technet. microsoft.com/en-au/library/gg681958.aspx.*

Configuration items

Configuration Manager supports the following types of configuration items for assessing the compliance of computers:

- **Application configuration item** Use this type of configuration item to determine application compliance, including whether the application is installed and whether it is configured in a specific manner.
- **Operating system configuration item** Allows you to determine operating system configuration compliance, such as whether particular roles or features are installed and particular registry keys are configured.

- **Software updates configuration item** Available when you manage software updates with Configuration Manager, and allows you to assess whether a computer has specific software updates installed.

For example, to create a configuration item related to whether Remote Desktop is enabled on a target computer running the Windows Server 2012 R2 operating system, perform the following steps:

1. In the Assets And Compliance workspace of the Configuration Manager console, select the Configuration Items node under the Compliance Settings node. On the ribbon, click Create Configuration Item.

2. On the General page of the Create Configuration Item Wizard, provide a name and ensure that the type of configuration item is set to Windows, as shown in Figure 5-1.

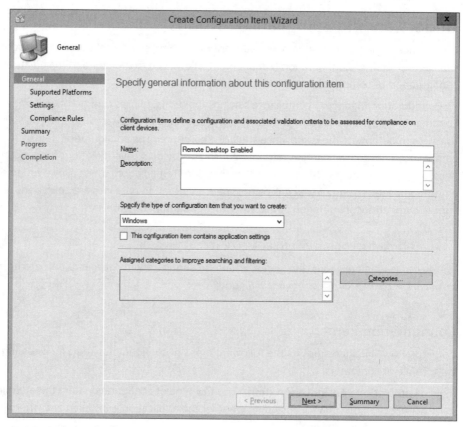

FIGURE 5-1 Create Configuration Item Wizard

3. On the Supported Platforms page, ensure that Windows Server 2012 R2 is selected, as shown in Figure 5-2. You should only select the operating systems that you want the configuration item assessed for on this page.

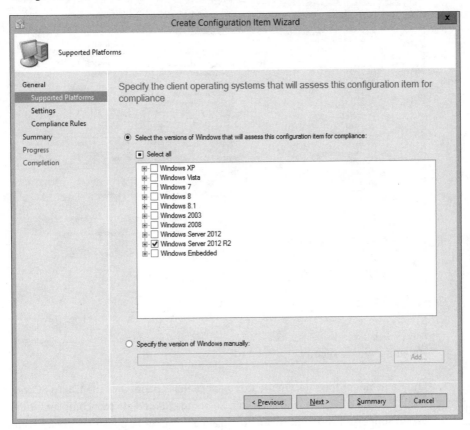

FIGURE 5-2 Select Windows versions

4. On the Settings page, click New. This will launch the Create Setting dialog box.

5. In the Create Setting dialog box, click Browse.

6. In the registry tree, navigate to HKEY_LOCAL_MACHINE\SYSTEM\CurrentControlSet\Control\Terminal Server, and select the fDenyTSConnections registry value. In this scenario, the value is set to 0, which allows Remote Desktop connections. Enable the This Registry Value Must Satisfy The Following Rule If Present Equals 0, as shown in Figure 5-3.

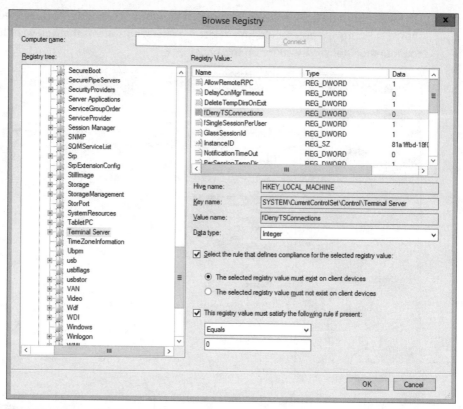

FIGURE 5-3 Browse Registry

7. Enter a name for the rule. On the Compliance Rules page, click the fDenyTSConnections Equals 0 condition, and click Edit. Select the Remediate Noncompliant Rules
   When Supported and Report Noncompliance If This Setting Instance Is Not Found
   check boxes, and set the Noncompliance Severity For Reports to Critical, as shown in
   Figure 5-4.

8. Complete the wizard to create the configuration item.

MORE INFO CONFIGURATION ITEMS

You can learn more about configuration items at *http://technet.microsoft.com/en-us/li-
brary/gg712331.aspx.*

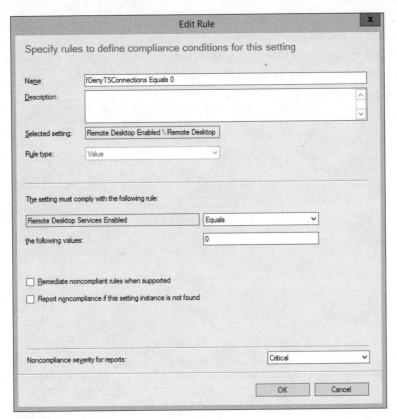

FIGURE 5-4 Edit Rule

Configuration baselines

Configuration baselines can include configuration items, software updates, and other configuration baselines. To create a configuration baseline that includes the Remote Desktop configuration item configured earlier, perform the following steps:

1. In the Assets And Compliance workspace of the Configuration Manager console, select Configuration Baselines under Compliance Settings.

2. On the ribbon, click Create Configuration Baseline. This will launch the Create Configuration Baseline dialog box.

3. On the Create Configuration Baseline dialog box, specify a name for the baseline, and then click Add, and then click Configuration Items.

4. On the Add Configuration Items dialog box, click the Remote Desktop Enabled configuration item, and click Add, as shown in Figure 5-5.

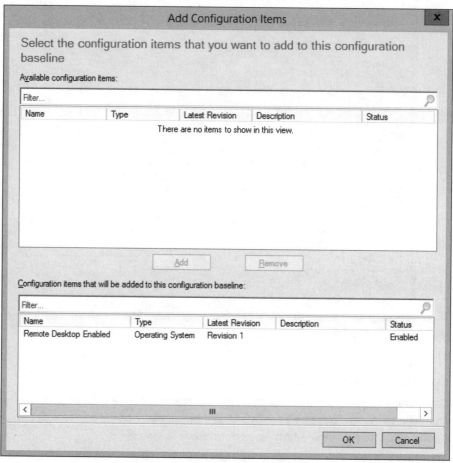

FIGURE 5-5 Add Configuration Items

5. Verify that the configuration item is present, as shown in Figure 5-6, and then click OK.

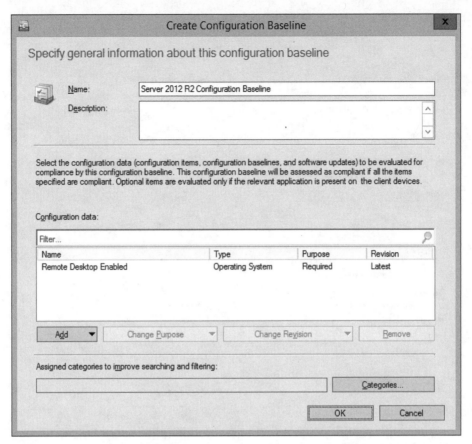

FIGURE 5-6 Create Configuration Baseline

To deploy the configuration baseline to a collection, select the configuration baseline, and click Deploy on the ribbon. When deploying the baseline, select the collection to which you want to deploy the baseline, and also choose whether you want to enable remediation. Figure 5-7 shows the Server 2012 R2 Configuration Baseline deployed to the Windows Server 2012 R2 Servers collection with the remediation option enabled.

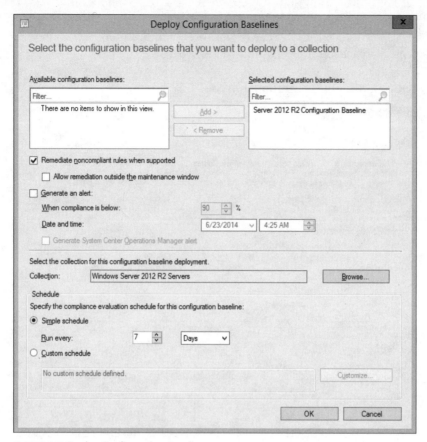

FIGURE 5-7 Deploy Configuration Baselines

Once the configuration baseline has been deployed, you'll be able to view a list of compliant and non-compliant computers from the Configuration Baseline node, by selecting the
baseline in Deployments node in the Monitoring workspace, or by viewing reports in the
Compliance And Settings Management report category.

> **MORE INFO** **CONFIGURATION BASELINES**
>
> You can learn more about configuration baselines at *http://technet.microsoft.com/en-us/
> library/gg712268.aspx.*

Remediation

Certain types of configuration items can be remediated, but only when the item is included
in a baseline deployment that you have also configured for remediation. Remediation is only
available for the following types of computer related configuration items:

- Registry value

- Scripts
- WQL query configuration items

You can configure remediation to be performed, either by creating a value if it is not present, altering a value if it exists but is not compliant (for example, changing a registry value), or by running a remediation script. The remediation script will need to alter the setting to the desired state.

Using Desired State Configuration

Desired State Configuration (DSC) is a feature new to Windows PowerShell 4.0 that allows you to manage the configuration of computers, accomplishing many of the objectives with Windows PowerShell that you could otherwise accomplish using compliance settings with Configuration Manager. You can use DSC to perform the following tasks:

- Ensuring that server roles and features are either enabled or disabled
- Managing registry settings
- Managing files and directories
- Managing service and the state of processes
- Managing user and group accounts
- Software deployment
- Managing environment variables
- Assessing configuration state
- Remediating configuration drift

When using DSC, you define a Windows PowerShell script block using the configuration keyword. This script block allows you to specify the desired configuration for each computer (termed nodes in DSC). Within the script block, you can define resource blocks as a way of configuring specific resources. When you invoke the configuration, a MOF file is created in a new directory that is a child of the current directory with the same name as the configuration block. The newly created MOF file stores configuration information about the target computers. You can enforce the configuration by running the Start-DscConfiguration cmdlet.

> **MORE INFO DESIRED STATE CONFIGURATION**
>
> You can learn more about Desired State Configuration at *http://technet.microsoft.com/en-us/library/dn249912.aspx.*

Understanding System Center Advisor

System Center Advisor is a cloud-based service that collects data from computers and generates alerts based on that data. For example, System Center Advisor can generate alerts about missing security updates, or where the configuration of a computer deviates substantially from best practice. The knowledge used to raise these advisory alerts comes from Microsoft's engineering support team, and reflects direct customer experiences running the products in production environments.

System Center Advisor includes the Advisor web service, hosted in Microsoft's cloud, an on premise gateway, and one or more agents, which you deploy to computers in your environment. The agent functions in a way that is similar to the Operations Manager agent. By connecting to the web portal, you can view alerts and advise on how to remediate those issues. Figure 5-8 shows a typical System Center Advisor deployment, with agents installed on local computers communicating with a gateway, that forwards collected data that is stored and analyzed in the cloud.

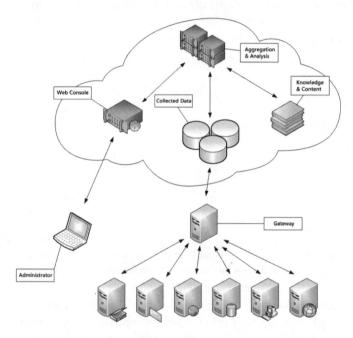

FIGURE 5-8 System Center Advisor

MORE INFO **SYSTEM CENTER ADVISOR**

You can learn more about System Center Advisor at *http://onlinehelp.microsoft.com/en-us/advisor/ff962512.aspx.*

> ### *Thought experiment*
> ### System Center Advisor at Adatum
> You are planning on deploying System Center Advisor to a client named Adatum, who has a small number of servers as a way of monitoring whether those servers are current with the latest software updates. You deploy the System Center Advisor agent on to the servers on the internal network.
>
> 1. What server should you deploy on the perimeter network?
>
> 2. How will you review the status of the monitored servers?

Objective summary

- The System Center Process Pack for IT GRC allows you to perform compliance activities using Service Manager, Configuration Manager, and Operations Manager.
- A Configuration Manager compliance setting is a setting, such as an application or registry setting that can be checked.
- A configuration baseline is a collection of compliance settings, software updates, and other configuration baselines.
- Some compliance settings can be automatically remediated.
- Desired State Configuration allows you to check and remediate a computer's configuration using Windows PowerShell.
- System Center Advisor is a cloud-based monitoring service that can provide advice on how to better configure monitored servers.

Objective review

Answer the following questions to test your knowledge of the information in this objective. You can find the answers to these questions and explanations of why each answer choice is correct or incorrect in the "Answers" section at the end of this chapter.

1. Which of the following can you add to a Configuration Manager configuration baseline?

    A. Configuration item

    B. Compliance baseline

    C. Software updates

    D. Update baselines

2. Which System Center products are required to support the System Center Process Pack for IT GRC?

   A. Configuration Manager

   B. Operations Manager

   C. Service Manager

   D. Virtual Machine Manager

3. Which of the following connectors must you configure in Service Manager to support the deployment of the System Center Process Pack for IT GRC?

   A. Active Directory

   B. Orchestrator

   C. Operations Manager

   D. Configuration Manager

Objective 5.2: Manage Updates

This objective deals with the various methods you can use for managing software updates for your organization's private cloud deployment. The most basic method of managing software updates is to use Windows Server Update Services (WSUS). In a Microsoft private cloud environment, you are likely to use both Configuration Manager and VMM, both integrated with WSUS, to manage updates. You use VMM to manage updates for the servers involved in the virtualization infrastructure, and Configuration Manager to manage the updates for the virtual machines running within the private cloud.

> **This section covers the following topics:**
> - Managing updates with WSUS
> - Managing updates with Configuration Manager
> - Integrating WSUS with VMM
> - Updating offline VMs

Managing updates with WSUS

WSUS is a Windows Server 2012 and Windows Server 2012 R2 role service that allows you to manage and deploy Microsoft operating system and application updates. Rather than having each computer in your organization connect over the Internet to acquire software updates, you can configure a server with the WSUS role installed to acquire these updates, and then to serve as a central distribution point. You can also integrate the WSUS role with Configuration Manager and with VMM, topics that are covered later in this section.

Configuring the WSUS server

Once you've installed the WSUS server role, you need to run the WSUS Server Configuration Wizard to configure how the WSUS server functions. The WSUS Server Configuration Wizard allows you to configure WSUS server settings. Running this wizard involves performing the following steps:

1. Choose whether the WSUS server will synchronize with Microsoft update, or synchronize with another WSUS server. If you synchronize with Microsoft update, the WSUS server will obtain updates from Microsoft's servers through the Internet. If you choose to synchronize with another WSUS server, you can choose to synchronize updates from that server, or configure the WSUS server as a replica, in which case you will synchronize approvals, settings, computers, and groups from the server. You configure replica servers in scenarios where you want to deploy multiple WSUS servers, but have them all use the same settings. Figure 5-9 shows a WSUS server configured to synchronize as a replica. When you configure a WSUS server as a replica, you don't need to choose languages, products, or classifications.

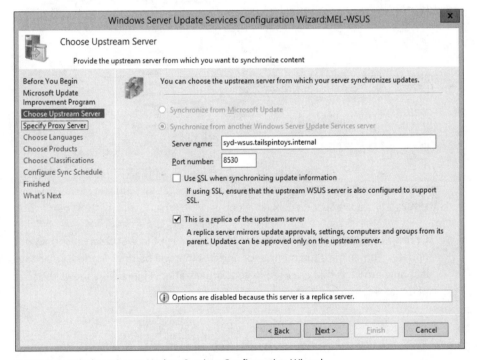

FIGURE 5-9 Windows Server Update Services Configuration Wizard

2. Next, you configure whether the WSUS server will use a proxy server during synchronization. If required, you can configure proxy server credentials.

3. The next step requires the WSUS server to synchronize with either Microsoft Update, or the upstream server. This allows the WSUS server to obtain a list of update types, language options, and products that the WSUS server will provide.

4. Once synchronization has completed, select whether to download updates in all languages, or updates in a specific language. Most organizations will only require updates in their local language. Figure 5-10 shows a configuration where only English is selected as the language.

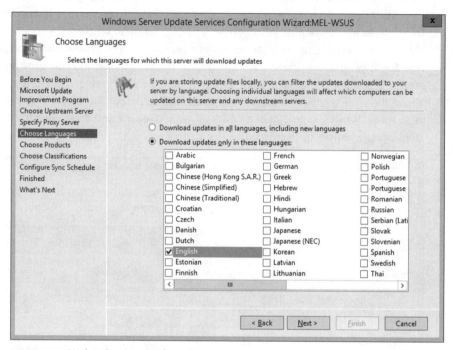

FIGURE 5-10 Update Services Configuration

5. On the Products page, select the products for which the WSUS server should obtain updates. To minimize the number of updates that will be downloaded, you should select only products that are used in your organization. Figure 5-11 shows the selection of updates for several System Center 2012 R2 products.

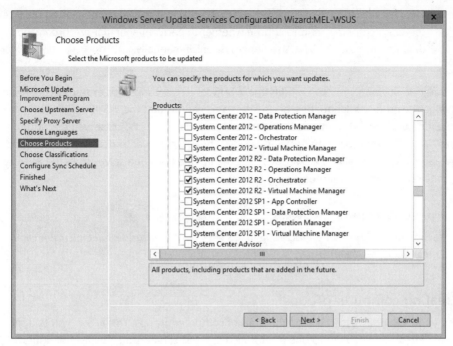

FIGURE 5-11 Product Selection

6. On the Classifications page, select which update classifications you want the WSUS server to synchronize. Figure 5-12 shows updates of all the classifications selected.

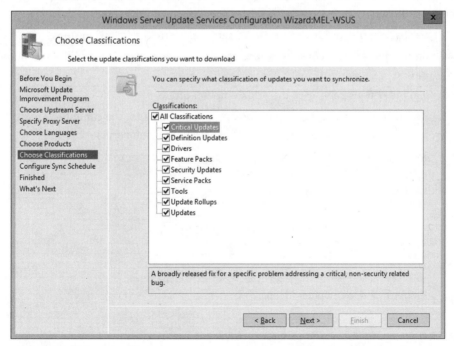

FIGURE 5-12 Choose classifications

7. The final step to take in configuring a WSUS server is to choose how often the WSUS server synchronizes, and to choose whether to perform an initial synchronization. The default is to have the WSUS server synchronize manually.

After deployment, you can modify the WSUS server's settings. For example, you might change the products, languages, or update classifications that the WSUS server uses when obtaining updates. You can also configure an "approvals only" WSUS server. An "approvals only" WSUS server is one where clients contact the WSUS server to determine which updates are approved for installation, but download the update files themselves from the Microsoft update servers on the Internet.

> **MORE INFO** **CONFIGURING WSUS**
>
> You can learn more about integrating WSUS with VMM at *http://technet.microsoft.com/ en-us/library/hh852346.aspx*.

Creating computer groups

You approve updates in WSUS on the basis of computer groups. This allows you to approve an update for deployment to one group, such as a test server group, whilst not deploying the update to every computer in your organization. You can assign computers to computer groups manually, or by using Group Policy. You should create the computer groups on the WSUS server prior to configuring WSUS computer group assignment through Group Policy. You'll only be able to manually assign computers to groups that have contacted the WSUS server for updates.

To create computer groups on the WSUS server, perform the following steps:

1. In the WSUS Server console, expand the Computers group, and then the All Computers group.
2. On the Actions pane, click the Add Computer group.
3. On the Add Computer Group dialog box, enter a name for the computer group. Figure 5-13 shows a computer group named Melbourne Infrastructure.

FIGURE 5-13 Add Computer Group

Once you've created the group, you can manually assign computers that have contacted the WSUS server to the group by moving them from the Unassigned Computers group. Computers assigned to groups through Active Directory will automatically be added to the appropriate group.

Group Policy settings

In domain environments, you use Group Policy to configure computers with the address of the WSUS server, as well as other configuration settings. Windows update related group policies are located in both the Computer Configuration and User Configuration nodes. Figure 5-14 shows Windows update related group policies.

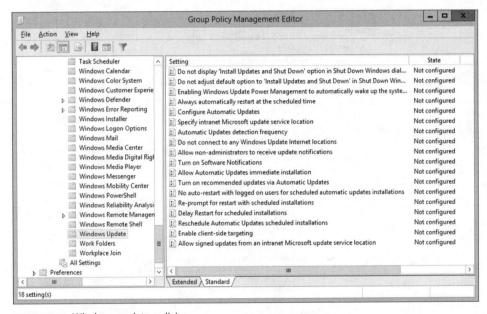

FIGURE 5-14 Windows update policies

> **MORE INFO WSUS GROUP POLICY SETTINGS**
>
> You can learn more about WSUS related Group Policy settings at *http://technet.microsoft. com/en-us/library/dn595129.aspx.*

You use the Specify Intranet Microsoft Update Service Location policy to configure a computer with the address of the WSUS server. Figure 5-15 shows this policy configured so that the computer subject to this policy will use the update server at *http://mel-wsus.tailspintoys.internal* on port 8530, which is the default port used by WSUS on Windows Server 2012 and Windows Server 2012 R2.

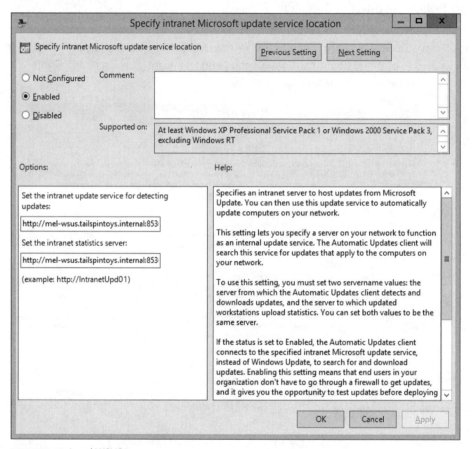

FIGURE 5-15 Local WSUS server

You assign computers to WSUS computer groups using the Enable client-Side Targeting policy. Figure 5-16 shows this policy configured for membership of the Melbourne Infrastructure WSUS computer group.

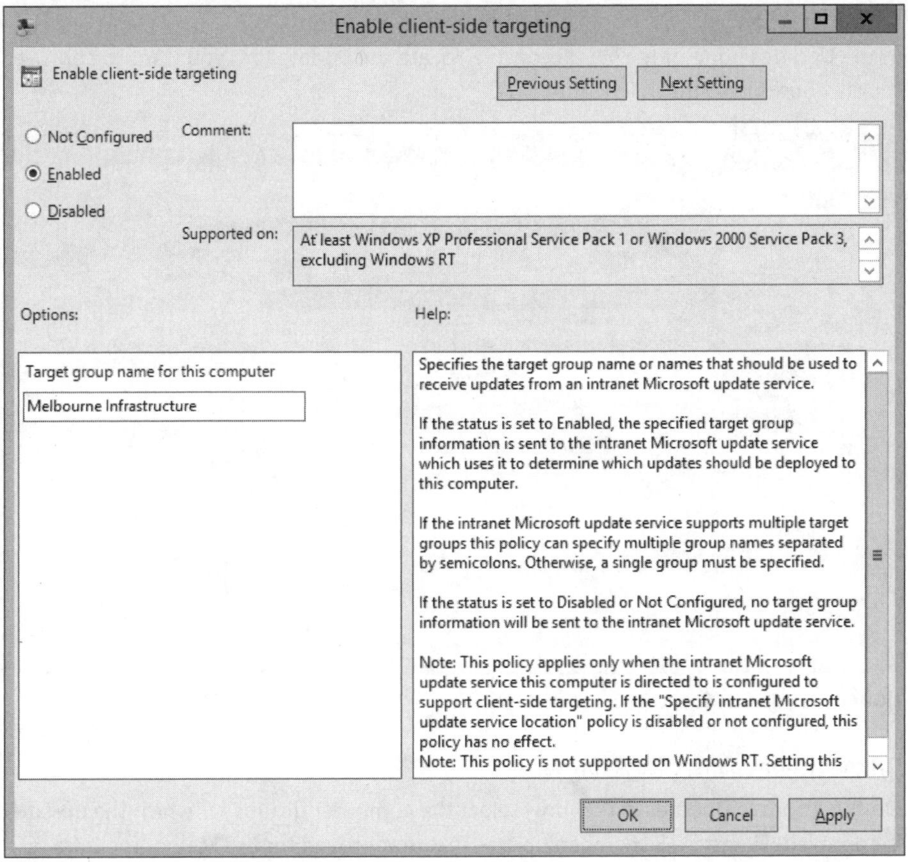

FIGURE 5-16 Client-side targeting

Approving updates

You can choose to manually approve WSUS updates, or configure auto-approval rules. You approve updates on a per-computer group basis. When you approve an update, you can have that update apply to the computer group and any computer groups that are nested members of that computer group. You can also choose to apply an update to a computer group, and exclude any computer groups that are nested members of that group.

To manually approve an update, perform the following steps:

1. In the Updates node of the WSUS console, locate the update that you want to approve for distribution, as shown in Figure 5-17.

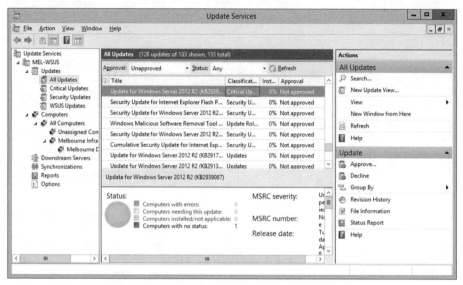

FIGURE 5-17 Update Services

2. On the Actions pane, click Approve.

3. On the Approve Updates dialog box, select the computer groups for which the update is approved. Figure 5-18 shows an update that is approved for the Melbourne Infrastructure group, but not approved for the Melbourne DHCP Servers group.

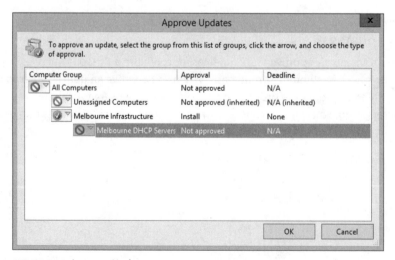

FIGURE 5-18 Approve Updates

Rather than manually approve updates, you can configure automatic approval rules so that new updates are automatically approved based on their properties. A default automatic approval rule, which is not enabled, will automatically approve critical and security updates to all computers that report to the WSUS server. To configure an automatic approval rule, perform the following steps:

1. In the Options node of the WSUS console, click Automatic Approvals.

2. On the Automatic Approvals dialog box, shown in Figure 5-19, click New Rule.

FIGURE 5-19 Automatic Approvals

3. On the Add Rule dialog box, select from the following options:

- Update Classification
- Update Product
- Approval Deadline
- Computer Groups

4. Figure 5-20 shows a rule that will automatically approve critical updates, security updates, update rollups, and updates for Windows Server 2012 R2 if a computer is a member of the Melbourne Infrastructure group, with an installation deadline of 7 days after the approval.

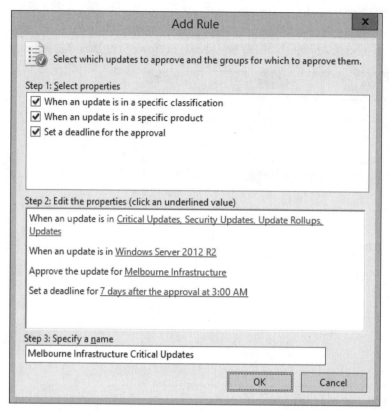

FIGURE 5-20 Add Rule

MORE INFO **DEPLOY WSUS UPDATES**

You can learn more about deploying updates at *http://technet.microsoft.com/en-us/library/ hh852348.aspx*.

Verifying update deployment

You can verify update deployment and computer compliance either by viewing the properties of individual computers, or by viewing information on a per-update basis. Figure 5-21 shows that computer Mel-demoserver requires 59 updates and has 69 updates either installed or not applicable. It is important to note that the WSUS server doesn't scan a computer to determine what updates are installed. Instead, the client computer contacts the WSUS server and provides information about which updates have been installed. The WSUS server then uses this information to determine which updates need to be installed given the current configuration of the WSUS client.

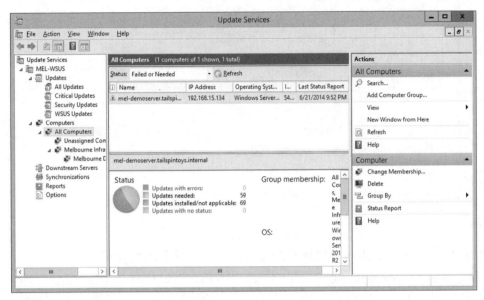

FIGURE 5-21 Update status

The WSUS server also provides the following reports, shown in Figure 5-22, that you can use to determine the update status of computers that report to the WSUS server:

- Update Status Summary
- Update Detailed Status
- Update Tabular Status
- Update Tabular Status For Approved Updates
- Computer Status Summary
- Computer Detailed Status
- Computer Tabular Status
- Computer Tabular Status For Approved Updates
- Synchronization Results

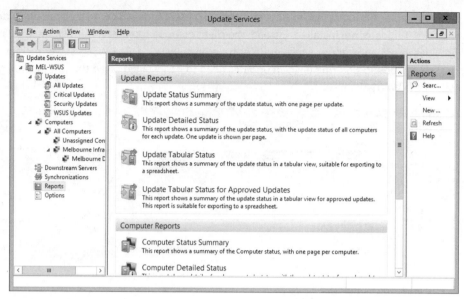

FIGURE 5-22 Report

Managing updates with Configuration Manager

WSUS provides basic update management functionality, but does not provide advanced functionality such as maintenance windows, configuration baselines, support for Network Access Protection, and support for Wake On LAN. You can integrate WSUS with System Center 2012 R2 Configuration Manager to provide advanced software update management functionality for computers in your private cloud environment. When you integrate WSUS with Configuration Manager, you perform update management tasks using the Configuration Manager console.

Integrating WSUS with Configuration Manager

Integrating WSUS with Configuration Manager involves installing and configuring a software update point and synchronizing the software update point's metadata with Configuration Manager. To deploy a software update point when WSUS has been deployed and configured on another computer, perform the following steps:

1. In the Administration workspace of the Configuration Manager console, select Servers And Site System Roles under the Site Configuration node.

2. On the Home tab of the ribbon, click Create Site System Server.

3. On the General page of the Create Site System Server Wizard, specify the name of the server that hosts WSUS, the site code, and the account used for deploying the site system. Figure 5-23 shows the server CBR-WSUS.tailspintoys.internal being configured for this role.

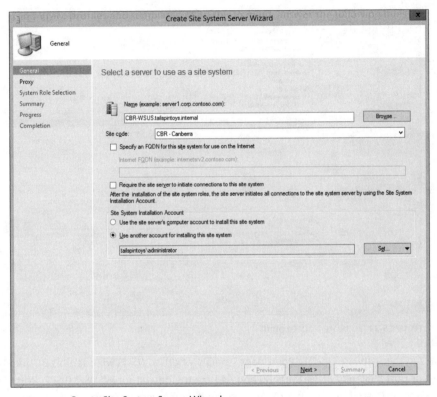

FIGURE 5-23 Create Site System Server Wizard

4. On the Proxy Server page, you can specify the details of any proxy server required to allow the computer that hosts the site server role the ability to connect to hosts on the Internet.

5. On the System Role Selection page, select Software Update Point, as shown in Figure 5-24.

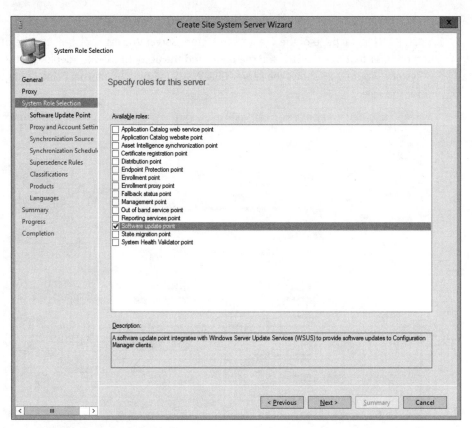

FIGURE 5-24 Software update point

6. On the Software Update Point page, specify whether WSUS will use port 80 and 443, or port 8530 and 8531. Ports 80 and 443 are the default for WSUS 3.0 SP2. Ports 8530 and 8531 are the default for WSUS on Windows Server 2012 and Windows Server 2012 R2. You can also specify whether connections will be limited to Internet, intranet, or both intranet and Internet clients. Figure 5-25 shows this page of the wizard.

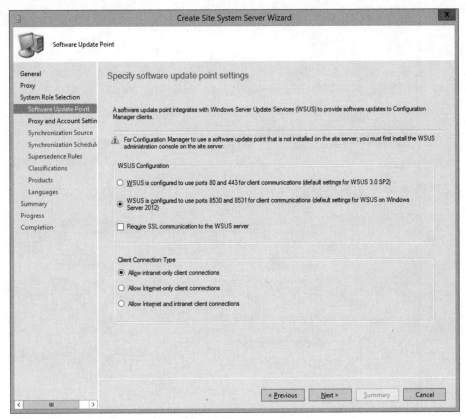

FIGURE 5-25 Software Update Point settings

7. On the Proxy And Account Settings page, specify the account that will be used to connect from the Configuration Manager site server to the WSUS server.

8. On the Synchronization Source page, specify whether the WSUS server will synchronize updates from Microsoft update, or from another WSUS server. You can also use this page to specify whether WSUS will continue to generate reports. If you are using Configuration Manager's more sophisticated reporting functionality, you do not need to enable WSUS reporting. Figure 5-26 shows the Synchronization Source set to Microsoft Update.

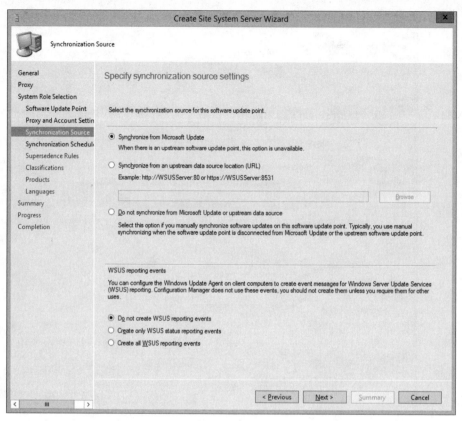

FIGURE 5-26 Synchronization Source

9. On the Synchronization Schedule page, specify how often synchronization should occur. You can also perform synchronization manually.

10. On the Supersedence Behavior page, specify how to treat superseded updates. You
    can configure superseded updates to expire immediately, or after a specific number of
    months.

11. On the Classifications page, shown in Figure 5-27, specify which updates Configuration
    Manager will use the WSUS server to obtain.

12. On the Products page, specify which product you wish to provide updates for.

13. On the Languages page, specify the product language versions that you want to sup-
    port, and then complete the wizard.

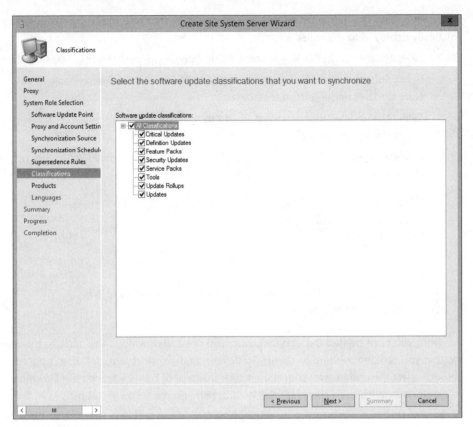

FIGURE 5-27 Update classifications

Once you have configured the Software Update point, you can trigger a manual synchronization by performing the following steps:

1. In the Software Library workspace of the Configuration Manager console, click All Software Updates under Software Updates.

2. On the ribbon, click Synchronize Software Updates. You can view the status of the synchronization by checking the SMS_WSUS_SYNC_MANAGER segment in the Component Status node of the Monitoring workspace.

Software update groups

Software update groups allow you to collect together updates. You can add software updates to software update groups manually, or automatically configure new software updates to be added to a software update group through an automatic deployment rule. You can deploy software update groups to Configuration Manager collections. Configuration Manager collections are groups of configuration manager clients or users, though you can only deploy software updates to client collections. You can deploy software update groups to collections either manually, or automatically through an automatic deployment rule. When you deploy a software update group to a collection, any new updates that you add to the group are automatically deployed to the collection.

To add software updates to a new software update group, perform the following steps:

1. In the Software Library workspace of the Configuration Manager console, click All Software Updates under Software Updates.

2. Select the updates that you want to add to the new software update group, and then click Create Software Update Group on the ribbon.

3. Provide a meaningful name for the update group, and then click Create. Figure 5-28 shows the Create Software Update Group dialog box.

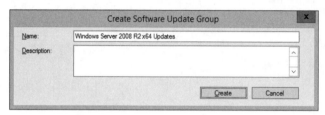

FIGURE 5-28 Update group

Once you have created the update group, you need to download the updates themselves, so that you can deploy them to clients. To download the constituent files of an upgrade group, select the update group, and then click Download. This will launch the Download Software Updates Wizard. To complete this wizard, perform the following steps:

1. On the Deployment Package page of the Download Software Updates Wizard, shown in Figure 5-29, choose either to use an existing deployment package, or to create a new deployment package. If you choose an existing deployment package, any updates that have been previously downloaded will not be downloaded again. If you choose to deploy a new deployment package, you'll need to provide the following information:

   ■ **Name** A unique name for the deployment package.

   ■ **Package Source** A unique shared folder location to host the software update source files. You need to create and specify this folder prior to clicking Next.

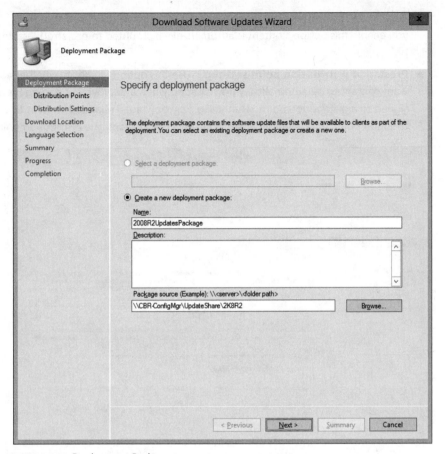

FIGURE 5-29 Deployment Package

2. On the Distribution Point page, choose the Configuration Manager distribution points that will host the software update files.

3. On the Distribution Settings page, shown in Figure 5-30, configure the following settings:

   - **Distribution Priority** This determines the priority when the package is sent to distribution points at child sites. Priority is only used if there is a backlog of packages being sent to distribution points.

- **Distribute the content for this package to preferred distribution points**   If you enable this option, content is automatically distributed to preferred distribution points.
- **Prestaged distribution point settings**   Use this option to specify whether you want content to be automatically downloaded when a deployment package is assigned to a distribution point, whether to only download changed content to a distribution point, or whether you will manually copy content to a distribution point.

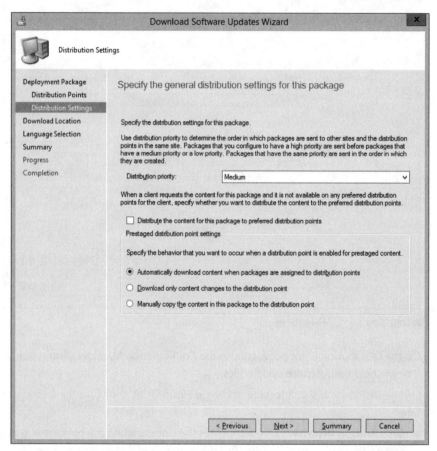

FIGURE 5-30 Distribution Settings

4. On the Download Location page, shown in Figure 5-31, choose how Configuration Manager will obtain software update source files. Choose between having Configuration Manager download software updates from the Internet, or from a location on the local network.

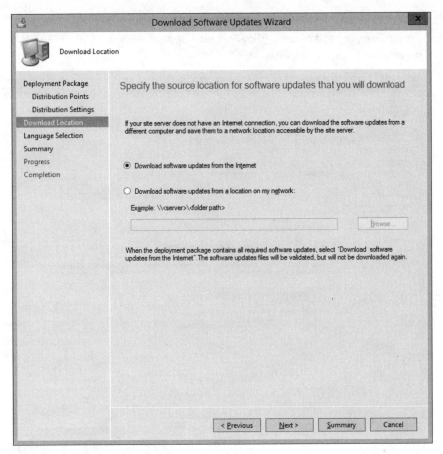

FIGURE 5-31 Download Location

5. Select which language the update files will be downloaded in. Most organizations will only need to download updates for the language version of the software that they use

Deploy software updates

Once software updates have been obtained, you need to deploy them to Configuration Manager clients. The clients that you will deploy the updates to need to be part of a Configuration Manager collection. You can configure maintenance windows on a per-collection basis. Maintenance windows allow you to specify the time of day that operations such as update installation occur.

To deploy a software update group package to a Configuration Manager collection, perform the following steps:

1. In the Software Library workspace of the Configuration Manager console, click Software Update Groups under Software Updates, and then select the software update group that you want to deploy.

2. On the ribbon, click Deploy. This will launch the Deploy Software Updates Wizard.

3. On the General page of the Deploy Software Updates Wizard, shown in Figure 5-32, provide the following information:

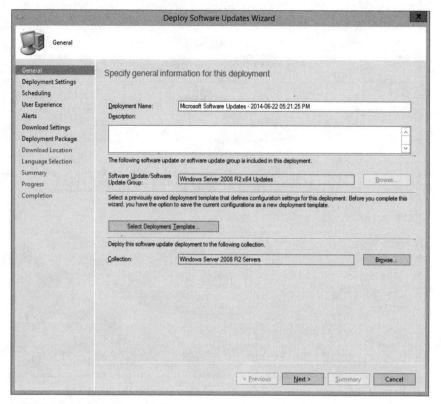

FIGURE 5-32 Deploy Software Updates

- **Name**   The name of the deployment.

- **Collection**   The collection to which you want to deploy the software update group package.

- **Deployment Template**   These templates allow you to save commonly used properties. Rather than configuring similar settings each time you use the wizard, you can instead save those settings as a deployment template, and select that template when you run the wizard.

- **Software Update/Software Update Group**   This setting will be pre-populated with the details of the software update group you are intending to deploy.

4. On the Deployment Settings page, provide the following information:

   - **Type of deployment** Here you select between Required and Available. When you select Required, software updates install automatically on clients before the configured installation deadline.

   - **Use Wake-on-LAN to wake clients for required deployments** If you have configured, and your clients support Wake-on-LAN, special packets will be sent to client computers that are in a low power state to wake them for update installation. This option is only available for the Required deployment type.

   - **Detail level** This configures the level of detail for state messages reported back to Configuration Manager by clients.

5. On the Scheduling page, configure the following information:

   - **Schedule Evaluation** This setting determines whether the deadline time is calculated using UTC, or the computer's local time.

   - **Software Available Time** Use this setting to specify whether the updates will become available at a particular time, or that the client will be aware of them when it next polls the Configuration Manager server.

   - **Installation Deadline** Allows you to specify a deadline for update installation. You can also choose for updates to be installed as soon as possible.

6. On the User Experience page, specify the type of notification users will receive about software update download and installation. You also configure what happens when the deadline is reached, and what happens if the computer requires a restart to complete installation.

7. On the Alerts page, specify how Configuration Manager and Operations Manager will generate alerts related to this deployment. This option is only available if the deployment type is set to Required.

8. On the Download Settings page, shown in Figure 5-33, you configure whether the clients will download the software locally and then install them if connected to a slow network, whether to use BranchCache when obtaining content, and whether to use the Microsoft Update servers to obtain updates if a distribution point is not available.

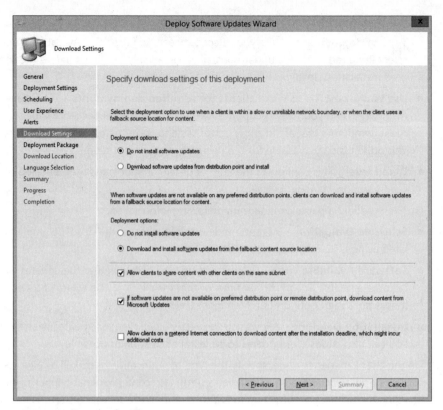

FIGURE 5-33 Download settings

9. On the Deployment Package page, shown in Figure 5-34, select the deployment package that contains the updates you want to deploy.

10. On the Download Location page, select whether updates will be downloaded from the Internet or over the local network. Download only occurs for updates that are not already present in the deployment package.

11. On the Language selection page, ensure that the product language used in your organization is selected.

12. On the Summary page, you get the chance to save this information as a template, so you don't have to go through the process of configuring all of these deployment settings in the future.

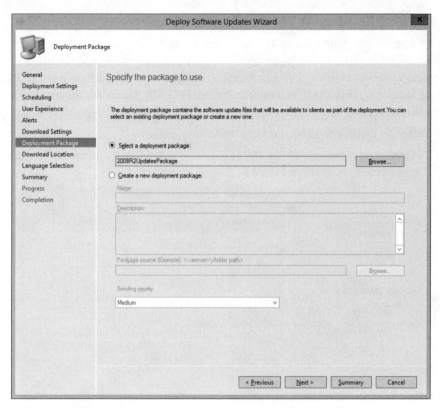

FIGURE 5-34 Select deployment package

> **MORE INFO** **MANAGING SOFTWARE UPDATES WITH CONFIGURATION MANAGER**
>
> You can learn more about managing software updates with Configuration Manager at
> *http://technet.microsoft.com/en-us/library/gg712304.aspx.*

Integrating WSUS with VMM

You can integrate WSUS with VMM as a way of centrally managing updates for your organization's virtualization servers and VMM infrastructure servers. Integrating WSUS with VMM allows you to:

- Collect updates together in baselines
- Determine update compliance.
- Remediate update compliance.
- Automatically evacuate VMs off of host cluster nodes that require a reboot to install updates.

Configuring WSUS with VMM

While it's possible to deploy the WSUS role on the computer that hosts VMM, Microsoft recommends that WSUS be deployed on a separate computer. You should run the WSUS Configuration Wizard to perform preliminary WSUS configuration, and perform a synchronization prior to integrating with VMM. You can run the WSUS Configuration Wizard and perform a synchronization using the default settings.

To integrate WSUS with VMM, perform the following steps:

1. In the Fabric workspace of the VMM console, click the Update Server Node under Infrastructure, as shown in Figure 5-35.

FIGURE 5-35 Update Server

2. On the Ribbon, click Add Resources, and then click Update Server. This will launch the Add Windows Server Update Services Server dialog box.

3. In the Add Windows Server Update Services Server dialog box, provide the following information, as shown in Figure 5-36, and then click Add.

   - **Computer Name** The FQDN of the WSUS server.
   - **TCP Port** The WSUS server's TCP port. By default, this is port 8530 (or port 8531 if using SSL) when you deploy WSUS on computers running Windows Server 2012 or Windows Server 2012 R2.
   - **Credentials** An account with local Administrator privileges on the WSUS server. You can also use a Run As account for this task.

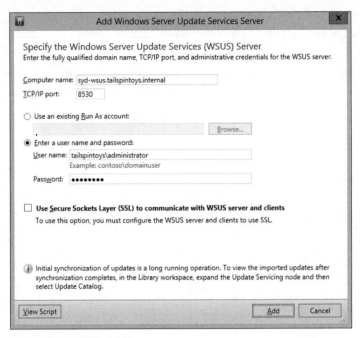

FIGURE 5-36 Add Update Server

4. Once the installation completes, verify that the update server is listed when the Update Server node is selected. The Agent Status is set to Responding, and Synchronization Result is listed as Succeeded, as shown in Figure 5-37.

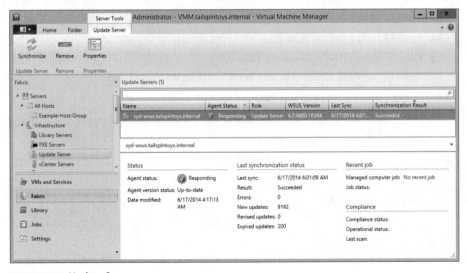

FIGURE 5-37 Update Server

5. To check which updates are available, in the Library workspace, select Update Catalog under Update Catalog And Baselines, and verify that updates are listed, as shown in Figure 5-38.

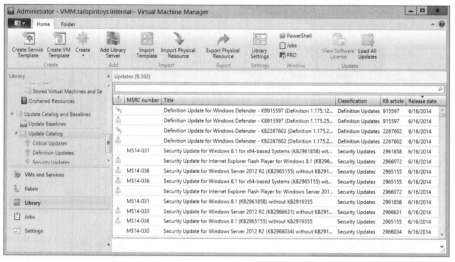

FIGURE 5-38 Update Catalog

After the initial synchronization is performed to gather the current list of available updates, VMM will not perform subsequent synchronizations automatically. This means that you need to either perform them manually, or configure a scheduled task using the Start-SCUpdate-ServerSynchronization Windows PowerShell cmdlet. To trigger a synchronization using the VMM console, perform the following steps:

1. In the Fabric workspace of the VMM console, select Update Server under the Servers\ Infrastructure node.

2. Select the WSUS server that you want VMM to synchronize.

3. On the ribbon, click the Synchronize icon.

To trigger synchronization from the Virtual Machine Manager Command Shell, issue the following command, where WSUSServerName is the name of the WSUS server.

```
SCUpdateServerSynchronization WSUSServerName
```

> **MORE INFO INTEGRATING WSUS WITH VMM**
>
> You can learn more about integrating WSUS with VMM at *http://technet.microsoft.com/ en-us/library/gg675099.aspx.*

Update baselines

An update baseline is a collection of software updates. You can use update baselines as a way of assessing computers and applications to determine whether or not they are up-to-date. A computer that has all of the updates that are in an update baseline collection installed is said to be compliant. A computer that does not have all of the updates that are in an update baseline collection installed is said to be non-compliant.
ment Scope

> **MORE INFO** **UPDATE BASELINES**
>
> You can learn more about update baselines at *http://technet.microsoft.com/en-us/library/gg675110.aspx.*

You assign baselines to computers performing the following VMM roles:

- Host group
- Individual hosts
- Library servers
- PXE servers
- Update server
- VMM Management server

Figure 5-39 shows the Assignment Scope page of the Update Baseline Wizard.

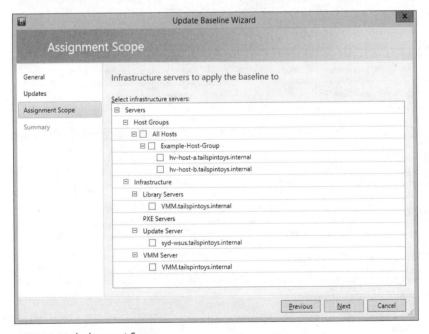

FIGURE 5-39 Assignment Scope

Assigning an update baseline does the following:

- When you assign a baseline to a host group, the baseline will apply to all stand-alone hosts and host clusters that are members of the group. The baseline also applies to any stand-alone costs and host clusters that are members of child host groups.

- When you move a host or host cluster between host groups, the host or host cluster will use the update baseline associated with its new host group.

- If you assign a baseline to a host or a host cluster directly, the host or host cluster will use that update baseline when moved between host groups.

To create a new update baseline, perform the following steps:

1. In the Library workspace of the VMM console, click Update Baselines under Update Catalog And Baselines.

2. On the ribbon, click Create, and then click Baseline. This will launch the Update Baseline Wizard.

3. On the General page of the Update Baseline Wizard, provide a name and description for the baseline.

4. On the Updates page of the Update Baseline Wizard, click Add. This will launch the Add Updates To Baseline dialog box. You use this dialog box to add updates to the baseline. Figure 5-40 shows a security update for Windows Server 2012 R2 selected for addition to the baseline. Select all of the updates that you want to have in the baseline, and click Add.

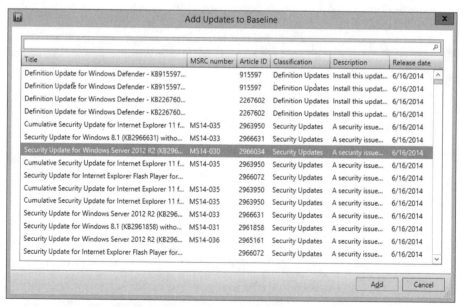

FIGURE 5-40 Add Updates To Baseline

5. On the Updates page of the Update Baseline Wizard, shown in Figure 5-41, review the list of updates in the baseline, and then click Next.

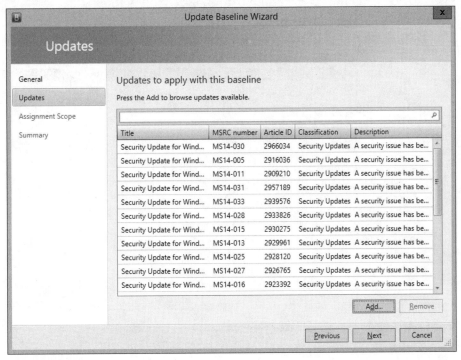

FIGURE 5-41 Updates

6. On the Assignment Scope page, select the servers, host clusters, and host groups to which you wish to assign the baseline. You don't have to assign the baseline at this time. You can do it after you have created the baseline.

7. Complete the wizard to create the update baseline.

To assign computers to a baseline, edit the properties of the baseline and select the host groups, hosts, or infrastructure server to which you want the baseline to apply. Figure 5-42 shows the TailspinToys Baseline update baseline being assigned to the Example-Host-Group host group.

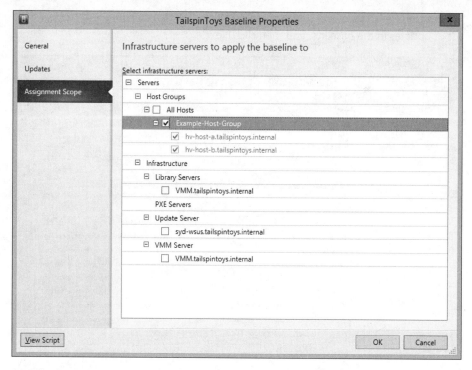

FIGURE 5-42 Assign

Update compliance

After assigning an update baseline, you can perform a scan to determine the compliance status of the computers subject to the baseline. A compliance scan checks whether each update in the baseline is applicable to the computer and, if the update is applicable, whether that update is installed. After a compliance scan, each update will have one of the following statuses:

- Compliant
- Non Compliant
- Error
- Pending Reboot
- Unknown

The unknown status often applies when hosts are moved between host groups, when updates are added or removed from baselines, or when computers are added to the scope of the baseline. Viewing compliance properties will provide additional information.

To scan a computer to determine whether or not it is compliant, perform the following steps:

1. In the Fabric workspace of the VMM console, select the server on which you want to perform the compliance check.

2. On the Home tab of the ribbon, click Scan.

3. On the Home tab of the ribbon, click Compliance Properties to view the compliance state of the computer. Figure 5-43 shows the compliance state of Hv-host-a.tailspin-toys.internal against the TailspinToys Baseline.

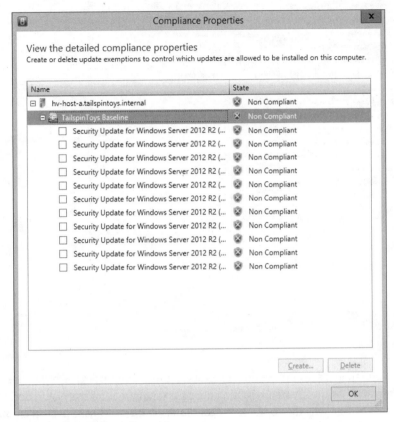

FIGURE 5-43 Compliance Properties

You can use the Compliance Properties dialog box to exempt a particular computer from a specific update. Figure 5-44 shows two updates exempted from a particular baseline for host Hv-host-a.tailspintoys.internal.

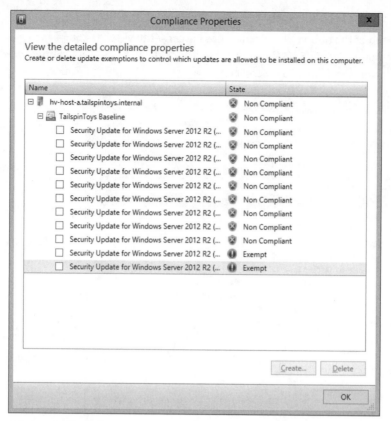

FIGURE 5-44 Exemption

To create an exemption, select those updates you want to exempt from the baseline, and click Create. This launches the Create Exemption dialog box. When using this dialog box, provide notes that explain why the computer or computers in question have been exempted from the updates being applied, as shown in Figure 5-45.

> **MORE INFO** **UPDATE COMPLIANCE**
>
> You can learn more about VMM update compliance at http://technet.microsoft.com/en-us/library/gg675093.aspx.

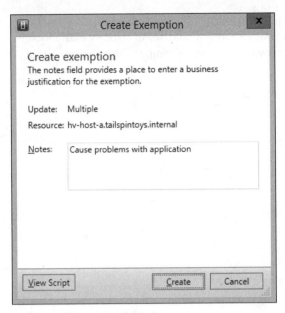

FIGURE 5-45 Create Exemption

Update remediation

Remediating a computer applies updates that are relevant but have yet to be applied to a computer. To remediate a computer, select the update baseline under the computer Compliance view in the Fabric workspace, as shown in Figure 5-46, and then click Remediate on the ribbon.

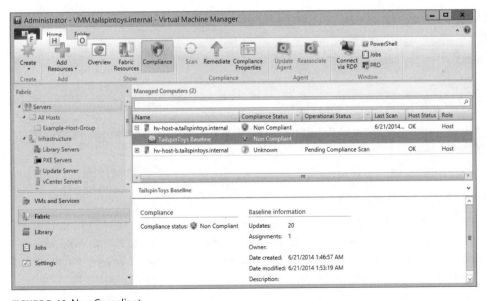

FIGURE 5-46 Non Compliant

On the Update Remediation dialog box, shown in Figure 5-47, select whether to restart servers to complete update installation. If you are applying updates to Hyper-V cluster nodes, you can also select whether virtual machines will be evacuated from the node, or placed into a saved state.

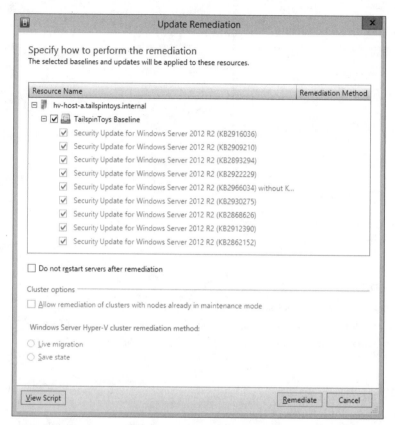

FIGURE 5-47 Update Remediation

MORE INFO **UPDATE REMEDIATION**

You can learn more about VMM update remediation at *http://technet.microsoft.com/en-us/library/gg675081.aspx*.

Updating offline VMs

Prior to the release of System Center 2012 R2 Virtual Machine Manager, administrators used the Virtual Machine Servicing Tool (VMST) to apply software updates to offline VMM virtual machines. Since the release of System Center 2012 R2 Virtual Machine Manager, the recommended method of updating offline virtual machines is to use a service management automation runbook that is available on Microsoft's website. The service management automation runbook performs the following tasks:

1. Locate all images stored in the VMM library.
2. Mount each virtual machine hard disk image on the VMM server.
3. Locate updates that are made available through WSUS.
4. Perform a check to determine if the update is applicable.
5. Perform a check to determine whether the update has been applied.
6. Apply updates to the mounted virtual hard disk image.
7. Commit the changes to the virtual hard disk and dismount.

MORE INFO **UPDATE OFFLINE VMS**

You can learn more about updating offline VMs at *http://blogs.technet.com/b/privatecloud/archive/2013/12/07/orchestrated-vm-patching.aspx.*

EXAM TIP

Remember that while VMM manages updates for virtualization hosts and VMM servers, it does not manage updates for virtual machines.

Thought experiment

WSUS at Fabrikam

You are in the process of deploying WSUS at a medium sized enterprise that will be deploying Configuration Manager and VMM to manage software updates within the next 12 months. You have created several computer groups and automatic deployment rules to allow for automatic update approval. You want to ensure that client computers at Fabrikam automatically contact the WSUS server rather than the Microsoft Update servers. You also want to ensure that WSUS computer group membership occurs through Group Policy.

1. Which Group Policy do you need to configure so that servers know the location of the WSUS server?
2. Which Group Policy do you need to configure to assign computers to WSUS computer groups?

Objective summary

- WSUS is a Windows Server server role that allows you to manage and centralize the deployment of updates.
- You can configure automatic approval rules that allow updates to be automatically approved based on update classification, product being updated, and the computers being updated.
- You can integrate WSUS with Configuration Manager. When you do this, you create software update groups that contain multiple updates and then deploy these updates to Configuration Manager computer collections.
- You can perform compliance checks to determine whether updates have been deployed on specific Configuration Manager clients.
- You can integrate WSUS with VMM. This allows you to manage the updates for your virtualization hosts as well as your VMM infrastructure.
- With VMM, you collect updates into baselines. You can then assess hosts against the baseline and remediate any hosts that are missing updates.

Objective review

Answer the following questions to test your knowledge of the information in this objective. You can find the answers to these questions and explanations of why each answer choice is correct or incorrect in the "Answers" section at the end of this chapter.

1. You are using Configuration Manager with WSUS to manage software updates in your environment. You have performed and updated synchronization and located five updates that you want to deploy to a collection of computers running the Windows Server 2012 R2 operating system. Which of the following steps should you take before performing deployment?

   A. Create a software update group.

   B. Create an Update baseline.

   C. Download the updates and create a deployment package.

   D. Create an automatic approval rule.

2. You have integrated VMM with WSUS. You want to check whether several virtualization hosts have several recently released updates installed. Which of the following steps should you take to accomplish this goal?

   A. Add the updates to an update baseline.

   B. Add the updates to a Software Update Group.

   C. Assign the update baseline to the virtualization hosts and assess compliance.

   D. Assign the software update group to the virtualization hosts and assess compliance.

3. You have deployed System Center 2012 R2 Virtual Machine Manager. Which of the following tools can you use to automatically apply software updates to VM images stored in the VMM library?

   A. Virtual Machine Servicing Tool

   B. Service management automation runbook

   C. WSUS

   D. Configuration Manager

Objective 5.3: Implement backup and recovery

Although it is likely that the fabric upon which you are running your private cloud is highly redundant, with VMs hosted on failover clusters that use redundant storage and network resources, it's still important to ensure that you regularly back up important workloads. This is because while redundant resources minimize the chance that you'll lose important data to hardware failure, it's still possible to lose data due to data corruption, malware, or an administrator making an unforced error.

> **This section covers the following topics:**
> - Understanding Data Protection Manager
> - Deploying DPM agents
> - Configuring DPM storage
> - Creating DPM protection groups
> - Performing recovery
> - Integrating Microsoft Azure Online Backup
> - Using DPM Orchestrator integration pack

Understanding Data Protection Manager

System Center 2012 R2 Data Protection Manager (DPM) is Microsoft's data protection and recovery solution. You can use DPM to backup and recover workloads including Exchange, SQL Server, SharePoint, Windows server role services and features, and virtual machine running under Hyper-V. DPM supports backup to disk, to take, and to Microsoft Azure.

When discussing DPM, it's important to understand the following terms:

- A recovery point objective (RPO) is the point in time to which you want to recover data. For example, you might need to recover a database to a specific RPO that represents the state it was in 45 minutes ago.
- A recovery time objective (RTO) is the amount of time you have to recover to the RPO. This is the amount of time it would take to recover the database to the state it was in 45 minutes ago.

Deploying DPM agents

DPM requires that an agent be installed if it is going to be configured to protect a computer. The agent identifies which data on the computer can be protected, tracks changes that occur to that data, and manages the process of forwarding protected data from the protected computer to the DPM server. You need to configure any firewall on the DPM server to allow inbound TCP port 135 traffic, as well as allowing traffic to the DPM service (msdpm.exe) and the protection agent (dpmra.exe).

To deploy the DPM agents, perform the following steps:

1. In the Management workspace of the DPM console, click Install. This will launch the Protection Agent Installation Wizard. On the Select Agent Deployment method, shown in Figure 5-48, choose Install Agents, or Attach Agents. You select Attach Agents for computers that already have the agent software installed, for example those that have the DPM agent as part of their installation image, or for computers that might be on the perimeter network.

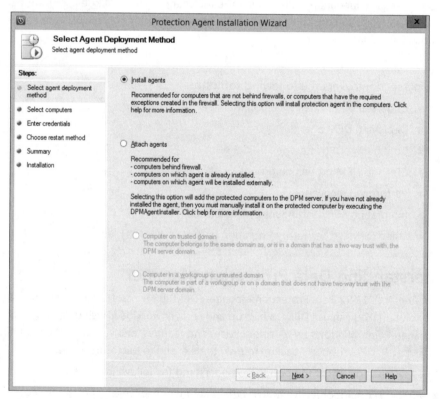

FIGURE 5-48 Install DPM agent

2. On the Select Computers page, either select computers that are in the same domain as the DPM server, which are presented in a list, as shown in Figure 5-49, or enter the FQDN of the computer.

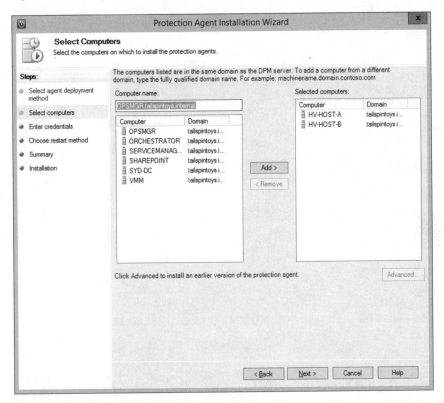

FIGURE 5-49 Select Computers

3. On the Credentials page, specify the credentials of an account that has local administrator access on the computers on which you want to deploy the DPM agent.

4. On the Choose Restart Method page, select whether restart will occur automatically or manually. Restart is only required on computers running the Windows Server 2003 or Windows Server 2003 R2 operating systems.

5. To complete the wizard, click Install. This will deploy the agent.

Figure 5-50 shows the DPM agent installed on HV-HOST-A and HV-HOST-B.

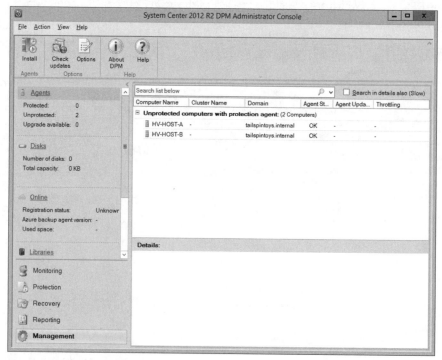

FIGURE 5-50 Agents

MORE INFO **DPM AGENT DEPLOYMENT**

You can learn more about deploying the DPM agent at *http://technet.microsoft.com/en-us/library/hh758075.aspx*.

Configuring DPM storage

DPM uses disk as the primary short-term storage location, whilst allowing long-term storage using tape. A DPM storage pool is a collection of disks that DPM uses to store replicas and recovery points for protected data. DPM requires at least one disk in the storage pool before it can begin protecting data. Additional disks can be added to the storage pool as necessary.

To add a disk to the DPM storage pool, perform the following steps:

1. In the Management workspace of the DPM console, click Disks.

2. On the ribbon, click Add. This will launch the Add Disks To Storage Pool dialog box. The disks must be online and initialized before you can add them to the DPM storage pool. Figure 5-51 shows two disks being added to the storage pool.

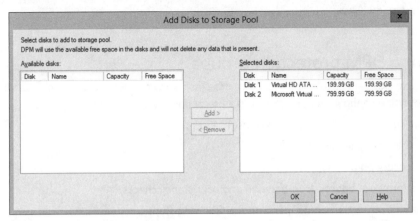

FIGURE 5-51 Adding disks to storage pool

3. Click OK to add the disks to the storage pool. DPM will convert any disk you add to dynamic, and convert any volumes to simple volumes. Best practice is to allocate new, unformatted, empty disks to the storage pool, and allow DPM to manage and prepare them. Figure 5-52 shows two disks added to the DPM storage pool.

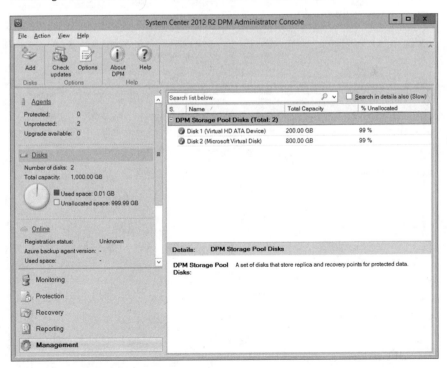

FIGURE 5-52 Storage pool disks

Creating DPM protection groups

Protection groups are collections of data sources (also known as workloads) that have a common protection configuration. Members of a protection group share the following:

- Backup targets (disk, tape, or Microsoft Azure)
- Protection schedule
- Recovery point schedule
- Performance options (compression and consistency checks)

To create a protection group, perform the following steps:

1. In the Protection workspace of the DPM console, click New.

2. On the Select Protection Group Type page of the Create New Protection Group Wizard, shown in Figure 5-53, select Servers. You can also configure DPM to protect clients.

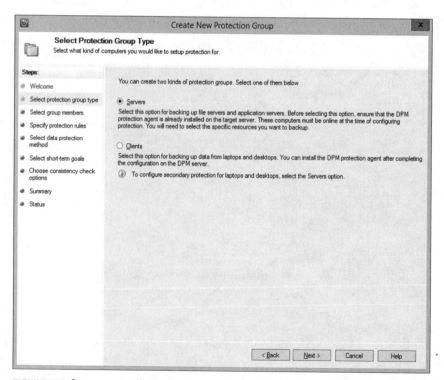

FIGURE 5-53 Servers protection group

3. On the Select Group Members page, specify which data you want to protect. For example, Figure 5-54 shows the selection of an online Hyper-V virtual machine named Live-Hyper-V-VM. When configuring protection group members, you specify what you will protect, from individual files and folders, through to VMs, databases, and even entire servers.

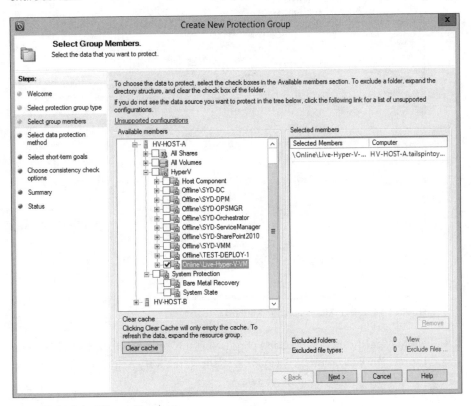

FIGURE 5-54 Select Group Members

4. On the Select Data Protection Method page, provide a protection group name, and then specify the protection methods. You can choose to have short-term protection using Disk, online protection using Microsoft Azure, and long-term protection using tape. The Azure and Tape options are only available if they have previously been configured. Figure 5-55 shows the selection of short-term protection using Disk.

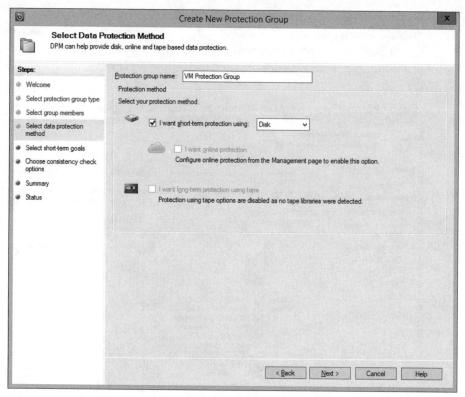

FIGURE 5-55 Select Data Protection Method

5. On the Specify Short Term Goals page, select the Retention Range and how often an Express Full Backup is taken. Figure 5-56 shows recovery points created every half an hour with a Retention Range of 3 days.

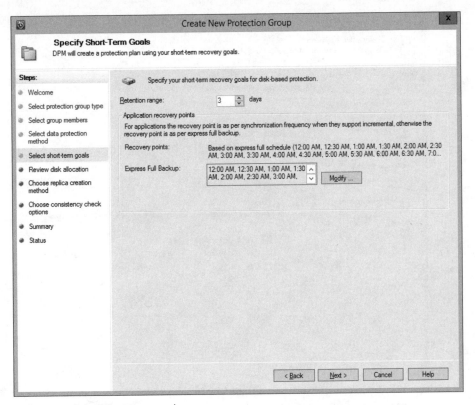

FIGURE 5-56 Select short-term goals

6. The Review Disk Allocation page allows you to view the allocation of storage in the storage pool. You also have the option to grow volumes as required. Figure 5-57 shows the Review Disk Allocation page.

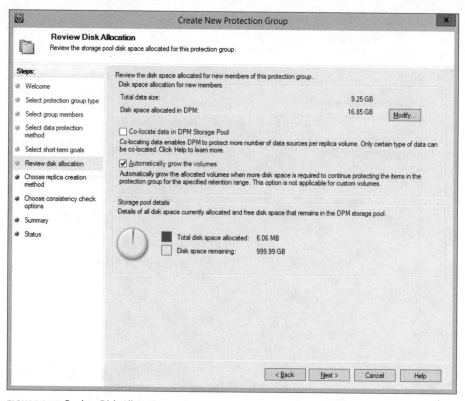

FIGURE 5-57 Review Disk Allocation

7. On the Choose Replica Creation Method page, select how the first replica should be created. Options include creating the replica immediately, creating the replica at a scheduled point in the future, or creating a replica manually using removable media.

8. On the Consistency Check Options page, shown in Figure 5-58, configure how often a consistency check is run to verify the integrity of the protected data.

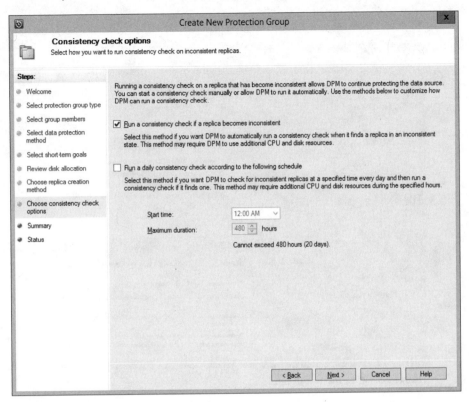

FIGURE 5-58 Consistency check options

9. Complete the wizard to finish creating the new protection group. Figure 5-59 shows the protection group that protects the online VM with an OK protection state.

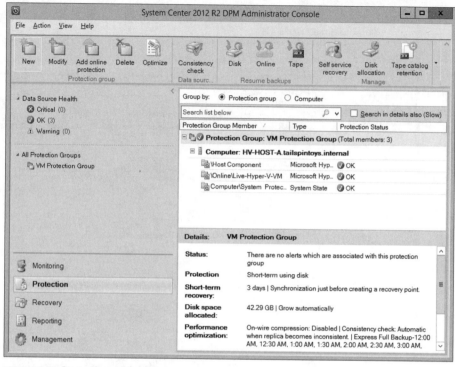

FIGURE 5-59 Protection workspace

> **MORE INFO** **DPM PROTECTION GROUPS**
>
> You can learn more about configuring DPM protection groups at *http://technet.microsoft. com/en-us/library/jj628070.aspx*.

Performing recovery

You can use DPM to recover data from any available recovery point. A recovery point, also termed a backup snapshot, is a consistent point-in-time copy of a DPM-protected item, be that a file, folder, database, virtual machine, or an entire computer. The type of data being protected determines your options when it comes to performing recovery. For example, you can recover a SQL Server database to another SQL Server as long as the destination SQL Server has the DPM agent installed. Similarly, you can recover Exchange mailbox databases or Hyper-V virtual machines if they are properly protected to a separate host, as long as the destination host is running the same version of Exchange, SQL, or Hyper-V, and has the DPM agent installed. You also have the option of performing recovery to an alternate location. For example, you might want to only recover a specific file from a protected VM. Rather than re-store the entire VM, you can restore the protected file to an accessible file share or local disk.

To recover the contents of protected VM, perform the following steps:

1. In the Recovery workspace of the DPM console, select the item and the recovery point that you wish to restore. Figure 5-60 shows the selection of the 7.00 AM recovery point of the Live-Hyper-V-VM virtual machine. When you have located the recovery point that you wish to restore, click Recover on the ribbon.

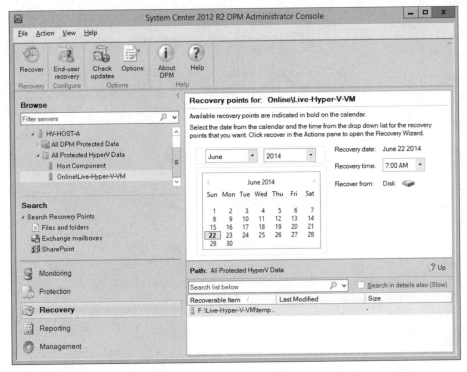

FIGURE 5-60 Recovery workspace

2. On the Select Recovery Type page of the Select Recovery Wizard, select Copy To A Network Folder. If the DPM server has the Hyper-V role installed, you could perform a recovery directly to another server running Hyper-V.

3. On the Specify Destination page, specify the location of a shared folder that will host the recovered files. The destination location must have the DPM agent installed.

4. On the Specify Recovery Options page, select whether you want to apply the security settings of the destination computer or the security settings of the recovery point. You can also configure bandwidth throttling, SAN recovery, and email notification. Figure 5-61 shows the Specify Recovery Options page.

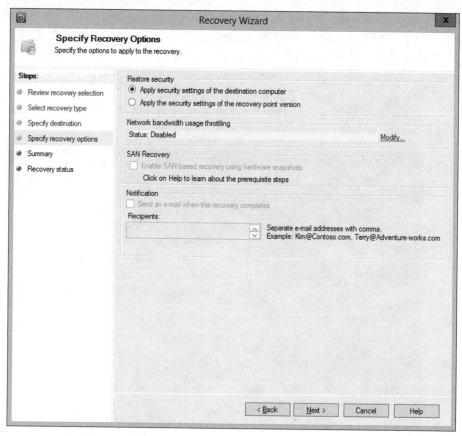

FIGURE 5-61 Specify Recovery Options

5. Complete the wizard by clicking Recover.

> **MORE INFO RECOVERY OPTIONS**
>
> You can learn more about DPM recovery options at *http://technet.microsoft.com/en-us/library/jj628056.aspx*.

Integrating Microsoft Azure Online Backup

Microsoft Azure Online Backup is Microsoft's cloud-based subscription backup service. Microsoft Azure Online Backup can be integrated with DPM, providing a secure off-site data storage and recovery location. Microsoft Azure can store data from DPM for 120 days if you synchronize data every 24 hours, and 60 days if you synchronize data every 12 hours. Your Azure subscription will be charged based on the amount of data stored in the backup vault, but you will not be charged for the bandwidth consumed transferring the data.

To configure DPM to work with Microsoft Azure Online Backup, you need to have performed the following steps:

- Have created a Microsoft Azure account.
- Have created a backup vault within the Microsoft Azure account. Backup vaults allow you to store backup data. Figure 5-62 shows the creation of a backup vault named ExampleVault.

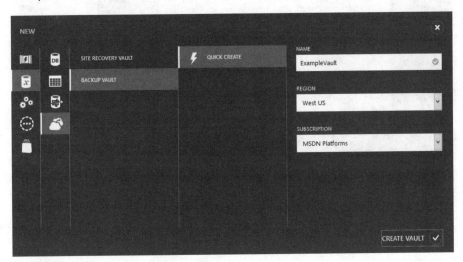

FIGURE 5-62 Create backup vault

- Upload a specially-created certificate that will identify the server to the backup vault, and secure the backup process. You can create this certificate with the makecert.exe utility, generate it using an internal certificate authority, or obtain it from a trusted third party CA.
- Download and install the Microsoft Azure Backup agent to the DPM server. This agent works for both Microsoft Azure Backup, a stand-alone server-based backup solution, and when installed on a System Center 2012 R2 DPM server, integrates with DPM, allowing protected data to be stored in the cloud.

To create a self-signed certificate, download the makecert.exe utility from Microsoft's website and run the following command.

```
.\makecert.exe -r -pe -n CN=SYD-DPM -ss my -sr localmachine -eku 1.3.6.1.5.5.7.3.2 -len
2048 -e 01/01/2018 SYD-DPM.cer
```

You replace SYD-DPM with the name of the computer for which you are creating the certificate, and where 01/01/2018 is an appropriate certificate expiry date. Once you've created the certificate, upload it to Microsoft Azure, as shown in Figure 5-63.

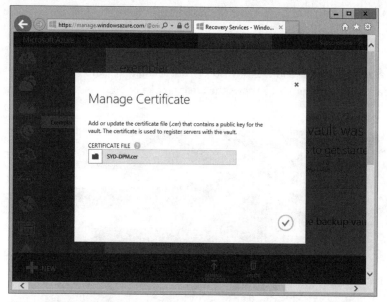

FIGURE 5-63 Manage Certificate

Once the certificate is uploaded, you download the agent and install it on the DPM server, as shown in Figure 5-64.

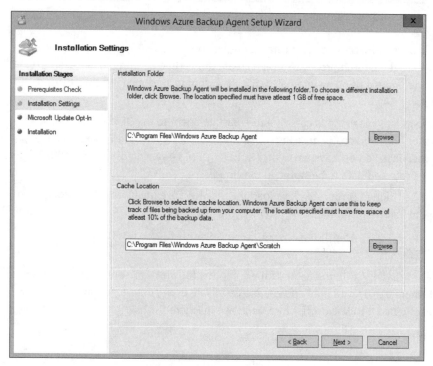

FIGURE 5-64 Windows Azure Backup Agent Setup

Once the agent is installed, you'll need to register the DPM server with Microsoft Azure. To register the DPM server with Microsoft Azure, perform the following steps:

1. In the Management node of the DPM console, click Online. In the ribbon, click Register. This will launch the Register Server Wizard.

2. On the Backup Vault page of the Register Server Wizard, select the management certificate that you uploaded to Microsoft Azure, and then select the name of the backup vault, as shown in Figure 5-65.

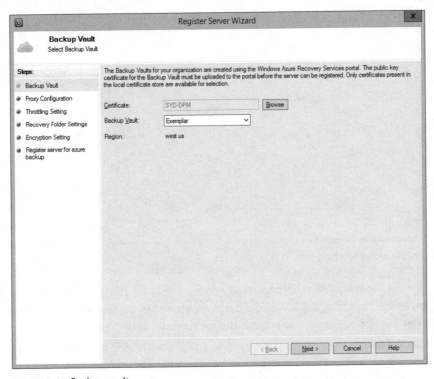

FIGURE 5-65 Backup vault

3. On the Proxy Configuration page, configure any proxy server settings that are required for the DPM server to make a connection to Microsoft Azure.

4. On the Throttling Setting page, shown in Figure 5-66, specify any bandwidth throttling settings that should apply when protected data is being transferred to Microsoft Azure. You can configure throttling settings for work hours and non-work hours.

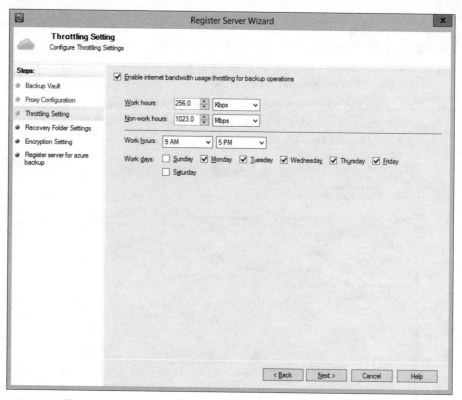

FIGURE 5-66 Throttling Setting

5. On the Recovery Folder Settings page, specify a location that the DPM server can use as temporary storage space before being transferred to the final recovery location. This location needs to have enough storage space to store this temporary data.

6. On the Encryption Settings page, provide a 16 character long passphrase. This passphrase will be used to encrypt backed up data. You need this passphrase to recover data from Microsoft Azure when recovering using a difference instance of DPM. The Encryption Setting page of the wizard is shown in Figure 5-67.

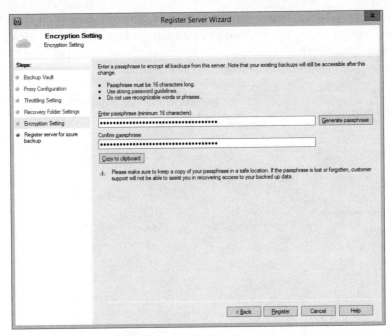

FIGURE 5-67 Encryption Setting

Once you have registered the DPM server with Microsoft Azure, you will be able to select the online protection option when creating or modifying a protection group, as shown in Figure 5-68.

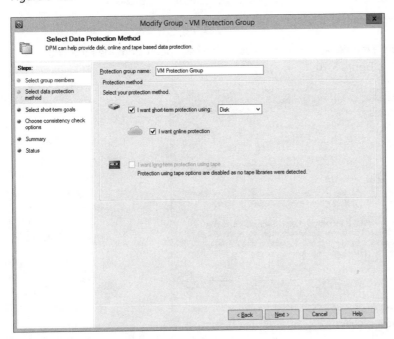

FIGURE 5-68 Select data protection method

Once you select the online protection option, you'll be able to configure which protection group data you want to protect. You can protect only a subset of the data protected by the protection group, rather than having to replicate all of the protected data to Microsoft Azure. Figure 5-69 shows the Online Protection Goals page of the wizard.

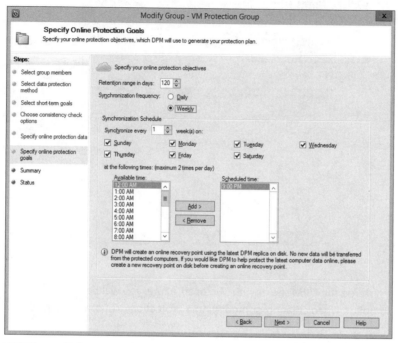

FIGURE 5-69 Online protection goals

You can force the creation of an online protection recovery point from the Protection workspace, as shown in Figure 5-70.

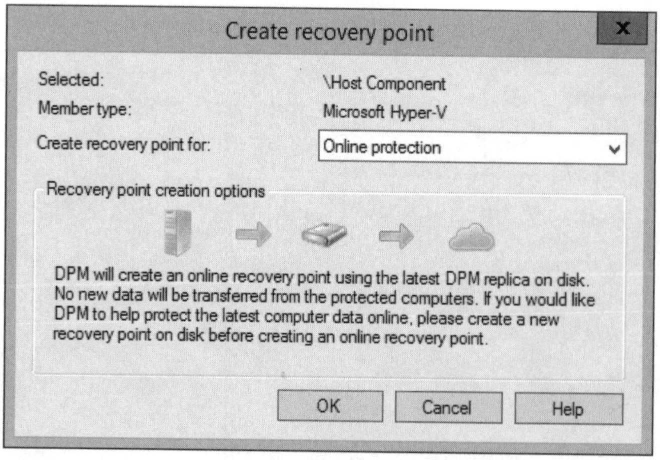

FIGURE 5-70 Create Recovery Point

To recover from Microsoft Azure backup, specify an online recovery point, as shown in Figure 5-71, and perform recovery normally.

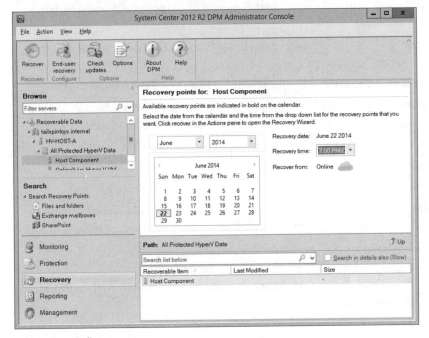

FIGURE 5-71 Online recovery

MORE INFO **AZURE BACKUP**

You can learn more about configuring Microsoft Azure Online Backup at *http://technet. microsoft.com/en-us/library/jj728752.aspx.*

Using DPM Orchestrator integration pack

You can use the DPM integration pack for Orchestrator, shown in Figure 5-72, to create DPM specific runbook automation. These activities allow you to automate the following tasks when creating an Orchestrator runbook:

FIGURE 5-72 Orchestrator activities

- **Create Recovery Point**   Use this activity to create a recovery point for a specific data source.

- **Get Data Source**   Use this activity to determine information about available data sources.

- **Get Recovery Point**   Use this activity to determine which recovery points exist for a specific protected data source.

- **Get DPM Server Capacity**   Use this activity to determine a DPM server's capacity.

- **Protect Data Source**   Use this activity to put a data source into protection. Use the Get Data Source activity to determine the identity of eligible data sources.

- **Recover Sharepoint**   Use this activity to recover Sharepoint data.

- **Recover SQL**   Use this activity to recover SQL data.

- **Recover VM**   Use this activity to recover a protected virtual machine.

- **Run DPM PowerShell Script**   Use this activity to run a DPM PowerShell script. You can use the information returned from this script in the Orchestrator runbook.

> **MORE INFO DPM INTEGRATION PACK**
>
> You can learn more about the DPM integration pack at *http://technet.microsoft.com/en-us/library/hh830694.aspx.*

EXAM TIP

Remember what steps you need to take to configure a DPM server so that it can write protected data to Microsoft Azure.

Thought experiment
Data protection at Contoso

You are in the process of planning data protection infrastructure for Contoso's private cloud deployment. You are researching how you will deploy and configure System Center 2012 R2 Data Protection Manager. As part of your planning, you want to know what steps you should take after deploying the DPM server before you can create protection groups. You're also interested in moving data to the cloud or another offsite location.

1. What steps do you need to take before adding virtualization hosts to DPM protection groups?

2. What steps could you take to ensure protected data is stored offsite?

Objective summary

- DPM requires agents to be deployed to servers that host data requiring protection.
- You need to add disks to a DPM storage pool before you can configure a protection group.
- DPM protection groups determine what is backed up, to where it is backed up, how often it is backed up, and how long it will remain backed up.
- You can integrate DPM with Microsoft Azure, allowing you to store protected data off site in the Microsoft Cloud.
- You can use the DPM integration pack for Orchestrator to create runbooks with DPM activities.

Objective review

Answer the following questions to test your knowledge of the information in this objective. You can find the answers to these questions and explanations of why each answer choice is correct or incorrect in the "Answers" section at the end of this chapter.

1. Which DPM integration pack activity would you use with an Orchestrator runbook to generate a list of recovery points?

   A. Create Recovery Point

   B. Get Data Source

   C. Get Recovery Point

   D. Protect Data Source

2. You are planning on synchronizing data from a DPM protection group to a Microsoft Azure backup vault. You want to perform one synchronization per day. What is the maximum data retention period available given these conditions?

   A. 60 days

   B. 90 days

   C. 120 days

   D. 150 days

3. You have been using DPM to protect several Hyper-V virtualization hosts, as well as the VMs that they host. You want to recover a protected VM to a different Hyper-V virtualization host than the one it was originally hosted on. Which of the following conditions must the destination Hyper-V host meet?

   A. The host must have the DPM agent installed.

   B. The host must be running the same version of Hyper-V.

   C. The host must have the Operations Manager agent installed.

   D. The host must have the Configuration Manager agent installed.

Answers

This section contains the solutions to the thought experiments and answers to the lesson review questions in this chapter.

Objective 5.1: Thought experiment

1. You should deploy a System Center Advisor gateway server to collect traffic from servers on the internal network and forward it to the System Center Advisor servers in the cloud.

2. You need to connect via web browser to the System Center Advisor console hosted in the cloud.

Objective 5.1: Review

1. **Correct answers:** A, B, and C

   A. **Correct**: You can add configuration items to compliance baselines.

   B. **Correct**: You can add existing compliance baselines to new compliance baselines.

   C. **Correct**: You can add software updates to configuration baselines.

   D. **Incorrect**: Update baselines are used with VMM and not with Configuration Manager baselines.

2. **Correct answers:** A, B, and C

   A. **Correct**: The System Center Process Pack for IT GRC requires an existing deployment of Configuration Manager, Operations Manager, and Service Manager.

   B. **Correct**: The System Center Process Pack for IT GRC requires an existing deployment of Configuration Manager, Operations Manager, and Service Manager.

   C. **Correct**: The System Center Process Pack for IT GRC requires an existing deployment of Configuration Manager, Operations Manager, and Service Manager.

   D. **Incorrect**: The System Center Process Pack for IT GRC requires an existing deployment of Configuration Manager, Operations Manager, and Service Manager.

3. **Correct answers:** A, C, and D

   A. **Correct**: The System Center Process Pack for IT GRC requires that Service Manager be configured with the Active Directory, Operations Manager, and Configuration Manager connectors.

   B. **Incorrect**: The System Center Process Pack for IT GRC requires that Service Manager be configured with the Active Directory, Operations Manager, and Configuration Manager connectors.

   C. **Correct**: The System Center Process Pack for IT GRC requires that Service Manager be configured with the Active Directory, Operations Manager, and Configuration Manager connectors.

D. **Correct**: The System Center Process Pack for IT GRC requires that Service Manager be configured with the Active Directory, Operations Manager, and Configuration Manager connectors.

Objective 5.2: Thought experiment

1. You configure the Specify intranet Microsoft update service location policy to configure a computer with the address of the WSUS server.

2. You assign computers to WSUS computer groups using the Enable client-side targeting policy.

Objective 5.2: Review

1. **Correct answers:** A and C

   A. **Correct**: You need to create a software update group.

   B. **Incorrect**: You create update baselines when using software updates with VMM, not with Configuration Manager.

   C. **Correct**: You need to download the updates and create a deployment package prior to deploying the updates.

   D. **Incorrect**: You don't need to create an automatic approval rule prior to deploying the updates.

2. **Correct answers:** A and C

   A. **Correct**: You add software updates to update baselines in VMM.

   B. **Incorrect**: You use Software Update Groups with Configuration Manager, not with VMM.

   C. **Correct**: You can assess compliance by assigning update baselines to virtualization hosts.

   D. **Incorrect**: You don't assign software update groups in VMM, you deploy them in Configuration Manager.

3. **Correct answers:** B and C

   A. **Incorrect**: The VMST is not supported for System Center 2012 R2 Virtual Machine Manger. Instead, you use a service management automation runbook to update offline VM images in the VMM library.

   B. **Correct**: You use a service management automation runbook to update offline VM images in the VMM library.

   C. **Correct**: The service management automation runbook interacts with WSUS to obtain updates that can be applied to offline VM images in the VMM library.

   D. **Incorrect**: You don't use Configuration Manager to perform offline updates of virtual machine images in the VMM library.

Objective 5.3: Thought experiment

1. You need to deploy protection agents to the virtualization hosts. You also need to create a storage pool.

2. You could connect the DPM instance to Microsoft Azure, which allows you to store a copy of protected data in an offsite location. Although not discussed in the text, you can also create a DPM replica in another site.

Objective 5.3: Review

1. **Correct answer:** C

   A. **Incorrect:** The Create Recovery Point activity allows you to create a new recovery point.

   B. **Incorrect**: The Get Data Source activity provides information about available data source.

   C. **Correct**: The Get Recovery Point activity allows you to generate a list of recovery points.

   D. **Incorrect**: The Protect Data Source activity allows you to protect a specific data source.

2. **Correct answer:** C

   A. **Incorrect**: With one synchronization per day, Microsoft Azure, when integrated with DPM, supports a maximum data retention period of 120 days.

   B. **Incorrect**: With one synchronization per day, Microsoft Azure, when integrated with DPM, supports a maximum data retention period of 120 days.

   C. **Correct**: With one synchronization per day, Microsoft Azure, when integrated with DPM, supports a maximum data retention period of 120 days.

   D. **Incorrect**: With one synchronization per day, Microsoft Azure, when integrated with DPM, supports a maximum data retention period of 120 days.

3. **Correct answers:** A and B

   A. **Correct**: You can only restore a VM in its entirety to a Hyper-V host that has the DPM agent installed.

   B. **Correct**: You can't restore a VM to a host if it is running an earlier version of Hyper-V.

   C. **Incorrect**: Only the DPM agent is required.

   D. **Incorrect**: Only the DPM agent is required.

Index

A

M

N

S

Y

yellow (warning) health state 180

About the author

ORIN THOMAS is an MVP, an MCT and has a string of Microsoft MCSE and MCITP certifications. He has written more than 25 books for Microsoft Press and is a contributing editor at Windows IT Pro magazine. He has been working in IT since the early 1990's. He regularly speaks at events like TechED in Australia and around the world on Windows Server, Windows Client, System Center and security topics. Orin founded and runs the Melbourne System Center, Security, and Infrastructure Group. You can follow him on twitter at *http://twitter.com/orinthomas*.

Free ebooks

From technical overviews to drilldowns on special topics, get *free* ebooks from Microsoft Press at:

www.microsoftvirtualacademy.com/ebooks

Download your free ebooks in PDF, EPUB, and/or Mobi for Kindle formats.

Look for other great resources at Microsoft Virtual Academy, where you can learn new skills and help advance your career with free Microsoft training delivered by experts.

Microsoft Press

Now that you've read the book...

Tell us what you think!

Was it useful?
Did it teach you what you wanted to learn?
Was there room for improvement?

Let us know at http://aka.ms/tellpress

Your feedback goes directly to the staff at Microsoft Press,
and we read every one of your responses. Thanks in advance!

 Microsoft